EXPERT SYSTEMS AND ARTIFICIAL INTELLIGENCE
IN DECISION SUPPORT SYSTEMS

EXPERT SYSTEMS
AND
ARTIFICIAL INTELLIGENCE
IN
DECISION SUPPORT SYSTEMS

PROCEEDINGS OF THE SECOND MINI EUROCONFERENCE, LUNTEREN, THE NETHERLANDS, 17-20 NOVEMBER 1985

edited by

HENK G. SOL
Department of Mathematics, Technical University, Delft, The Netherlands

CEES A. TH. TAKKENBERG
BSO/Partners, Utrecht, The Netherlands

PIETER F. DE VRIES ROBBÉ
Academic Hospital, Groningen, The Netherlands

D. Reidel Publishing Company

A MEMBER OF THE KLUWER ACADEMIC PUBLISHERS GROUP

Dordrecht / Boston / Lancaster / Tokyo

Library of Congress Cataloging in Publication Data

CIP DATA APPEAR ON SEPARATE CARD

Expert systems and artificial intelligence in decision support systems.

Includes index.

ISBN 90-277-2437-7

Published by D. Reidel Publishing Company,
P.O. Box 17, 3300 AA Dordrecht, Holland.

Sold and distributed in the U.S.A. and Canada
by Kluwer Academic Publishers,
101 Philip Drive, Assinippi Park, Norwell, MA 02061, U.S.A.

In all other countries, sold and distributed
by Kluwer Academic Publishers Group,
P.O. Box 322, 3300 AH Dordrecht, Holland.

TABLE OF CONTENTS

PREFACE

In 1985 it was 20 years since Nobel Laureate Herbert A. Simon published: 'THE SHAPE OF AUTOMATION: For Men and Management'.

This short but important and still topical book dwells on three subjects:
- The Long-Range Economic Effects of Automation;
- Will the Corporation be Managed by Machines?
- The New Science of Management Decision.

In contrast with George Orwell, who was a critic of contemporary political systems rather than a prophet, Simon portrays a far more rosy picture of our 'brave new world'. Simon's work breathes optimism.
First, computer technology; looking back it is doubtful whether even the professor expected the hardware development we have wittnessed.
Secondly, our ability to 'tame the beast'; there is now not much reason for complacency and satisfaction. Offices and factories can by no means be called automated, at most semi-automated.
Thirdly the organizational and social implications of these rapid technological developments; referring to what he then called: 'The Computer and the new decision making techniques ...'
Concerning this last point, there is little need to emphasize that had been less practical application in organizations than the often impressive theoretical developments would lead one to believe.
In Europe this situation is even more accute than in the USA and Japan. The ESPRIT programme of the ECC and many similar national programs intend to bridge the gap.

NSOR's November 1985 Mini Euro Conference has been devoted to those promises contained in Simon's seminal work that just now, some ten to fifteen years late, are beginning to appear above the practical horizon.

The Second Mini Euro Conference looked at Expert Systems, Artificial Intelligence, and Decision Support Systems from a 'traditional' Operations Research/Management Science point of view: 'as methodologies, techniques and tools to improve Management Decision making!

This conference was a platform for the exchange of information among theoreticians and practitioners who share a common interest in this subjects.

PROGRAMME COMMITTEE

Chairman : C.A.Th. Takkenberg
Members : H.G. Sol
           P. de Vries Robbé

ORGANIZING COMMITTEE

Chairman : H. van Gelder
Secretary: W.P.A. van der Heijden
Treasurer: A.G.W. Termeulen
Members : E.A. van Doorn
           C.A.Th. Takkenberg
         : E.P.C. van der Wel
Conference Manager: C. van Bremen

SPONSORS

The Netherlands Society for Operations Research expresses it's gratitude
for the financial support received from various Dutch authorities and
companies.

Shell Nederland BV
IBM Nederland BV
Hewlett Packard Nederland NV
Hollandsche Beton Groep NV
Bank Mees & Hope NV
BSO/Buro voor Systeemontwikkeling BV
Centrale Directie PTT
Delta Lloyd Verzekeringsgroep NV
Ministry of Economic Affairs
Heineken NV
Hoogovens Groep BV
Fysisch en Electronisch Laboratorium TNO
NCM
Digital Equipment BV
Dow Chemical (Nederland) BV
Interpolis
Euro III Foundation
KLM, Royal Dutch Airlines
NV Electriciteits-Maatschappij IJsselcentrale NV
Nederlandse Gasunie
Nederlandse Unilever Bedrijven BV
Storkdata BV
De Tombe/Melse & co., accountants

2 anonymous sponsors

by Dr. Henk G. Sol, Professor of Information Systems,
Delft University of Technology, Dr. Cees A.Th. Takken-
berg, Partner, BSO/Partners, Utrecht, Dr. Pieter de Vries
Robbé , University of Groningen

Support for managerial decision making in organizations is attracting a lot
of interest. Numerous researchers and practitioners have no hesitations in
putting the label Desision Support Systems (DSS) on their work. With the
same ease Expert Systems (ES) and Artificial Intelligence (AI) are put
forward as tracks to improve organizational efficiency and effectiveness.
Various contributing disciplines are jumping on the label DSS to sell their
products for academia and practice. Clearly the basis for defining DSS has
been migrating from an explicit statement of what a DSS does to some ideas
how the DSS objective can be accomplished. This migration during the years
can be shown in the following descriptions for DSS:

1. In the early 1970's DSS was described as 'a computer based system to aid
   in decision making'. The starting point was found in the application of
   interactive technology to managerial tasks in order to use computers for
   better decision—making. There was a strong cognitive focus in this DSS
   concept, viz. that of a single decision—maker.
2. In the mid to late 1970's the DSS **movement** emphasized 'interactive
   computer—based systems which help decision—makers utilize data bases and
   models to solve ill—structured problems'. The emphasis lies not so much
   on the **decision** process, but rather on the **support** for personal computing with fast development tools and packages, e.g. for financial planning.
3. In the later 1970's to early 1980's the DSS **bandwagon** provides **systems**
   'using suitable and available technology to improve effectiveness of
   managerial and professional activities'. User—friendly software is produced almost unexceptionally under the label DSS. Disciplines like
   operations research and cognitive psychology are jumping on the bandwagon. Concepts like information center and prototyping are put forward in
   the same flavour as DSS.
4. By now we face a new technical base for DSS: the convergence on **intelligent workstations.** Telecommunications put forward the issues of organisational versus personal computing and distributed DSS. We see new

1

H. G. Sol et al. (eds.), Expert Systems and Artificial Intelligence in Decision Support Systems, 1–7.

technologies emerging as expert systems and document-based systems. This is expressed by Elam et al. (1985) in the need for a new vision on DSS. They propose to confine the notion DSS to 'the exploitation of intellectual and computer-related technologies to improve creativity in decisions that really matter'.

A useful framework for research on DSS is introduced in Sprague (1980). He discusses the perspective of the end-user, the builder and the toolsmith from which a DSS can be viewed. In accordance with this distinction the concept of a DSS-generator is put forward to bridge the gap between general tools and specific DSS. Sprague distinguishes as the main components of a DSS a data base, a model base, and an intermediate software system which interfaces the DSS with the user.

Within the data base for decision support one can distinguish between external data from public data sources, administrative data produced by the transaction processing system, and internal data created by personal computing.
The models in the model base as envisaged by Sprague are mostly of the equation type: A great number of so called corporate models or financial models consists of definition equations and behavioural equations. Econometric models also consists of equation models. Another category is formed by optimization models based on (non)linear, dynamic or stochastic programming.
A first generation of so-called DSS generators focuses on equation models with data base and interactive facilities like data-, model- and text manipulation, cf. Klein and Manteau (1983) and Berquist and McLean (1983). By now, the integrated facilities are not only offered on mainframes, but also on micro-computers together with facilities for 'down-loading from and uploading to central computer systems through data communication'.
A conceptual framework is put forward by Bonczek et al. (1981). They replace the components mentioned, by the concepts of a language system, a knowledge system and a problem processing system. A language system is the sum of all linguistic facilities made available to the decision maker by a DSS. A knowledge system is a DSS's body of knowledge about a problem domain. The problem processing system is the mediating mechanism between expressions of knowledge in the knowledge system and expressions of problems in the language system.

The framework put forward by Bonczek et al. makes it easy to relate the

work in the field of articifial intelligence to DSS. We define an 'expert
system as a computer system containing organised knowledge, both factual
and heuristic, that contains some specific area of human expertise, and
that is able to produce inferences for the user', see Chang, Melamud and
Seabrook (1983).

When one looks upon an inference system as a special kind of problem
processing system and upon the knowledge base as the knowledge system, then
expert systems fit neatly into the framework. Along this line a school of
researchers focuses on the representation of knowledge for decision support, cf. Fox (1984), Bonczek et al. (1983). The relevance of epistemology
to improve decision—making processes is addressed by e.g. Lee (1983).
However, as Stamper (1984) remarks: 'Our growing technical capacity to
produce, store and distribute information is no guarantee of the information's organisational and social usefulness. The trend towards intelligent,
knowledge—based systems cannot solve the problem: instead it could well make
the problem worse by disguising poor information under a cloak of logical
self—consistency'.

Although DSS may provide a link on the path from traditional information
processing towards knowledge engineering, we may recall that expert systems
are always based on historical expertise. The search for expertise should
not detract attention from grasping creativity—processes in new, unexperi-
enced problem situations.

Although the interest for DSS should be welcomed, a clearer delineation of
the concept of DSS is needed in order to make it a potentially rich research track. Rich, in the sense that it can foster the effectiveness and
efficiency of organisational decision—making. Keen has questioned the role
of modelling and quantitative models in stimulating creative thinking. If
the OR discipline is taking up the DSS line, it should pick up this challenge and focus on creative dicision—making and learning on the merge of
MIS and OR/Management Science.

One line is to focus on heuristics from an AI perspective. Another melting
point could be model management and model representation. A third line is
to take up the process of problem solving in a knowledge—based framework.
Therefore, Sol (1985) extended the frameworks presented by Sprague and
Bonczek into a new one, see Figure 1.

Sol proposes to direct DSS—research to the concept of DSS—generators or, more generally, DSS design environments. One of the main reasons for this choice is the lack of generalizability in dealing with specific decision support systems. Another reason is that one has to address all stages in the process of problem solving, not only at the conceptual level.

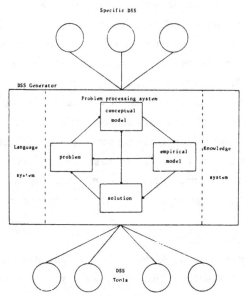

Figure 1. Extended framework of the one presented by Sprague and Bonczek

The trends mentioned above are clearly reflected in this proceedings of the Second Mini Euro Conference, held in Lunteren, The Netherlands, 17—20 November 1985.

The developments on the edge of DSS and Operations Research are depicted by D.B. Hertz by addressing the virtues of Models: Operations, Expert and Intelligent Manifestation. He sees a hybrid merge of rule—based, knowledge—based, algorithm—based and heuristic—based systems to provide advice, diagnosis and analysis for decision—makers.

Philosophical and methodological issues around the conference theme are addressed broadly by A. Bosman when he asks whether DSS is a vision or a discipline. He argues that DSS can only become a discipline when we focus on the process of decision—making as a separate field of study.
H.J. Lüthi and R. Pfeifer discuss the question: ˊDSS and ES: A Complemen-

tary Relationship? They provide a conceptual framework to compare the two in the context of management problems. They conclude that DSS and ES should be considered as complementary concepts.

H.A. Kurstedt illustrates that expert systems with their replicative orientation are of a lower order than responsive, intelligent management tools.

Another important theme is modeling and model management.

R.M. Lee presents 'A logic Programming Approach to Building Planning and Simulation Models'. He shows that this approach is able to represent to dynamic programming, decision trees, Pert—networks and discrete event simulation.

A knowledge based formulation of linear planning models is presented by M. Binbasiogen and M. Jarke. They express that under current AI—technology, model formulation cannot be made fully general and user—friendly at the same time. A problem—solving approach seems fruitfull.

H. Koppelaar illustrates how shortcomings of quantitative models can be overcome by linguistic explanatory analysis of decision support situations. The issue of specific modelling support environments is taken up by U. Maschtera. Useful support environments may contain natural language interfaces, abstraction aids, coupling operators, modelling expertise, and validation aids.

The conference theme clearly heads to various design issues: The efficiency of parallel knowledge processing is addressed by H.J. van de Herik et al. through the example of 'Heuristics in the Abbot Mark Problem'.

R.M. O'Keefe et al. present 'Microcomputer Based Expert Systems Shells: the spreadsheets of Artificial Intelligence'. They argue that declarative programming and knowledge based methods have applications far beyond expert systems, as illustrated by spreadsheets.

Extensions to the Expert System Shell 'Delfi—2' are presented by H. de Swaan—Arons et al. They show that shells should enable various formalisms for knowledge representation.

G.L. Doukidis and R.J. Paul put forward ASPES as a skeletal Pascal Expert System. It consists of a general purpose inference engine to which the user adds his domain specific knowledge base.

Important applications are emerging:

J.C.R. Pomerol et al. describe 'An Intelligent Support System for Strategic Decisions'. The main feature of this system is a scenario developer which is connected to various expert systems.

P. Gallo et al. elaborate a knowledge-based approach to business planning.
They highlight critical conditions for the correct and effective design of
support systems.
J. Kazimierczak addresses 'Knowledge Acquisition from User Programs by
Computers'
J.J.J. van Beek presents a prototyping approch to the 'Analysis of Estab-
lishment Potential'. The system developed combines knowledge on esta-
blishment assessment with heuristics to look for new establishments.

Finally Ch.H. Kriebel evaluates the evidence created by these contributions.
He discusses the shaping of management decision science with intelligent
technology. He illustrates that the shape of management decision science has
emerged through the discipline of mathematics and the medium of information
technology towards closer linkages between the fields of operations research
and psychology/computer science-based problem solving paradigms in artificial intelligence.
The contributions clearly show that the potential for impact and payoff is
great.

References

Berquist, J.W., and McLean, E.R. (1983), 'Integrated data analysis and
    management systems: An APL-based decision support system', in: H.G. Sol,
    (ed), Processes and Tools for Decision Support, North-Holland, Amster-
    dam.

Bonczek, R.H., Holsapple, C.W., and Whinston, A.B. (1981), Foundations of
    Decision Support Systems, Academic Press New York.

Bonczek, R.H., Holsapple, C.W., and Whinston, A.B. (1983), 'Specification
    of modeling and knowledge in decision support systems', in: H.G. Sol,
    (ed), Processes and Tools for Decision Support, North-Holland, Amster-
    dam.

Elam, J. et al. (1985), 'A vision for DSS', Proceedings DSS-85.

Fox, M.S. (1984), 'Knowledge representation for decision support', Pro-
    ceedings of the IFIP 8.3 Working Conference on Knowledge Representation
    for Decision Support Systems, Durham.

Ginzberg, M.J., and Stohr, E.A. (1982), 'Decision support systems: Issues
    and perspectives', in: M.J. Ginzberg, W. Reitman and E.A. Stohr (eds.),
    Decision Support Systems, North-Holland, Amsterdam.

Klein, H.K., and Hirschheim, R. (1985), 'Consequentialist perspective of decision support systems´, Decision Support Systems 1 (1).

Klein, H.K., and Manteau, A. (1983), Optrans: A tool for implementation of decision support systems´, Decision Support Systems 1 (1).

Sol, H.G. (1983), Processes and Tools for Decision Support: Inferences for Future Developments, North—Holland, Amsterdam, 1983.

Sol, H.G. (1985), DSS: Buzzword or OR Challenge?, European Journal of Operational Reseach 22 (1985), 1—8.

Sprague, R.H. (1980), ´A framework for research on decision support systems´, in: G. Fick, and R.H. Sprague, (eds.), Decision Support Systems: Issues and Challenges, Pergamon Pres, Oxford.

MODELS: OPERATIONAL, EXPERT, AND INTELLIGENT

David Bendel Hertz
Distinguished Professor, University of Miami
Director, Intelligent Computer Systems
Research Institute
P.O. Box 248235, Coral Gables, FL 33124, USA

ABSTRACT. Operations research (OR) has developed both formal and heuristic solutions to a broad spectrum of real-world issues.   Artificial intelligence (AI) through its expert systems (ES) approaches has recently begun to attack similar problems. I believe that AI/ES and OR applications have similar objectives to permit the executive or decision maker to improve his understanding of, and take desirable actions in a particular operational domain. Both must build computable models which have an equivalent model structure. The surface differences are programming devices that may be stripped away. In the not too distant future, all significant programs intended to provide advice, diagnosis and analysis to aid decision-makers will be hybrid. That is, AI rule-based, knowledge-based and OR algorithm-based, heuristic-based expert systems will be joined to accomplish the desired end-result as efficiently as possible. This will be achieved through the construction of programming languages calling on the combined knowledge of AI, OR, and the computer science communities.

1. INTRODUCTION

As many of my colleagues and long-time friends in this audience know, my connections with operations research go back to the early days of OR, to the Operations Research Society of America, of which I was a founding member, and to the first IFORS conference at Oxford.

Almost twenty years ago I wrote:

Computer technology permits the creation of an information network which, like the human central nervous system, is not merely a network of communicating cells but essentially a unifying mechanism for the organization of experience. This means increasing coordination of operations, revising the historical tendency toward progressive fragmentation and subdivision that

9

H. G. Sol et al. (eds.), Expert Systems and Artificial Intelligence in Decision Support Systems, 9–22.

made mechanization and rationalization of
production possible in the past.

Consequently, top management comes under the
greatest pressure. "The senior executives are
among the hardest pressed and persistently
harassed groups in human history. Electronics not
only requires far deeper knowledge and faster
interplay, but has made the harmonizing of ...
schedules ... as rigorous as that demanded of the
members of large symphony orchestras. And, the
satisfactions are often just as few for the
manager as for symphony instrumentalist, since a
player in a big orchestra can not hear the music
that reaches the audience. He only gets noise." (1)

In the intervening years I have been exposed to most
of the arguments regarding the dividing lines between
applied and pragmatic operations research model building and
the mathematical development of formal solutions to the
problems posed by these applied models and their peculiar
and particular solution spaces. In recent years these
arguments have begun to include research and model building
in cognitive science and what is known as artificial
intelligence and expert systems (AI/ES). The models,
whether built in FORTRAN, PL1, or ADA with OR algorithms
and heuristics, or in LISP, PROLOG, or OPS5 with AE/ES
algorithms and heuristics, are usually intended to deal with
an area of the world that poses a user more or less
realistically about some aspects of the problem. The users
of the model may or may not act on the information supplied
by the model.

2. THE COMPUTER AND THE BRAIN

In her book, _Machines Who Think_, Pamela McCorduck
reports on a conference held at Dartmouth in the summer of
1956 supported by the Rockerfeller Foundation on the basis
of a proposal which read, in part:

We propose that a two-month, ten-man study of
artificial intelligence be carried out .... The
study is to proceed on the basis of the conjecture
that _every aspect of learning or any other feature
of intelligence_ can in principle be so precisely
described that a machine can be made to simulate
it. (2)

The mathematicians, psychologists, electrical
engineers, and computer experts who attended came away from
that conference with the feeling that there was a community

of people who were seriously interested in tackling the
challenges this premise presented. McCorduck writes,
"Artificial intelligence, if it wasn't quite a legitimate
scientific field, had at least emerged as an entity about
which one could ask questions: 'Was it a science? High
jinks? Both?'" (2a) The immediate results were the
initiation of a number of projects along with lots of
prophecies suggesting that anything the brain could do could
also be done by an appropriately programmed computer.
Twenty-five years was considered the time scale for
significant results: in language translation, world
championship chess, creative thinking.

        The twenty-five years have passed; we now know that
these tasks are much harder than had been thought or
predicted. Most of the more sweeping predictions have not
come to pass (no world computer chess champion, just
checkers; no significant success in language translation).
But we've also learned that AI is not a joke or a passing
fancy. What has happened is that the continuing work in
developing computer hardware and software, along with
studies of human cognition, speech and language, has led to
the conclusion that for now, "real" thinking is beyond the
capabilities of machines and programmers. But something
close to it is feasible, and that something turns out not to
be "high jinks" or trivial. This "something" -- AI -- has
begun to achieve results that are sufficiently serious and
significant to alert corporate, institutional and
governmental executives to real opportunities.

        The artificial science researchers have constructed
various kinds of computer languages to help build models
that, it is suggested, emulate some forms of mental
behavior. These are intended to assist in undertaking and
diagnosing various kinds of difficult thought problems, and
assist in making decisions in a wide variety of situations,
and to contribute to the implementation planning process for
computerization of intelligent activity. There are those
who think that artificial intelligence/expert systems and OR
are one and the same -- just with a different point of view.
On the other side of the debate there are those who believe
that the two viewpoints are irreconcilable: so different as
to practically obviate any connections or bridges between
the two. Having decided several years ago that AI (there was
then no ES, except those supplied in operational models,
which were indeed expert, and even called such), was going
to be of considerable significance to the further
development of OR, I began serious study of its subject
matter.(3) One partial result has been, as some of you may
know, that IFORS president, Dr. Heiner Muller-Merbach and I
have written a joint letter to the IFORS membership, in
which we suggest common roots for AI/ES and OR.(4) So you
know my own as we begin. But in this presentation I wish to

deal with the heart of both the dialectic argument and the
more informal possibilities that more useful models could
contribute to both sides by analyzing the kinds of models we
might term OPERATIONAL, INTELLIGENT and EXPERT.
    The new computer technologies of hardware, firmware,
and "smart" software can provide the eyes and ears to change
the customary ritual and put the executive in front of this
"orchestra". I assume that AI/ES and OR have similar
objectives: to permit the executive or decision maker, who
may be a commander, analyst, or diagnostician, to improve
his understanding of, and take desirable actions in some
domain or part of his world.(5) These model-building
processes, at bottom, are about behavior _and_ about science
applied to thought. With these assumptions in mind I shall
assert:

    (a) that these objectives require model building
    processes whether the end results are intended for
    decision makers, analysts or diagnosticians.

    (b) that all such models have the same formal
    structure.

    (c) that the differences that appear on the
    surface are programming devices that may be
    stripped away to leave the underlying framework
    bare.

    Parenthetically, the results of these processes will, I
indicate that none of these programs, OR or AI/ES, reveal
very much, if anything, about the human brain's
methodologies for accomplishing the same kinds of ends.
    In the event, the three assertions lead me to make a
prediction, possibly rash, but certainly worth putting
forward here. I suggest that in the not too distant future
all significant programs that are intended to accomplish the
purposes of advice, diagnosis and analysis to aid humans will
be hybrid: that is, there will be expert systems, rule-
based, knowledge-based; and there will be expert systems,
algorithm-based, heuristic-based; these systems will be
joined to accomplish the end result as efficiently as
possible. Simulation programs, along with dynamic
allocation programs, along with production rules, frames,
and schemas will form a network that will solve a higher
order of operational problems than any of these alone.
FORTRAN 77 will join with OPS5, PASCAL with PROLOG, among
others to make the task of aiding human thought faster, more
understandable, more useful, and more complete. Let us see
how this is an inevitable consequence of thirty of forty
years of parallel thought.
    It is as though we were able to hold our problem-

solving thought processes up to a strangely constructed mirror that produced a set of deformed and transformed "programs" which came close to giving us what we believed were "intelligent" or "operational" answers to questions.

I should note, of course, that some of these models may represent purely formal constructions, even mathematical theorems and proofs, in addition to the more pragmatic descriptions of the human designs of a brain or thought emulation process for depicting some part of the outside world to itself and others. Such models, of course, may also describe organization, competition, or the use of computers for decision analysis, command, communications, and control in the institutions of our society.

3. BUILDERS OF OPERATIONAL, EXPERT, AND INTELLIGENT MODELS

OR has given attention to OPERATIONAL models, i.e., those that describe the expected consequences of alternative actions taken in the real world along with estimates of possible benefits, and costs of such actions. Inventory, queuing, resource allocation, among others are well known examples of such operational models that offer suggestions and analyses for action. The models may be based upon algorithmic and/or heuristic formulations.

AI, on the other hand has attempted to construct models that would deal with the symbol-oriented world of human mental behavior, psychology, language, and thought. Such models have, perhaps unhappily been designated as artificially INTELLIGENT. If the models are designed to help the user take actions in the domains to which they applied, they are called EXPERT SYSTEMS. Dreyfus, in discussing the difficulties involved in building such systems writes:

> All everyday problems [for which we try to build models in OR, AI/ES] -- whether in language translation, problem-solving or pattern recognition -- come back to these two basic problems: (a) how to restrict the class of possibly relevant facts while preserving generality, and (b) how to choose among possibly relevant facts those which are actually relevant.(6)

Both AI/ES and OR scientists try to accomplish this objective by thinking about how the human mind might choose and process perceived sensations and turns them into new facts or reinforces old facts, in order to arrive at useful conclusions. The outcome of such thought is a model that can be formally or intuitively related to some domain in which the particular observed mind is working. If it were

to be sufficiently formal the model might achieve some
results that the brain working <u>directly</u> on the problem might
not be able to accomplish.

Let us juxtapose two models. A useful OR example that
we will all immediately understand is linear programming.
An example from AI/ES, less familiar perhaps to the OR
practitioner, is production rule-based programming. Both of
these models have formal aspects; both have been developed
from pragmatic examples; both have similar objectives: to
provide assistance to decision makers, analysts and
diagnosticians, in difficult problem-solving environments.
Except for the very simplest of problems posed in terms
appropriate to these models, it is unlikely that the human
brain would provide quick and correct solutions (e.g., in a
linear program with many thousands of variables and
constraints; in a production rule diagnostic, or fault-
finding system with many thousands of rules).

To a certain extent, these examples strongly support
the first of my assertions: that objectives such as "doing
the work of experts" requires the construction of models.
For example, application systems created with production-
rule models or systems are "expert systems" or "knowledge-
based systems." It is the usual intention of those who
design such systems that there be sufficient domain-specific
knowledge (representations of the real world, if you will) and
rules about how the world operates, so that, when programmed
in this production system structure (language) it will
perform tasks in that domain at the level of a human
expert.(7)

4. THE UNIFICATION OF PROBLEM-SOLVING PROCESSES

The distance between the development of a mathematical
algorithm, as Danzig's for the linear programming problem
(and thence a model for solving classes of problems in this
domain) and developing some languages for computer
programming that permit such achievements as expertly
diagnosing bacterial infections and prescribing treatment
for them as a consultant to a physician, (as Shortliffe has
done in MYCIN), lies more in the mind of man than in the CPU
of a computer.(8)(9) The linear programming model has
proliferated into a variety of more-or-less open
formulations that no longer guarantee an optimum solution
(e.g., non-linear, and chance-constrained models) that
become relatively close to the AE/ES end result. Although
significantly different on the surface, as I indicated in my
earlier assertion the differences that appear on the
surface are programming devices that may be stripped away to
leave the underlying framework bare.

Building models for solving problems confronts the

human brain with a broad set of tasks. Building models of
the behavior of the human brain clearly means that the brain
is attempting to model itself. If we define the brain's
capability to do this sort of thing as "intelligence," then
we are devising the concept of "intelligence" to explain
itself, since the devices by which we propose to understand
intelligent behavior must themselves be products of that
very behavior. Although scientists know a good deal about
the anatomy of the human brain, very little is understood
about the way it actually goes about dealing with the
complexities of problem solving. The situation is familiar
to all of us who have had to communicate with computers. A
computer accepts as inputs only symbols from a given list
that has been constructed in advance, by the user or others.
The symbols must be used in accordance with certain given
rules. This is accepted as given in computer languages.
But what we call "natural" language, as used in human
communication, is also subject to rules. But what rules?
We are far from understanding exactly how we do understand
one another in the face of noise and ambiguity: we have not
yet been able to make the rules explicit.

   The computer acts on its given inputs just as the human
does -- that is, it follows grammatical rules in parsing its
language, <u>except</u> that we recognize that it is "stupid,"
precisely because we know that the computer language has a
specific, given, fully specified vocabulary with rules that
are, or can be, completely stated. (But, one may certainly
add here, even then the computer and programmer separately
or together manage to construct and run programs with bugs
and glitches).

   Now, because the computer language is a formal one, as
we might expect, it can be represented mathematically.
Mathematics, of course, is a human activity, like
linguistics, or designing computer languages. "At the same
time mathematics has, as a special feature, the ability to
be well described by a formal language, which in some sense
mirrors its contents precisely.... The possibility of
putting a mathematical discovery into a formal language is
the test of whether it is fully understood."(10)

   It is true, in general, that knowledge is cumulative
and, as far as can be determined, to a certain extent self-
corrective. For example we have continuously improved our
mathematical tools for dealing with the world of stochastic,
fuzzy, or uncertain events or processes. "Real-life
knowledge bases are very complex. They are built of
propositions, production rules, and frames (of information)
that, together capture the knowledge of the field (domain)
as data structures in the memory of the computer" See,
e.g., Negoita, (11). Polya distinguishes between
demonstrative and plausible reasoning from what we know call
knowledge bases.(12) Demonstrative reasoning is

"impersonal, universal, self-sufficient, and
definitive....final, machinelike." By contrast, plausible
reasoning (for which in computer programs we would use
inductive inference engines) is, in Polya's words, "vague,
provisional, specifically `human'.... plausible reasoning
leaves indeterminate a highly relevant point: the `strength'
or `weight' of the conclusion. This weight may depend not
only on the clarified (logically justified) grounds such as
those expressed in the premises, but also on unclarified
unexpressed grounds somewhere in the background of the
person who draws the conclusion." (13) Polya suggests that
"a person has a `background,' a machine has not. His own
(somewhat clouded) plausible inference (in 1953) was "that
you can build a machine to draw demonstrative conclusions
for you, but I think that you can never draw a machine that
will draw plausible inferences." Indeed: this is precisely
what inventory theory does in OR, and what medical
diagnostic and similar programs do in AE/ES.

The fundamental issue is that life confronts us with
the problem of devising mental or machine models for
operational systems, that is, systems of interacting
physical, human, and animal behavior in the real world. The
utility of the so-called inference engine (to be used in an
AI/ES model) hinges on the way we approach this problem.
How many (alternate) inference engines are available? Real
systems usually contain probabilistic and decision-making
elements, so that the resulting models are necessarily quite
complex and often require enormous simplifications --
literally, in the chess players' sense of that term -- if
the "game" is to become tractable. In a well-known OR
example that attempted to deal with this kind of problem,
Bellman proposed a recursive formal "engine" to deal with
dynamic decision problems in which the outcomes (e.g.,
stability or disaster) dependent upon the recursive
interactions of the probabilistic variables.(14) But this
model simply posed the larger question of how to deal with
the very large set of problems that could be formulated in
the dynamic programming technique than could be solved.

Naturally, questions like this have been faced in many
ways. At about the same time that Bellman was offering
dynamic programming John McCarthy proposed that all human
knowledge be given a formal, homogeneous representation, the
first-order calculus. And J. A. Robinson followed with a
logical, machine-oriented theorem that many thought would be
the "engine" which would turn this ideal into practical
computer programs.(15)(16)

But, of course, the world always seemed to turn out to
be more complex and less amenable to attack. New and more
effective languages for new formalizations (mathematical) of
real world problems and for programming machines (e.g. LISP,
FORTRAN, ADA, OPS5, among others) to attack these problems

were visualized to the the key to attacking this complexity.
Some linguists hypothesized that a language may indeed
control the way one thinks, indeed on what one can
think.(17)
      For these reasons I assert that models both in OR
and in AI/ES have the same "formal" structure -- that is
they represent a unified problem-solving process, either
logically deductive or inductive. But, you will say, so
what; these are entirely different approaches to different
kinds of problems. We must examine this objection from the
point of view of the problem solver and the programmer.
Models are constructed to solve problems. Programming
languages for computers are themselves "models" built to
solve the problem of directing a machine to act in a way
that will carry out a series of steps dictated by models
that have been constructed to attack certain classes of
problems. As we have indicated, different languages set in
motion different thought patterns regarding methods of
solving particular problems. But this does not necessarily
prevent the formal structures from being equivalent so long
as they are languages intended to operate a digital
computing device. The wired machine has "predispositional"
characteristics that "look for" a processing language in
order to perform its functions, in a general sense similar
to the readiness of the brain to undertake tasks that are
describable in one or another human language, as Chomsky and
others have suggested. (18)
      Of course, this does not mean that language A may be as
efficient as language B in attacking a specific problem
class (or even that it may be able to solve that kind of
problem). But if it can do so, then, it can be shown to be
formally equivalent with respect to that class of problem
solving. Thus, "A programming language is a notation, and,
as such serves to record and assist the development of human
thought in a particular direction -- the formulation of
processes to be carried out on a computer."(19)   Ledgard
and Marcotty illustrate the application of very different
language types to a specific problem, the "Eight Queens
Problem."(20)
      The Eight Queens problems requires that eight chess
queens (with the usual powers) be arranged on a standard
chess board so that no queen can capture any other. (One
queen can capture another if the two are in the same row,
column, or diagonal). There are 4.4 billion ways of
arranging eight queens so a brute force solution would be
quite inefficient. Thus, there are various approaches to
the solution. Ledgard and Marcotty show how two completely
different types of programming languages, one based on
PASCAL, the other on LISP, can be used to program one such
approach. In the PASCAL case, the components of the arrays
describing the status of the board, as a queen is added or

moved, are established by assignment, and then maintained by
procedures and functions utilizing global variables.
Boolean valued arrays are introduced and looping statements
are used to iterate over the various board configurations.
    By contrast a LISP type program that finds the same
configuration as a solution, with approximately the same
efficiency. In this case there is no use of assignment,
looping control structures, or global variables. Rather the
solution is a sequence of function definitions. A list of
integers giving row positions of queens that are safely
placed in each column represents the board configuration,
starting with an integer list placing the first queen in the
first column and proceeding to add queens until the
objective is reached. The lesson here is illustrated by
Chomsky's assertion:

> The human mind is endowed with some set of
> principles that can be put to work when certain
> questions are posed, a certain level of
> understanding has been achieved, and certain
> evidence is available, to select a narrow class
> of possible theories.... Evidently the scope and
> limits of knowledge are intimately related. Thus,
> if there are principles that make possible the
> acquisition of rich systems of knowledge and
> belief, then these very principles limit the class
> of accessible theories.(21)

5. THE WORLD OF MODELS AND MODELS OF THE WORLD

    Laplace has cautioned us that "It is difficult to
estimate the probability of the results of induction." But
this is an extremely difficult issue in real life modeling
of anything. And the usual OR and AI/ES models are either
largely deductive (in which case, assuming no errors in the
processing, the answer is in the inputs and is guaranteed to
follow from them), or where inductive, is at best, very
fuzzy indeed.
    Zadeh, the developer of fuzzy set theory, raises the
the underlying problem of production-rule, knowledge-base
systems, that applies just as well to OR non-stochastic
models. He states that where the "fuzziness" of the
knowledge base is ignored (since neither predicate logic nor
probability based methods provides a satisfactory basis for
dealing with it), the "fuzzy" facts are generally
manipulated as if they were nonfuzzy, the methodologies lead
to questionable conclusions.(22) In his view the certainty
factors that may be assigned to the facts must be treated as
distributed (i.e., "fuzzy") rather than some crisp set of
numbers. However, Zadeh's algorithms for dealing with such

distributions of uncertainty yields less than satisfactory
end results for decision makers and diagnosticians.
Embedded simulations operating on knowledge based systems
using formal dynamic type models and production-rule systems
may be the only effective solution for the long run. Thus,
I visualize, the development of hybrid-system language,
constructed to run on Class VI and parallel processing type
supercomputers, that will permit the model builder to
construct pragmatic approximations to his domain or world
and run this program in reasonable time frames to achieve
"plausible inferences" about that world.

6. CONCLUSIONS: MODELS OF THE FUTURE AND THE FUTURE OF MODELS

        Successful executives certainly understand how to
apply their mental skills to attack and resolve problems;
how to challenge and direct people toward management
objectives; how to determine what objectives ought to be
achieved. They know that people learn and acquire knowledge
by obtaining and manipulating information. The processes
and capabilities involved in all these activities require
intelligent behavior, or just generally intelligence.
        Enlarging the scope of intelligent executive behavior
throughout history has been accomplished with new technical
devices -- the telegraph, telephone, bookkeeping machine,
among many others come to mind. Each has affected
management style significantly. A revealing example of what
leaders must do when they do not have adequate technology is
the fact that not until the second half of the seventeenth
century did senior military commanders start taking their
place behind, rather than in front of their men. Martin van
Creveld notes in his excellent book on the evolution of
modern command structures:

        Taken as a whole, present-day military
    forces, for all the imposing array of electronic
    gadgetry at their disposal, give no evidence
    whatsoever of being one whit more capable of
    dealing with the information needed for the
    command process than were their predecessors a
    century, or even a millennium ago. ... To believe
    that the wars of the future, thanks to some
    extraordinary technological advances yet to take
    place in computers or remotely controlled sensors,
    will be less opaque and therefore more subject to
    rational calculations than their predecessors is
    sheer delusion.... The quest for certainty will
    logically end only when there is nothing left to
    be certain about.(23)

Obviously, a commander who wielded a spear in the front ranks of his army cannot have exercised much more than the -- admittedly very important -- moral functions of his job. Armies that were commanded in this way either could not be subjected to close control during battle or else were so simple in structure and function that no such control was required. This simplicity, in turn, was both cause and effect of the fact that millennia passed without the technical means of communication undergoing any fundamental change. The telegraph, the telephone, and now the computer have turned that simplicity into what some now call the nightmare, and others the magnificent vistas of computerized command, control, and communications.

The pragmatic requirement is that we must use computers to operate along side the human mind: reasoning using computers; computer assisted decision-making; computer programs that can augment the most important problem solving resource of all -- knowledge. We must address getting at and codifying know what and know how that resides in human (expert) heads in order to use that natural intelligence to develop computer systems that can help attack and resolve significant business and institutional problems. For this purpose we must construct models that will permit deeper understanding and improved decision making in our increasingly complex world.

This can only be achieved, in my opinion, through the construction of languages that call on the combined knowledge of the artificial intelligence, operations research, and computer science communities.

MODELS: OPERATIONAL, EXPERT, AND INTELLIGENT
David Bendel Hertz

REFERENCES

) Hertz, David B., NEW POWER FOR MANAGEMENT, McGraw-Hill, New York, 1969 pp. 184-185.

) McCorduck, Pamela, MACHINES WHO THINK, W. H. Freeman & Company, San Francisco, 1979, p.93, emphasis added.

a) Id., p. 109.

) Hertz, (1) p. 78.

) Muller-Merbach, Heiner, and Hertz, David B., "Letter to Members of IFORS", IFORS Bulletin, 1985.

) Newell, Allan and Simon, Herbert, Human Problem Solving, Prentice-Hall, Englewood Cliffs, NJ 1973.

) Dreyfus, Herbert, What Computers Can't Do: A Critique of Artificial Reason, 1972, p.171, quoted in McCorduck, (2), p.185.

) Brownston, Farrell, Kant, and Martin, Programming Expert Systems in OPS5: An Introduction to Rule-Based Programming, Addison-Wesley, Reading, MA.,1985, pp.4-13.

) Dantzig, G. B., Linear Programming and Extensions, Princeton University Press, Princeton, N. J. 1963.

) Buchanan, Bruce G. and Shortliffe, Edward H., Rule-Based Expert Systems, The MYCIN Experiments, Addison-Wesley Press, Reading, MA, 1984.

0) Davis, Phillip J. and Hersh, Reuben, The Mathematical Experience", Birkhauser, Boston, MA, 1981, p.247.

1) Negoita, Constantin Virgil, Expert Systems and Fuzzy Systems, Benjamin/Cummings Publishing Co., Menlo Park, CA, 1985, p. 100.

2) Polya, G., Patterns of Plausible Inference, Vol. I, Princeton University Press, Princeton, NJ, 1954, Chapter XV, "The Calculus of Probability and the Logic of Plausible Reasoning," esp. pp.109-112.

3) Id.,pp.115-116.

(14) Bellman, R., _Dynamic Programming_, Princeton University Press, Princeton, NJ 1957.

(15) McCarthy, John, "Programs with Common Sense," in M. Minsky, ed., _Semantic Information Processing_, MIT Press, Cambridge, Mass. 1968, pp. 403-409.

(16) Robinson, J. A., "A Machine-Oriented Logic Based on the Resolution Principle," _Journal of the Association for Computing Machinery_, Vol. 12, no. 1, 1965.

(17) Whorf, Benjamin, _Language, Thought and Reality_, MIT Press, Cambridge, Mass. 1956.

(18) Chomsky, Noam, _Rules and Representations_, Columbia University Press, New York, 1980, Chap. 5.

(19) Ledgard, Henry and Marcotty, Michael, _The Programming Language Landscape_, Science Research Associates, Chicago, 1981, p.419.

(20) Id., pp. 298-311.

(21) Chomsky, (18) pp. 250-251.

(22) Zadeh, Lofti A., "The Role of Fuzzy Logic in the Management of Uncertainty in Expert Systems," _Fuzzy Sets and Systems_, Vol. 11, pp. 199-227, 1983.

(23) Van Creveld, Martin. _Command in War_, Harvard University Press, 1985, p.265-267.

DECISION SUPPORT SYSTEMS:
A DISCIPLINE OR A VISION?

A. Bosman
Information Systems Research Group
University of Groningen
P.O. Box 800
9700 AV Groningen
The Netherlands

ABSTRACT. Two instruments are being used to answer the question whether the problem area of DSS can be regarded as a discipline. These instruments are: a worldview and a construct paradigm. The construct paradigm is related to the model building process as used in DSS. After applying both instruments, we have come to the conclusion that the problem area of DSS cannot be regarded as a discipline. A conclusion that is valid for nearly all fields studying parts of organizational processes. Suggestions are given how to define the process of decision-making as a separate field of study.

1. INTRODUCTION.

A lot of discussion is going on about a problem area that is called decision support systems (DSS), see Elam et al. (1985), Klein and Hirschheim (1985), Dery and Mock (1985), Sol (1985) and Stamper (1985).
Some authors see this problem area as a discipline, others describe it as a buzzword for software of all types. As Sol (1985) points out: 'It is remarkable that the term DSS is much used without a very strict definition of its content. Many writers seem to approach DSS as a philosophy to seek a useful complementarity between technological tools and human judgement and discretion.' We do not wish to give another variant of a discussion about definitions of DSS in this paper. Instead we'll try to answer the question whether or not the problem area of DSS can be regarded as a discipline. We think it is useful to try and answer this question because the answer can be used to structure the discussion about the sense or nonsense of DSS.
The question whether a certain problem area can be regarded as a discipline can be described, using DSS terms, as ill-structured. To answer this question we use two instruments. These instruments are:

23

H. G. Sol et al. (eds.), Expert Systems and Artificial Intelligence in Decision Support Systems, 23–39.
© 1987 by D. Reidel Publishing Company.

a worldview or paradigm and the way descriptions of problems are made. This last instrument can also be described as the model building process used or as the content of a construct paradigm. In section 2 we give a survey of DSS definitions to enable us to find a set of attributes that is relevant for the definition of the problem area. We divided the set of attributes in two subsets, viz. the organizational and the information processing one. In section 3 we discuss the organizational set emphasizing the construct paradigm and therefore the model construction procedures used in the DSS problem area. We think that most of the attributes used to describe DSS are irrelevant and suggest to use other attributes in the organizational set. Section 3 covers the main part of this paper. Section 4 deals with the information processing set. To our opinion, the information processing set should be derived from the organizational one and not the other way round as is more or less common in literature. In section 5 we conclude that the problem area of DSS cannot be regarded as a discipline. We'll give a number of suggestions how to define a discipline of which DSS could be a specialization.

Visions on a problem area are always welcome, especially when a problem area is not recognized as a discipline. However, visions are difficult to recognize when a frame of reference about the problem area, e.g. in the form of a discipline, is lacking. Therefore, we do not deal with possible visions in this paper. (See for visions the authors mentioned at the beginning of this section). Our conclusion that the problem area of DSS cannot be regarded as a discipline, has been derived from a vision. Not a vision on DSS, but one of a methodological nature, viz. how to construct models in social sciences. (See for a more or less comparable approach, Mitroff and Kilmann (1978)). As other visions, ours might be incorrect. However, our approach has the advantage that we have restricted the discussion to two disciplines, viz. epistemology and methodology.

2. A SURVEY

There are numerous definitions of DSS. Surveys of these definitions are given and discussed by Ginzberg and Stohr (1982) and Bennett (1983). Some definitions will be presented in this section. These definitions are given to be able to distinguish the main attributes of DSS. Sets of these attributes are discussed in the following sections. Keen and Scott Morton (1978, p.1) state that DSS:' represent a point of view on the role of the computer in the management decision making process. Decision support implies the use of computers to:
1. Assist managers in their decision process in semistructured tasks.
2. Support, rather than replace, managerial judgment.
3. Improve the effectiveness of decisionmaking rather than its efficiency'.
According to Ginzberg and Stohr (1982, p.10), Alter (1980) defines DSS by contrasting it with traditional electronic data processing (EDP) systems on five dimensions:

1. Use: active (DSS) vs. passive (EDP).
2. User: line, staff and management (DSS) vs. clerk (EDP).
3. Goal: overall effectiveness (DSS) vs. mechanical efficiency (EDP).
4. Time horizon: present and future (DSS) vs. past (EDP).
5. Objective: flexibility (DSS) vs. consistency (EDP).

Thierauf (1982, p.79) gives a definition of DSS using attributes of the system that are necessary to accomplish the DSS objectives. He remarks: 'Decision support systems allow the decision maker to combine his or her judgment with computer output in a human/machine interface for producing meaningful information to support the decision-making process. They are capable of solving all types of problems (structured, semistructured and unstructured) and use query capabilities to obtain information by request. As deemed appropriate, they utilize mathematical and statistical models as well as data base elements for solving the problem under study. From an overall standpoint, decision support systems can be looked upon as an integral part of the decision maker's approach to problem solving that stresses a broad perspective by employing the 'management by perception' principle.'

By stressing the importance of attributes of DSS, it is possible to define the contents of a decision support system. A well known example: the components of a decision support system as specified by Sprague (1980) and Sprague and Carlson (1982). These components are: a dialog system, a data base system and a model base system.

Recently the emphasis in defining DSS has been changing to achieve the ultimate goal of DSS, viz. the decision-making process. Bonczek, Holsapple and Whinston (1981, p. 11) state: 'it must be stressed that information processing is not always an end in itself. Rather it is a means to an end, a means to decisions. Decisions, in the guise of information, are the 'finished products' of a human/machine information processing system. We refer to information-processing systems that yield that finished product as decision-making systems. Note that information is a raw material, an intermediate product, and a finished good of a decision-making process. The terms 'information processing' and 'decision-making' as used in this book are closely related. Various information-processing procedures (systems) might deal exclusively with the raw materials or intermediate products of decision making. But when these are combined with other information-prcessing procedures (systems) that involve the finished goods, the resultant and more global information-processing procedure (system) is a decisionmaking system. We refer to an information-processing system that is embedded within a decision-making system as a decision support system.'

They divide DSS in three components: a language system, a knowledge system and a problem-processing system as an interface between the two other components, see figure 1. The dialog system in the definition of Sprague has the same function as the language system in figure 1. The data base and model base system are part of the knowledge base system in figure 1. The problem-processing system is the new component. It is described by Bonczek et al. (1981, p. 71) as: 'The main function of a decision support system is to take strings of symbols organized according to language system syntax (problem) and to take strings of

symbols according to knowledge system representation rules (problem
domain knowledge) and to produce information that supports (enhances
or make possible) a decision process. To do so there must be an
interfacing mechanism between expressions of knowledge in the knowledge base and expressions of problems in the language system. We
refer to this interfacing mechanism as the problem processor or the
problem-processing system.'

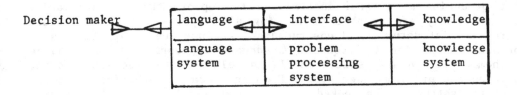

Figure 1. The three components of DSS as defined by Bonczek et al.

Belew (1985, p. 147) finally declares: 'What is required is a broader,
more robust conception of DSSs. This paper attempts to provide part of
this new perceptive by using the broadest possible definition of a
DSS-viz., a collection of information facilities.' He delivers this
new perspective through an extension of the three components of DSS in
the definition of Sprague by adding a text base and a rule base
system.

After analysing the various definitions, two different kinds of
attributes can be distinguished that are used to delineate DSS. The
attributes connected with the process of decision making in organizations are the most important ones. The other ones are the information processing attributes of DSS. I shall refer to the first set of
attributes as the organizational set and to the other as the information processing set. I discuss the elements of these sets in section
3 and 4. The main problems, however, in the discussion of the attributes of DSS are:
- the lack of a general accepted mechanism for the conceptual specification of DSS;
- the differences in worldviews used for the specification of DSS.
Different worldviews result in different attributes. We will deal with
the differences in worldviews and their consequences for the construction of DSS in section 5.
Both sets of attributes are not independent and it is therefore
necessary to have a mechanism to describe the relations between them.
As supporting and improving decision-making is the issue in DSS, we
propose to use as a mechanism for the description of decision processes the well known distinction in three phases made by Simon (1960).
The three phases are: intelligence, design and choice. The contents of
these three phases and their interconnections are sketched in figure
2. The line on the right of the figure refers to certain disciplines
and/or computer applications as described by Sprague (1980, p. 12).

3. THE ORGANIZATIONAL SET

A consensus has been established with regard to the following key

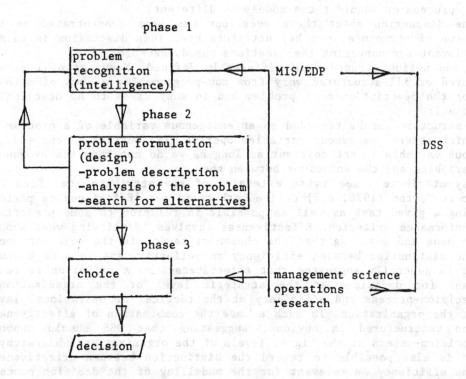

phase 1

problem
recognition
(intelligence)   MIS/EDP

phase 2

problem formulation
(design)   DSS
-problem description
-analysis of the problem
-search for alternatives

phase 3

choice   management science
                         operations
                         research

decision

Figure 2. A description of the three phases of a decision process

attributes of the organizational set, see Klein and Hirschheim (1985, p. 6). They mention the following attributes of DSS:
1. Deal with semi-structured tasks.
2. Draw on descriptive insights and normative models of decisionmaking.
3. An intent to improve effectiveness rather than efficiency.
4. Reflect an implementation strategy based on the use of skilled intermediates, responsive service and humanized software interfaces.
5. Employ an evolutionary and middle-out design strategy.
These key attributes can be divided into two kinds. The first three attributes deal with aspects of the process of decision-making, the other two with the implementation of such a process. I shan't deal with the last two attributes in this paper. For a comment on these attributes, see Ginzberg and Stohr (1982, p. 19-23).

Use of a mechanism to describe the process of decision-making gives an insight in the structure of that process. Should one relate such a mechanism to a worldview or paradigm, it still leaves unanswered the question what modelling facilities have to be used to make the description. In the case of modelling DSS various questions can be raised:

a. Does modelling of DSS mean a description of the whole decision
   process as depicted in figure 2 and suggested by Sprague, or of
   parts of it?
b. Are the models of a normative or a descriptive nature?
c. Can the same kind of model be used for every part of the decision
   process or should these models be different?

The discussion about these questions has been concentrated on the
issue of structure, see key attribute one. This discussion is hardly
relevant for answering the questions posed, because:
- the notion structure is differently defined. Meanings of unstructured or ill-structured vary from non-progammable, a lack of methods
for the description of a problem and in many cases to no description
at all;
- structure can be regarded as an endogenous variable of a process in
which several exogenous variables operate. The outcome of the endogenous variable is not relevant as long as we do not know the exogenous
variables and the relations between them.

Key attribute three is an extension of key attribute one. Keen and
Scott Morton (1978, p.7) define both terms as: 'Efficiency is performing a given task as well as possible in relation to some predefined
performance criterion. Effectiveness involves identifying what should
be done and ensuring that the chosen criterion is the relevant one.'
The distinction between efficiency and effectiveness is made because
it is generally suggested that effectiveness as a criterion is relevant for decisions at the strategic level of the organizational
decision-process and efficiency at the tactical or operational level
of the organization. In such a case the combination of effectiveness
and unstructured is obvious, suggesting that DSS should support
decision-makers at the higher levels of the organizational hierarchy.
It is also possible to regard the distinction between effectiveness
and efficiency as relevant for the modelling of the decision process
as described in figure 2. Effectiveness as a criterion deals with more
phases and their interrelations of the process than efficiency. In
that case effectiveness can also be used to model decision-processes
at the tactical or operational levels of an organization.

Key attribute two deals explicitly with the modelling process of DSS.
However, the distinction between normative and descriptive models is
not always made and in most cases it is not clear what the consequences of the distinction for the modelling process are. The three
key attributes discussed, do not give an image of what DSS are.
Depending on the person using these attributes different DSS can be
defined and designed. As far as the goal for the construction of DSS
is concerned this is not a drawback. It would be, however, if we wish
to answer questions as raised in section 1 and if we wish to instruct
people and compare results of research. That DSS can be used for
different purposes is relevant but not important to structure the
discussion about DSS. To implement a structure it will be necesssary
to find a common denominator. It is our opinion that such a denominator can be found in the process of constructing models necessary for
the design of DSS. These models define the way we look at problems and
specify, next to some other factors, the set of information processing
attributes.

To be able to specify attributes of the modelling process in the organizational set we will discuss two points relevant for the distinction that has to be made in the process of modelling. In these two points we describe the construct-paradigm, see section 1, we use.
I. We first define a number of notions, see table I. Models are being built for the solution of problems. The output of the model building process is a design for the solution of a problem. The model building process consists of two stages.
a. A general description of the problem, mostly in the form of hypotheses. At this stage the conceptual model is being constructed defining the problem by specifying relationships between endogenous and exogenous variables. Conceptual models are data-void, they do not directly refer to a specific problem in reality. Their main purpose is of a heuristic nature, viz. to give a description of the problem to be able to find an algorithm that can produce a solution or solutions. The relation between variables are specified as equations.
b. If in reality a problem has to be solved, the conceptual model has to be transformed into an empirical model. The empirical model defines reality through:
- a specification of the relevant variables,
- a specification of the relationships between the relevant variables, and
- a numerical specification of the parameters.

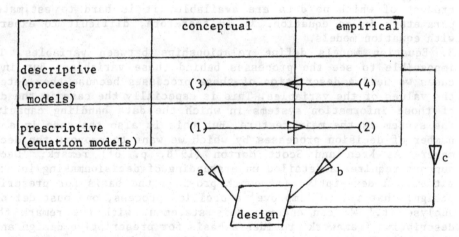

Table I. A distinction between models

It is rather common in science and methodology to proceed in the model building process from the conceptual stage to the empirical one, see the relation between element (1) and (2) in table I. This procedure is rational because, as Kuhn (1961) remarks: 'The route from theory or law to measurement can almost never be travelled backwards. Numbers gathered without some knowledge of the regularity to be expected

almost never speak for themselves. Almost certainly they remain just numbers.' Furthermore this procedure gives an efficient division of labour because conceptual models have a relatively high degree of generality. The relations with the design process are therefore twofold.
- Arrow a in table I delivers the algorithm to find a solution. In the model base of DSS one of the main components are the algorithms of operations research, see e.g. Thierauf (1982).
- A description of the problem and a possibility to apply an algorithm, arrow b in table I.

The term descriptive can be used in two ways. All empirical models are descriptive, they all give a description of a problem occurring in reality. Descriptive can also be used in a sense of giving a description of a problem, arrow c in table I. In that case element (4) bears a relation to element (3) in table I, because a conceptual descriptive model of a problem is regarded as a contradiction in terms. Therefore, in many cases, also in DSS, we use descriptive empirical models, arrow c in table I, to influence and/or specify the design process. These models are used to describe reality because prescriptive empirical models (equation models) fail to do so. There are a number of reasons for this failure.
1. The variables in the equation models cannot be measured.
2. Given a measurement of the variables the equation specifies what has happened. If a new problem arises, e.g. the introduction of a new product of which no data are available, it is hard to estimate the parameters in an equation. It is therefore, difficult to experiment with equation models.
3. Equation models define relationships between variables. It is impossible to see the processes behind these variables. But in many cases we need a description of these processes because they determine the values of the variables. This is especially the case in the design of those information systems in which the data handling capacity of the system is the main feature. But this is also the case in a great number of decision processes by which we want to support the decision maker. As Keen and Scott Morton (1978, p. 61) remark: 'Decision support requires a detailed understanding of decisionmaking in organizations. A descriptive framework provides the basis for prescriptive design; that is, to 'improve' a decision process, one must define and analyse it.' We can endorse this statement with the remark that a descriptive framework provides a basis for prescriptive design and not the basis. That is in essence the difference between prescription and description. The algorithm as the basis for design is lacking in descriptive models. As already stated, the other difference is that generally a conceptual descriptive model is not available, see section 5. The means that are used for the construction of descriptive empirical models are quite different and come from several disciplines where they are generally used when everything else fails. We mention as examples: heuristic programming, simulation and scenario-analysis. Artificial intelligence can be regarded as a new discipline that tries to specify a conceptual descriptive model using also different kinds of models, see e.g. the differences between expert systems. Therefore, Bosman and Sol (1985) suggest to pay more attention to the construction of a common denominator. They propose to introduce the notion

process model and use it in the same way the notion of a black box is used in equation models. There are several differences between equation and process models. As Bosman and Sol (1985, p. 90) remark: 'Process models make it possible to open the black-box way of describing problems. By opening this black-box we are able to specify the language system, knowledge system and problem-processing system of individual decision-makers. As to the construction of a conceptual model of an individual decision-maker, we have to describe how scenario's of entities with their attributes are actualized. We may specify various psychological types of a decisionmaker in a multidisciplinary way by introducing entities with corresponding attributes and scenario's for processing data and making decisions.' Process models play an important role in the model building process of DSS. The last two definitions given in section 2 underline this statement.The idea of a problem-processing system can be specified by using inquiry systems for the construction of models, Sol (1982) and Bosman (1982). The problem-processing system can also be an inference system as a part of an expert system, see Bonczek et al.(1982). Rule based systems, see the definition of Belew in section 2, can be regarded as an example of a process model.

II. In figure 2 a description is given of the different phases of the decision-process. On the right side of this figure a partition of models as suggested by Sprague is depicted. In this partition three things are remarkable.
1. Sprague relates management science and operations research to the third phase of the decision process. We subscribe this point of view.
2. Sprague relates the first phase of the decision process to management information systems and/or EDP models. However, these models are, from a model building piont of view, not a separate class of models, see section 4.
3. Sprague suggests that there is a class of DSS models that describes the whole process of decision-making. A statement that is at least contradictory to the first one, especially because, as already concluded, the main part of the model base consists of operations research models.
It is our point of view that the different phases of the decision process cannot be represented by the same model. One of the main reasons for the dispute about the modelling of decision-processes is the fact that nearly all builders of models of decision making processes suggest that their model gives a correct description of the whole process. A survey of the models used for the description of the whole process delivers three different classes of models. Each of these classes can be connected with one of the phases of the decision process.
a. Management science, operations research and economic models are specifying the third phase of the decision process. The selection of the best alternative gets emphasis. How the alternatives are specified and how the problem is detected and described are not features these models deal with. Given these circumstances it is not surprising that these models are prescriptive with a heavy accent on the algorithmic aspect and using equations to define the problem. Given these characteristics Bosman and Sol (1982, p. 123) suggest to define the class of well-structured problems as the class of problems that can be solved

by using models of this kind. These models are, as Sprague suggests, especially relevant for the third phase of the decision process using the assumption that a set of relevant alternatives is available.

b. A number of authors, see e.g. Forrester (1968) and the technique of system dynamics he developed, suggest that the process of decision making can be described as a cause-effect relationship, and therefore as a system. A feedback system is influenced by its own past behaviour. A feedback system has a closed loop structure that brings results of the past action of the system back to control future action. An idea that is used to produce an image of the organization in a part of the organization literature. However, empirical models of systems, as well as feedback systems, only describe one part of the decision process, viz. the first phase. Feedback systems can produce information relevant for the recognition of problems. In most cases it does not produce a description of the problem, nor does it generate a set of alternatives, the second phase of the decision process.

As the models under point a and b are of a conceptual nature, the empirical models connected with them do not deliver additional features. Most of these models are of the equation type. In some cases it is possible to extend the usage of the models to the second phase of the decision process. An extension of the first phase is possible if the empirical model producing signals of an existing problem can also be used for a description or explanation of the problem, as sometimes can be done with econometric models. Models of the third phase of the decision process can be applied, especially if these are models using simulation, to experiment with several alternatives. However, what both kinds of models are missing is an adequate specification of the other phases of the decision process, especially the second phase.

c. Descriptive empirical models generally cover only a part of the decision process. Applications concentrate on the first two phases of the process, especially on the problem description part in phase 2, see figure 2. As already remarked, the main disadvantage of descriptive empirical models is a lack of a subject matter and its conceptual specification. Rational behaviour, see section 5, cannot be defined in general terms, e.g. by an algorithm, but must be specified using a description of a problem. A specification of rational behavior is therefore depending on a mixture of description and design principles, because without some design principles it is difficult to make a distinction between rational and non rational behavior. These design principles are, however, hardly defined in a systematic way and are generally based on: intuition, experience and expertise. Descriptions of a problem can be given with process models. These models can describe a situation in detail, opening the possibility to change parts of the description and study the results of these changes. Along this way alternatives can be generated and evaluated. In some cases expert systems can be used to generate an alternative without the necessity to construct an extensive description. Expert systems are descriptive empirical models that try to implement a kind of rationality in the form of the knowledge of an expert. As descriptive empirical models generally produce only a few relevant alternatives it is not necessary to have a seperate third phase available to make a choice. If a third phase is not necessary, descriptive empirical models can give a rather complete description of a decision process.

Disadvantages are:
- the model building process is expensive;
- the degree of generality is low;
- rationality as a design principle, with the exception of some expert systems, is not available in the modelling process.

Based on the two points we discussed, we shall try to specify a number of attributes of the organizational set.
1. Support can be given to every kind of decision process.
2. It is not feasible to construct or promote one model or modeltype to support any decision-maker.
3. The models supporting decision-makers should be differentiated. Differences have to be made according to the three phases of the decision process and the way a decisionmaker wants to be supported, see section 4.
4. The possibility to recognize and describe problems is the basic attribute of DSS. Description in a broad sense, comprising element (2) and (4) in table I, should be available. A clear distinction has to be made between the modelling facilities in element (2) and those in element (4).
5. Facilities to construct process models should be available, see also Belew (1985).
6. Knowledge representation as a mean to detect problems and generate alternatives should become a basic attribute of DSS in the future. With these attributes it is possible to answer the three questions raised at the start of this section. There is not an overall DSS model, DSS should provide facilities for the construction of different kinds of models. The distinction between normative and descriptive is relevant as far as the delivery of an algorithm is concerned, see arrow a in table I. However, an algorithm without a proper problem specification has no meaning and it is the combination of both, arrow b in table I, that gives a proper facility to assist in the construction of a design.

4. THE INFORMATION PROCESSING SET

The development of DSS has been driven by technology. The developments of hardware and software made it possible to use computers in different ways and for different applications. Especially in the former years this technology push resulted in a description of DSS in which attributes in the field of information processing were part of the definition of DSS. Statements like: DSS should have interactive facilities and a data base, are common (see for a more extensive survey Ginzberg and Stohr (1982)).
It is our point of view that information processing facilities cannot be defined as long as the attributes of the organizational set are not yet specified. Since these attributes can differ considerably it is impossible to describe in general terms the attributes of an information processing set. In a concrete case a description can be given but it should be derived from the attributes of the organizational set. This point of view is rather uncommon in the DSS world and we wish to support it with the following two points.

1. In many DSS publications it is or has been suggested that DSS applications differ from EDP and management information systems (IS) applications of computers. As far as decision making applications of IS are concerned it was not difficult to recognize that they were not a big success. However, this was the result of the kinds of models that were used in combination with technical constraints in the computer systems of that time. This situation was recognized by a great number of people and several solutions were formulated. To mention just one as an example: decision calculus proposed by Little (1970). DSS was another one, in which the basic idea of support had been implemented by using various new information processing facilities. As shown in section 3 the DSS world has paid little attention to reformulate the modelling facilities to be able to improve decision support. As Naylor (1982, p. 94) remarks: 'DSS is a redundant term currently being used to describe a subset of Management Science that predates the DSS movement. DSS is not based on any formal conceptual framework, and this lack casts serious doubts on its substantive underpinnings. ' What DSS supporters did was to regard management science models and management information systems as synonyms. However, the most applied definition, see Davis and Olson (1985, p. 6), of an IS is: 'an integrated, user-machine system for providing information to support operations, management, and decision-making functions in an organization. The system utilizes computer hardware and software; manual procedures; models for analysis, planning, control and decisionmaking; and a data base.' An IS is a concrete system and DSS are a part of this system. By using attributes of both sets to define DSS the real attributes of DSS, those of the organizational set, were not recognized.

2. The confusion about the term IS is also apparent in the case of DSS. Answers to the questions of the contents of DSS can differ by stressing the importance of a data base, a model base or a dialog system or using attributes of the information processing set. Sprague (1980) and Sprague and Carlson (1982) make a distinction in tools, DSS generators and specific DSS (SDSS). DSS generators fill the gap between tools and SDSS. These generators are important because a generator determines the possibilities decisionmakers have for the construction of SDSS and the quality of generators partly depends on the tools incorporated in it. DSS generators are the meeting place between technology and users and any discussion on the attributes of DSS should be conducted using DSS generators as object. This has several advantages.
- One can generalize the discussion when the different wishes of users and the technical possibilites of the tools in a generator have to be formulated.
- A DSS discipline should be an intermediary in the discussion and stimulate it by adding new ideas, like e.g. a problem-processing system, for applications and tools.
- It opens the possibility to compare the generators.

5. DISCIPLINE OR VISION - RATIONAL BEHAVIOUR

In numerous publications on DSS it has been suggested that the problem area of constructing and building DSS can be regarded as a discipline. Elam et al. (1985) state: 'In the course of the evolution of a discipline from a collection of related ideas to a set of established research programs, it is often essential to reevaluate its progress and direction. DSS is such a discipline.' Vazsonyi (1982, p. 34) remarks: 'There is certainly one good thing about Decision Support Systems: the discussions about them force us to reexamine the philosophy and outlook of our field. We have labels like Operations Research, Management Science, Management Information Systems, Decision Analysis, Simulation, Corporate Planning Models or just Planning Models, Scenario Writing, Subjective Expected Utility Theory, and even Management Support Systems. The differences between these fields have been stressed, but is there a commonality encompassing the approach, or at least part of the approach, to all these efforts? And if there is such a paradigm, is it useful to discuss it? I think so, but to reach such a common basis we need to go beyond our field to a higher level of abstraction.' We subscribe the suggestion made by Vazsonyi to use a higher level of abstraction to determine the availability of a common basis.

To determine a common basis upon which a separate problem area or discipline can be defined, we propose to use two instruments. These instruments, see Bosman (1977), are the existence of a worldview or paradigm and the existence of a construct paradigm that determines the methods to be applied for the construction of models. Table I can be regarded as an expedient to transform those two instruments into a concrete specification. The construct paradigm can be related to the distinction between conceptual and empirical models and the possibilities to construct these. The worldview can be related to the distinction between a descriptive and prescriptive approach to modelling. We regard a common basis for the determination of a separate problem area or discipline available when it is possible te detect a more or less general agreement using both instruments. In the terminology of Lakatos (1976) a hard core has to be defined. As concluded in section 3 such a hard core is not available in the case of DSS when we look at the instrument of a construct paradigm. There are major differences in the ways in which models are constructed and in the final product of this construction, viz. the models applied. These major differences cannot be explained by arguments from the problem area. As we showed in section 3 nearly all models constructed deal with a part of the decision process.

The lack of agreement on model building is not the major reason to conclude that the design and construction of DSS is not a discipline. We regard as the major reason the lack of a hard core on possible worldviews. DSS has this feature in common with all the other fields mentioned by Vazsonyi. We regard all these fields as specializations in a mother discipline, e.g. the organizational science. As organizations are object of study in several disciplines and a mother discipline is lacking, we are confronted with a variety of output

depending mainly on the different worldviews applied in various
sciences, as economics, administrative sciences, sociology and psychology. The study of organizations can be characterized as conceptual
descriptive modelling, element (3) in table I. In most cases these
models cannot be translated into empirical ones. This is one of the
reasons why many models in element (4) are regarded as conceptual and
some elements in the set of organizational sciences make a distinction
between macro and micro organizational research, see Pondy and Mitroff
(1979). To try and end the continuous discussion whether DSS is a
discipline or not, we think it necessary to search for a mother
discipline. Such a search is not only relevant to the problem area of
DSS but also to other 'fields' studying parts of the organizational
processes. Such a mother discipline should deliver a methodology in
which it will be possible to define the two instruments we used for
the classification and the relations between them as we did in table
I. For DSS and a number of other fields the object of this mother
science should be decision processes in organizations. The term used
for this mother discipline could be decision science. The plural,
decision sciences, has already been used for that purpose, but is not
commonly accepted. Without going into detail we wish to mention a few
of the main characteristics of this decision science, referring to the
two instruments we used to classify a science of DSS.
1. The object should be the whole process of decision making, as described in figure 2, and not only parts of it. There is a fast growing
interest in organization literature in such an object, as the following quotations may show.
'Organizations are not just groups of people; they are sets of organizing rules', Pondy and Mitroff (1979, p.29).
'In reply to the question 'what is an organization', we consider
organizations to be snapshots of ongoing processes, these snapshots
being selected and controlled by human consciousness and attentive-
ness', Weick (1979, p.42).
'Within this metastrategy, the goal shifts from solutions invented by
policy makers to combinations of hardware, software and people which
continually invent, revise, adapt, generate and modify their own solutions', Hedberg et al. (1977, p. 174).
The process as a whole is important because it opens possibilities to:
- take into account different considerations on the process of decision making, see the quotation of Weick;
- integrate micro and macro processes, see the quotation of Pondy and
Mitroff. The basic element should be the structure of the decision
process. These processes can differ according to the place in the
organizational structure where a decision is taken and the way the
organization is willing, able and capable to co-ordinate the decision
processes, Bosman (1982);
- regard decision processes from a multidisciplinary point of view. As
it is possible to use many of these views it is necessary to define
which combination of aspects in a certain view has been chosen and how
this combination is implemented in the modelling process.
2. The worldview to be used in the study of decision processes should
be the paradigm of bounded rationality as formulated by Simon (for an
extensive exposure on this paradigm, see Simon (1982)). As Weick (1979
a, p. 19/20) remarks:' Anyone who samples the literature on organizations will soon notice a term that occurs over and over again, <u>ratio-</u>

nality. This concept does not necessarily mean that organizational actions are logical or sensible, but rather that they are intended, thought about, planned, calculated, or designed for a purpose..... The fact that organizations typically exhibit a great deal of turbulence, disorder, and unpredictability does not necessarily disprove the theory that their origins were rational or that they are trying to be rational.' A statement on rational behaviour is a 'must' in every organizational study and this is certainly the case where decision processes are concerned. In most cases, however, rational behaviour is not explicitly defined and when it is, definitions varying from unbounded rationality to subjective rationality are possible. All these definitions have in common that they define rationality in general terms. The big advantage and at the same time disadvantage of bounded rationality is, that it is connected with individual decision processes and therefore demanding a descriptive approach of the problem. Description is necessary because otherwise a relation to a certain problem cannot be established and prescription of bounded rationality cannot be specified. In the construction of table I this implies that a description of a certain problem is necessary, elements (2) and (4) in table I. Where element (4) is used, the prescriptive element is missing, while in the case of element (2) in most cases the prescription of element (1) cannot be applied. The weakest point in applying the paradigm of bounded rationality is the lack of prescription in relation to the description of individual decision processes. One of the main fields of research for the future.

3. In section 3 we dealt with the problem of how to construct models of decision-processes. One of the problems we mentioned is the lack of conceptual descriptive models. This problem, however, can be solved by not emphazing in the conceptual model the description of a certain object but by paying special attention in these models to the instruments that can be used to give a description. The work of Simon, see Newell and Simon (1972), the idea of the problem-processing system of Bonczek et al. (1981) and the applications of rule-based systems as e.g. in expert systems, can be regarded as examples of an implementation of that suggestion. Bosman and Sol (1985), see section 3, propose to use the notion of process models to find a common denominator for a specification of element (3) in table I. This can be a second field of research which can be related to the one mentioned under point 2. The final purpose of this research is to make it possible to redirect the relation between elements (3) and (4) in table I.

4. DSS could be a specialization in a decision science with emphasis on design of information systems. Relevant in that case is the distinction made by Sprague between SDSS and DSS generators, see section 4. As already stated in section 4 we propose a relation between the organizational set of attributes and the information processing set in which the latter has been derived from the first. The main argument for this is, that the descriptive approach to prescribe bounded rationality makes it difficult to specify the design considerations in general terms. A third field of research should be the development of design considerations of a more general nature. However, in that case it is dangerous to start with the information processing attributes

because their general nature can easily lead to a domination of the design process. Especially in the case of the design of decision-processes the relevant features should be in the sphere of trans-forming data into information.

REFERENCES

Alter, S.L., Decision Support Systems: Current Practices and Conti-nuing Challenges, Reading, Addison-Wesley, 1980.

Belew, R.K., 'Evolutionary decision support systems', Knowledge Representation for Decision Support Systems, eds. L.B. Methlie and R.H. Sprague, Jr., Amsterdam, North-Holland, 1985.

Bennet, J.L., Building Decision Support Systems, Reading, Addison-Wesley, 1983.

Bonczek, R.H., C.W. Holsapple and A.B. Whinston, Foundations of Decision Support Systems, New York, Academic Press, 1981.

Bosman, A., Een Metatheorie over het Gedrag van Organisaties, Leiden, Stenfert Kroese, 1977.

Bosman, A., 'Decision support systems, problem processing and co-ordination', Processes and Tools for Decision Support, ed. H.G. Sol, Amsterdam, North-Holland, 1983.

Bosman, A. and H.G. Sol, 'Evolutionary development of information systems', Evolutionary Information Systems, ed. J. Hawgood, Amsterdam, North-Holland, 1982.

Bosman, A. and H.G. Sol, 'Knowledge representation and information systems design', Knowledge Representation for Decision Support Sys-tems, eds. L.B. Methlie and R.H. Sprague, Jr., Amsterdam, North-Holland, 1985.

Davis, G.B. and M.H. Olson, Management Information Systems, New York, McGraw-Hill, 1985.

Dery, D. and Th. J. Mock, 'Information support systems for problem solving', Decision Support Systems, vol. 1, nr. 2, 1985.

Elam, J.J., J.C. Henderson, P.G.W. Keen, B. Konsynski, C.L. Meador and D. Ness,' A vision for decision support systems', Proceedings DSS-85, 1985.

Forrester, J.W., Principles of Systems, Cambridge, Wright-Allen Press, 1968.

Ginzberg, M.J. and E.A. Stohr, 'Decision support systems: Issues and perspectives', Decision Support Systems, eds. M.J. Ginzberg, W.R. Reitman and E.A. Stohr, Amsterdam, North-Holland, 1982.

Hedberg, B.L.T., P.C. Nystrom and W.H. Starbuck, 'Designing organi-zations to match tomorrow', Prescriptive Models of Organizations, eds. P.C. Nystrom and W.H. Starbuck, Amsterdam, North-Holland, 1977.

Keen, P.G.W. and S. Scott Morton, Decision Support Systems, Reading, Addison-Wesley, 1978.

Klein, H.K. and R. Hirschheim, 'Fundamental issues of decision support systems: a consequentialist perspective', Decision Support Systems, vol. 1, nr. 1, 1985.

Kuhn, T.S., Quantification, ed. H. Woolf, Indianapolis, BobbsMerrill, 1960.

Lakatos, I., Proofs and Refutations, Cambridge, Cambridge University Press, 1976.

Little, J.D.C., 'Models and managers: the concept of a decision calculus', Management Science, vol. 16, nr. 8, 1970.

Mitroff, I.I. and R.H. Kilmann, Methodological Approaches to Social Science, San Fransisco, Jossey-Bass, 1978.

Naylor, Th. H., 'Decision support systems or whatever happened to MIS?', Interfaces, vol. 12, nr. 4, 1982.

Newell, A. and H.A. Simon, Human Problem Solving, Englewood Cliffs, Prentice-Hall, 1972.

Pondy, L.R. and I.I. Mitroff, 'Beyond open system models of organizations', Research in Organizational Behavior, ed. B.M. Staw, Greenwich, JAI Press, 1979.

Simon, H.A., The New Science of Management Decision, New York, Harper and Row, 1960.

Simon, H.A., Models of Bounded Rationality, vol.2, Behavioral Economics and Business Organization, Cambridge, MIT Press, 1982.

Sol, H.G., Simulation in Information Systems Development, Groningen, PH.D. thesis, 1982.

Sol, H.G., 'Paradoxes around DSS', Proceedings NATO Advanced Summer Institute, Berlin, Springer, 1985.

Sprague, R.H., Jr., 'A framework for research on decision support systems', Decision Support Systems: Issues and Challenges, eds. G. Fick and R.H. Sprague, Jr., Oxford, Pergamon Press, 1980.

Sprague, R.H., Jr. and E.D. Carlson, Building Effective Decision Support Systems, Englewood Cliffs, Prentice-Hall, 1982.

Stamper, R., 'Management epistemology: garbadge in, garbadge out', Knowledge Representation for Decision Support Systems, eds. L.B. Methlie and R.H. Sprague, Jr., Amsterdam, North-Holland, 1985.

Thierauf, R.J., Decision Support Systems for Effective Planning and Control, Englewood Cliffs, Prentice-Hall, 1982.

Vazsonyi, A., 'Computer-supported gedankenexperiments', Interfaces, vol. 12, nr. 4, 1982.

Weick, K.E., 'Cognitive processes in organizations', Research in Organizational Behavior, ed. B.M. Staw, Greenwich, JAI Press, 1979.

Weick, K.E., The Social Psychology of Organizing, Reading, Addison-Wesley, 1979 a.

Decision Support Systems And Expert Systems: A Complementary Relationship?

Rolf Pfeifer
Department of Computer Science
University of Zurich
Zurich, Switzerland

Hans-Jakob Lüthi
Institute of Operations Research
Swiss Federal Institute of Technology
Zurich, Switzerland

ABSTRACT. "Decision Support System" (DSS) and "Expert System" (ES) are two more buzzwords in the information technology community. Using the idea that DSS and ES are approaches rather than just systems, a conceptual framework is presented for comparing the two in the context of management problems. It consists of the following dimensions: general goals and paradigms, problem domain, model type, usage modality, and design and implementation. Given the state of the art in both fields it is shown that DSS and ES differ considerably along these dimensions. The ES approach can be viewed as an essential extension of the traditional quantitative modeling techniques. Although this represents a considerable enhancement of the domain of "programmable" decisions, those domains for which the construction of an ES is envisaged should meet certain rather strict criteria. Hence, an attempt to automate the whole range of management decision making with an ES is doomed to failure. In this paper it is argued that it may not be fruitful trying to *replace* management decision making by all means, but rather that DSS and ES should be considered as *complementary* concepts.

1. INTRODUCTION

In recent years an increasing number of software packages to support management decision making have been offered by many vendors under the fashionable label of Decision Support Systems (DSS) (see, for example, the list in Watson & Christy, 1983). This trend has been intensified by the increased availability of personal computers, advances in data base management systems, incorporation of "user-friendly" software interface techniques, color graphics, etc. But besides this general progress in information technology there are other reasons why there has been a sudden spur just lately. One of them -- an this is the one to be discussed in this paper -- has to do with the fact that the field of Artificial Intelligence has succeeded in demonstrating its usefulness in a number of practical applications. The buzz word is, of course, Expert Systems (ES). ES are capable of capturing a certain kind of human-like problem solving behavior. This problem solving behavior can also be viewed as a series of decisions the ES has to take to arrive at a solution. Moreover, managers, as well as ESs solve complex problems (an issue to be discussed in detail below), and therefore one

41

H. G. Sol et al. (eds.), Expert Systems and Artificial Intelligence in Decision Support Systems, 41–51.
© *1987 by D. Reidel Publishing Company.*

might want to develop an ES for management decision making. It is one of the goals of this paper to demonstrate that this view is biased and does not lead to fruitful research.

Towards this end it will be investigated in what ways DSS and ES are different and in what ways they are similar. A framework will be presented, enabling a characterization of the two approaches. This characterization is the second goal of the paper. The third goal will be to discuss the issues of where it is appropriate to apply a DSS or an ES approach, and in what ways they might be combined in the context of management decision problems.

The framework consists of the following dimensions:[1]

- general goals and paradigms,
- problem domains,
- types of models,
- usage modality, and
- design and implementation.

These will be discussed in turn with respect to similarities and differences.

Before going into the details, two observations should be made:
(a) *Terminology*. The terminology in both fields, ES and DSS, is confusing. For example, if the term "Decision Support System" is taken literally, most computer programs would in fact be DSSs: one way or another they "support decision" since they provide certain kinds of information used in a decision process. Then there is a host of names implying somehow that DSS and ES are indeed very similar concepts, e.g. ESM (Expert Systems for Management), suggesting that management (or substantial parts of it) can be done by ESs; IMS (Intelligent Management System), which suggests that management can be automated by applying techniques from Artificial Intelligence (e.g. ES), etc. Thus, the terminology in these fields should never be taken literally.
(b) *Software dominance*. With the event of ES a new programming methodology has emerged, namely the one of declarative specifications as opposed to procedural programs. Declarative specification is exemplified in production system languages (e.g. OPS5), and logic programming languages such as PROLOG. This has lead a number of authors to identify ES with logic programming. Any program employing logic programming (or other kinds of declarative) techniques is called an ES, a point of view the authors clearly reject. But the fact that DSS and ES may use a similar programming methodology does not imply that they are equal. Although we will discuss the software aspects, the present paper stresses concepts and not programming. Stamper's (1985) distinction between "information engineering" and "software building" accurately reflects the view of the authors.

2. GENERAL GOALS AND PARADIGMS

2.1. Paradigms for DSS

Historically the DSS approach was a reaction to the Management Information Systems (MIS) movement of the early seventies. It is commonly recognized that the issues central to DSS are (e.g. Keen & Morton, 1978) (a) the context and nature of management decision processes, (b) the computer support, and (c) the design and implementation strategies. (a) corresponds to "problem domain" in

---

1. Some of these dimensions are also used by Ford (1985) in a comparison of DSS and ES.

our framework, (b) to "usage modality and types of models", whereas (c) is the same.

Managers typically operate in complex situations under severe time constraints. Thus, one of the most important aspects of any system supporting a manager's decision making is to enable him to *learn* quickly about the kind of situation he is faced with. As has been pointed out by a number of authors (e.g. Keen & Morton, 1978; Sprague, 1980) a task which is at the same time multidimensional, multiobjective, and only partially defined (such as management decision making), cannot be automated. One of the reasons is that such tasks typically employ much of what one might call "common sense." Therefore, the goal of DSS is not to automate management decision making, but rather to *support the intuition of the decision maker.* Towards that end the basic question to ask is: Why is decision making so hard? Understanding this question would give us a clue as to what sort of support might be useful for managers facing a complex decision situation. However, since the question has obviously not been answered yet properly, the DSS field can be appropriately characterized by the following quote: "The battlefield of decision aiding is full with good ideas that did not quite pan out, after raising hopes and attracting attention." (Fischhoff & Johnson, 1985).

The DSS approach attempts to develop decision aids with a somewhat better chance of survival. Its hopes are based on the following two basic insights: First, any such system must be *interactive* and second, it must aim to support so-called *semi-structured problems*. The term "semi-structured problems" has its origins in the work of Simon (1960). It is used to characterize certain types of decision problems, namely those for which the information needed cannot be described in detail *before* making the decision (e.g. for lack of knowledge intrinsic to the problem, or lack of knowledge due to perceptual limitations, large search space, or other reasons). Keen & Morton (1978) wrote: "...(The semi-structured task) is where DSS can be most effective. These are decisions where managerial judgement alone will not be adequate, perhaps because of the size of the problem or the computational complexity and precision needed to achieve it. On the other hand, the model or data are also inadequate because the solution involves judgement and subjective analysis. Under this condition the manager *plus* the system can provide more effective solutions than either alone." (p.80)

Even if many concepts of DSS rely fundamentally on Simon's work on problem solving, there still lacks a systematic theoretical foundation. Whenever theory is missing, frameworks to organize the different issues may be helpful. An example of such a framework is the one presented by Sol (Sol, 1983; Bosman & Sol, 1985). It is aimed at describing the "ill-structured" problems faced in DSS research, and integrates the technological components of Sprague (1980) and the logical concepts due to Bonzek et al. (1981).

It is interesting to observe that it contains a *knowledge system*, i.e. a DSS body of knowledge about a problem domain. Up to date there is no practical system available having all components of his framework implemented in a nontrivial, i.e. *problem oriented* way (though they may well contain some logic programming software). In the traditional DSS approach two basic types of problem oriented resources are available, *databases* (which contain facts about the environment), and *models* which enable inferences to be made. Practically all of these models are quantitative in nature, typically providing optimization or statistical inferences.

2. Paradigm for ES

ESs have their origin in Artificial Intelligence research. In particular, the discipline grew out of the work of Newell and Simon (1972) who were among the first to develop profound models of human problem solving. They used a so-called production systems methodology which is still one of the main underlying ideas in most of today's ESs. While Newell and Simon analyzed human subjects doing mathematical proofs, or different sorts of puzzles, ES developers studied problem solving behavior in real-world domains, such as deducing chemical structures from mass spectrographic data (DENDRAL, e.g. Lindsay et al., 1980), medical diagnosis (MYCIN, Shortliffe, 1976; INTERNIST/CADUCEUS, Pople, 1982), analysis of geological formations (PROSPECTOR, Duda et al., 1979), configuring VAX computers (R1/XCON, McDermott, 1982), and many others.

The basic idea is to develop a model capable of solving problems from a particular domain. If there are no recognized methods available, the behavior of a human expert serves as a source of inspiration. Experts are analyzed and interviewed about how they go about in solving a particular problem: One would like to get at the know-how or heuristic knowledge of the expert. The process of extracting this knowledge from the expert, formalizing and coding it into a computer program is called knowledge acquisition or knowledge transfer (e.g. Hayes-Roth et al., 1983). Once the process of ES construction is finished the ES is capable of solving the problems it was designed to solve on its own, possibly requiring some additional data or information from the user. It is clear – given the state of the art in Artificial Intelligence and ES – that the tasks or task domains for which such systems can be built will be narrow and highly restricted. This point will be discussed in more detail in the next section.

One of the major goals of ES is the *dissemination* of expertise. A physician in his private practice has a patient with some kind of infectious disease. He might want to consult an expert on infections and this is where the ES comes in. Since in many areas, professionals, such as physicians, computer engineers, or scientists cannot keep up with the rapid developments in all domains relevant to their work, they will need the support of ESs more and more in the future. In other words, the ES helps to make the expertise available to many people. Another, subsidiary goal, is the *formalization* of expertise which is, of course, a prerequisite for the construction of a computer program.

For the sake of completeness, a definition of an ES is given. It is specific enough such that it can also be used to informally distinguish ES from other sorts of computer programs, e.g. from DSS. The definition has been compiled from several sources:

Definition: An *Expert System* is a computer program which
- solves real-world problems requiring an expert's interpretation,
- employs heuristic knowledge and/or qualitative models of the problem domain,
- reaches the same conclusions a human expert would if faced with a similar situation, and
- employs a programming methodology based on a separation between knowledge and its application.

2.3. Summary

In short, the paradigm for DSS is *improving* (management) decision making, the one of ES *problem solving*. Taking into account the different degrees of "formalizability", the general goal for DSS is to support the intuition of the decision maker, while the goal for ES is the dissemination and formalization of expertise.

3. PROBLEM DOMAIN

The problem domain of DSS is characterized by the following attributes which may partially overlap or depend on each other:[2]

---

2. A similar characterization can be found in Sprague & Carlson (1982).

- The problems are ill-specified, i.e. the goals are typically formulated in very general and vague ways (partial specification).
- Commonly more than one goal are to be achieved at any one time (multiobjective).
- The factors influencing the problems are from different domains (economics, engineering, psychology, politics, etc.) (complexity).
- The problems tend to require common sense.
- The situation in which the manager has to operate is not transparent and rapidly changing.

Although the application of DSSs to *management* decision making is predominant, DSSs are applicable to other types of decision making. Any sort of situation having some of the above characteristics, is a potential candidate for a DSS, in particular, the kinds of situations which are not transparent, ill-specified, influenced from many different sources, and rapidly changing. In all such situations, the primary goal is to learn quickly about the current situation, to "get a feel for it."

In contrast, areas for which it is reasonable to build ESs are characterized by a number of properties, pointed out by Davis (1982). Although this essay dates a few years back, the criteria are still valid and will probably remain so for a number of years to come.

1. Limited domain. Given the state of the art in the study of problem solving behavior (human and otherwise) the domains have to be clearly delineated and sufficiently narrow. Although it is frequently claimed that ES technology is applicable for ill-specified problems, their applicability is restricted to (more or less) well-defined problems. The fact that a problem is well-defined (e.g. a computer has broken down and should be fixed) does not mean that it is easy to solve, i.e. the solution path (or the solution paths) may not be obvious and highly complex.

2. Recognized experts. For many problems ESs are designed to solve, e.g. medical diagnosis and therapy recommendation, there may not be a "correct" solution, but one judged better, appropriate, not so well suited, etc. Thus, in evaluating an ES there are frequently no a priori criteria for appraising a solution, and therefore there must be a recognized human expert who does the evaluation. Moreover, while building an ES there must be someone available who can provide the heuristic knowledge, in particular what has been called "private knowledge", i.e. the knowledge acquired essentially through personal experience (in contrast to the "public knowledge" which can be extracted from text books, technical manuals, lectures at universities, etc.).

3. Duration. The typical ES task requires minutes to hours if performed by a human expert. This is a rule-of-thumb measure for the appropriate complexity of the task. If it takes weeks, months, or even years to do, such as drawing the construction plans of a new type of airplane, the task is clearly too complex. If it takes only a few seconds, it is too trivial and not worth the trouble of building an ES in the first place.

4. No common sense. The next requirement states that the task should require as little common sense as possible. This sounds somewhat strange, but there are profound reasons for this, all having to do, in essence, with formalizability. First, common sense frequently employs highly intuitive and emotional judgements. Although there have been a number of attempts at formalizing emotional processes (e.g. Pfeifer & Nicholas, 1985), they are still poorly understood. Thus, the tasks should require only cognitive activities, i.e. activities one might call "thinking". Second, common sense draws on knowledge from many different domains and uses analogies to personal experiences. And last, but not least, most of the processing going on in common sense reasoning is implicit, highly automated, and not accessible to conscious inspection.

5. High pay-off. The task should be repetitive. If this condition were not met it would not be worth the effort of building an ES. In other words, ES should only be developed if they can be frequently used.

Looking at these points it seems not surprising that the problem domains for which ESs have been developed in the past and for which ESs are mainly used today are medical, technical, or from the natural sciences. Of course, there may have been personal preferences of the knowledge engineers, who frequently have a mathematics, an engineering, or a science background, but it seems essential that the degree of formalizability in technical or scientific domains is much higher than in other domains, such as finance, management, or psychology. Criteria 1 through 4 in the above list are fulfilled better by technical domains than managerial ones. So, in some aspects ES and traditional OR approaches are similar (e.g. the limited domain), the main difference being that ESs employ Artificial Intelligence techniques which permit the representation of qualitative information as opposed to the purely quantitative ones in OR. Traditional OR disciplines, such as job shop scheduling, may be modeled more comprehensively if techniques from Artificial Intelligence are employed on top of the quantitative ones, as demonstrated in Fox's (1985) paper. One critical point is not discussed in Fox's paper, namely how completely the problem solving process is represented and how the system is used. We will start with a discussion of the latter point, the usage modality.

4. USAGE MODALITY AND TYPES OF MODELS

The usage modality is another important dimension differentiating DSS from other computer applications within an organization. To achieve the desired effects, the DSS must allow the user to confront a problem in a flexible, personal way by providing the ability to manipulate the data and models in a variety of ways while going through the decision making process. The a priori knowledge about the problem-solving process is sparse -- the system merely facilitates the potential usage of methods, models, and data, on an individual basis.

The most primitive support provides access to facts, or information retrieval systems to find relevant information in a slew of raw data. The second level of support involves the addition of filters and pattern recognition abilities, using statistical routines, graphical summaries, etc. The third level builds upon the previous ones and permits simple computations, comparisons, projections, and so on. The final level of support provides useful models to the manager (e.g. Elam & Henderson, 1983; Blanning, 1985).

The manager uses the DSS for certain specialized subparts of his task. The information from this sub-module is then processed by the manager in ways which typically cannot be specified in advance. The initiative is always with the user. He can "play" with the models to learn quickly about the current situation and the implications of his actions. He can then decide to use this knowledge in his decision process, or to ignore it. Normally the information gathered from the different modules can be trusted: the modules are developed using recognized techniques (such as OR models, statistics, etc.).

With ES the case is quite different. With minor exceptions, the initiative is always with the system: the system asks for data, performs all the reasoning steps, asks for more information, and in the end comes up with a solution. This is possible since an ES contains a more or less complete model of the problem solving process. The ES contains an implicit or explicit model of the kind of information needed and of how this information is processed. In contrast, the DSS only contains an implicit (and typically rather vague) model of the decision processes involved. The only hypothesis a DSS implies about the problem solving process of the manager is that the information it provides might be useful (or has been used in the past) to a decision maker. This is a *sparse* representation of the processes the decision maker deals with, as opposed to the *dense* one of an ES (see also Figure 1).

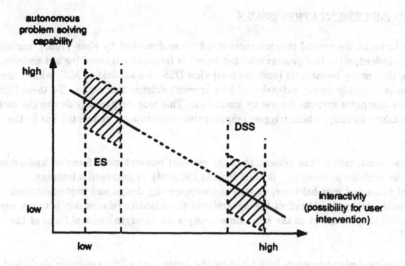

Figure 1: Usage modality and type of model. (a) ES: a dense representation of the
problem solving process enables a high autonomous problem solving capability, but the
possiblities for user intervention are only limited. (b) DSS: the situation is
complementary to ES.

The DSS user can normally trust the quality of the information produced by the individual modules
of the DSS, or he has some indication on how trustworthy it is. The whole process is under his
control and he can use the models or not. Again the situation is different for ES. The ES user,
typically an educated layperson (e.g. a physician, a general practitioner faced with a problem
requiring a specialist, say for bacterial infections, or a computer engineer faced with a specific kind of
failure in a part of the machine he is not entirely familiar with), gets a solution to his problem.
Should he believe the system? Is the solution given by the system to be trusted? The user is the one
who will suffer the consequences, but the ES has produced the solution. Clearly, what is needed is an
explanation facility. It is an essential part of the usage modality that the user must be able to ask
questions all along. If he understands the reasoning processes of the ES he can decide whether he
wants to trust the solution or not. Such an explanation facility is not really necessary for a DSS since
the whole process is under the decision maker's control. Today's ESs, in particular the relatively few
ones used commercially, are not equipped with good explanation facilities. They are "flat" or "surface
systems" (e.g. Hart, 1982) and their explanatory capabilities are usually restricted to providing trace
information (i.e. information on which rules have been applied), or to printing information previously
entered into the system. To generate a good explanation, the ES needs on the one hand a model of
the causal dependencies of the underlying problem domain, and on the other a model of the user,
since this determines what the explanation will look like.

5. DESIGN AND IMPLEMENTATION ISSUES

It is worthwhile to recall the central characteristic of a DSS as described by Keen (1980), namely the adaptive design. Indeed, since this process oriented aspect is frequently ignored (or not understood) it is not surprising that many researchers (and vendors) view DSS as a subfield of MIS, while others regard it as a technologically driven extension of Management Science techniques. To them DSSs are simply interactive computer systems for use by managers. This may be partially due to the fact that the term DSS is taken literally, which triggers inappropriate associations, as pointed out in the beginning.

If the essence is support, rather than system, then the relevant research must focus on understanding and improving the decision *process*, i.e. it must include the study of managerial learning, representation of tasks and user behavior, as well as corresponding design and implementation strategies. Those strategies should reflect the *dynamics* of the adaptive relationship between user, designer and technical system, but at the same time incorporate an organizational focus of the task to be accomplished.

Although the adaptive design process is facilitated by the concept of a DSS generator (technical perspective) the builder of a specific DSS is faced with the above tasks which are rarely addressed in an operational form. An operational method must include (operational) concepts for descriptive as well as prescriptive analysis of the problem, the perceived nature of ill-structuredness, the support functions, and the anticipated role of interactivity (man-machine synergy) in the solution process (e.g. Fuglseth & Stabell, 1985). The result of such an assessment should be the basis for ROMC-analysis (Sprague & Carlson, 1982) and similar techniques, which are — as of today — performed in a rather ad-hoc manner. Unfortunately, research is frequently driven more by the available technology than by an understanding of the support needed for improving the decision process.

ES can typically be used in one way only, namely to get the problems of the problem domain *solved*. This implies that many aspects in the design of the system, which have to be dealt with in a DSS approach, are currently not at issue. For example, the adaptive cycle: user-designer-technical system is, in the ES domain, essentially restricted to designing a user interface, possibly including a natural language and an explanation facility. This is mainly due to the many constraints of ESs pointed out previously. Nevertheless, understanding the user's needs is an essential point that has been largely neglected. This neglect is presumably one of the reasons the MYCIN system has never been routinely used by physicians. A recent research strand, called "user modelling" promises to provide substantial improvements in this direction.

One important design issue in the domain of ES concerns their extensibility. The process of knowledge acquisition requires much effort from knowledge engineers, as well as domain experts. It would therefore be desirable to reduce the knowledge aquisition phase to its minimum. The question is whether the system can be conceived such that it improves its behavior by being used. Or stated more pointedly: can (or should) the system be designed to learn? Although there has been much research on the subject in Artificial Intelligence in recent years, there is still no commercial ES available which performs any kind of nontrivial learning. Learning systems only exist in the form of laboratory prototypes. The only kind of incremental changes in today's ESs are performed via a so-called knowledge aquisition module, which is essentially an editing program enabling (relatively) easy changes and extensions to the knowledge base. Some of these knowledge aquisition modules can even be used directly by the domain expert without the assistance of a knowledge engineer.

There is a distinction in the literature between "first" and "second generation" ESs (e.g. Steels & Van de Velde, 1985). Most systems in existence today (MYCIN, R1/XCON, etc.) are "first generation" systems. They are characterized by the fact that they employ models of the heuristic problem solving behavior of a human expert. It has been pointed out that, in order to reason intelligently about a problem domain, and in order to be able to give good explanations, the ES should contain a model of the underlying problem domain (Clancey, 1982). For example, a system for repairing car engines should not only contain a heuristic model of what the mechanic does, but also of how the engine works. This model can be used whenever the behavioral model does not "know" how to proceed. The better this model, the less one has to rely on a human expert. However, causal models are hard to build, and for some domains the pertinent information may not be available (e.g. some domains in medicine, psychology, or economics).

Using the underlying domain model may imply extensive search and can be highly inefficient. Thus the "experience" gained from a special case should be preserved for later use, in other words, the system should do some kind of learning. In the system of Steels & Van de Velde (1985), whenever a solution has been found, heuristic rules which can be used in the future, are automatically generated to cover this case. (The issues involved here are intricate and one is only beginning to develop a basic understanding).

In this context it is intersting to note that this basic approach to work with causal models resembles the traditional OR approach in the domain of management.

3. CONCLUSIONS

In this paper we compared DSS and ES along the following lines: general goals and paradigms, problem domain, types of models, usage modality, and finally design and implementation. In Figure 2 the results of the comparision is summarized.

	Decision Support System	Expert System
Paradigm	Management decision making	Problem solving
Goal of system	Support of intuition	"Complete" solution
Goal type	"Ill-specified"	"Well-specified"
User	Manager	Educated layperson
Factors of influence	Not predictable From many domains	Predictable Restricted
Representation problem solving	Sparse representation	Dense representation
Control	With the user	With the system
Techniques	Tools in formalized subdomains	Artificial Intelligence Knowledge represe.

Figure 2: Summary of comparison of DSS and ES.

The observed characteristics lead to the following conclusions: ES and DSS differ considerably in a number of imporant ways and are by no means identical or even similar. They are in most respects complementary approaches for the domain of management. Whereas ES is a prototypical example of "programmable" decisions, DSS aims to capture the essence of the "man-machine synergy" in a decision process: It induces a learning process about the current situation and the possible space of actions. Traditionally OR and Management Science provided computer support using formal mathematical descriptions of the problem domain i.e. they were dealing with well-specified problems. In this regard ES, as it stands today, enhances and strengthens the problem solving capabilites of those disciplines. In particular heuristic as opposed to formal mathematical or logical reasoning has become amenable to formalization, and its application has proved successful in a number of cases. It follows immediately that many problems which are today perceived as "semistructured" may become formalizable due to a better understanding of the solution-process in terms of heuristic reasoning on the one hand, and to the availabilty of improved concepts for knowledge representation provided by Artificial Intelligence research, on the other. In such cases the DSS approach may and eventually will be replaced by an ES. It is precisely in this area where the two concepts (DSS & ES) are usually confused and the terms are used almost interchangeably. Certainly, the model base of a DSS may include appropriate ES-type models to enhance the user's modeling capabilities.

Given the state of the art, the authors clearly reject the idea of building ESs for management decisions - since those problems in general do not meet the tight constraints necessary for an ES-approach, but rather they are ill-specified, they employ common sense, etc. On the other hand the inclusion of a knowledge base in a DSS which complements the database by the knowledge of an organization (resources, production-processes, etc.) as (implicitly) used by managers for decision-making would indeed add a new dimension to the DSS approach (e.g. Fox, 1985).

REFERENCES

Blanning, R.W.: Expert systems for management: Research and applications. *Journal of Information Science*, 1985, *9*, 153-162.

Bonczek, R.H., Holsapple, C.W., & Whinston, A.B.: *Foundations of decision support systems*. New York: Academic Press, 1981.

Bosman, A., & Sol, H.G.: Knowledge representation and information systems design. In: L.B. Methlie & R.H. Sprague (eds.): *Knowledge Representation for decision support systems*. Amsterdam: North-Holland, 1985, 81-91.

Clancey, W.J.: The epistemology of a rule-based expert system - a framework for explanation. *Artificial Intelligence*, 1982, *20*, 215-251.

Davis, R.: Expert systems: Where are we? And where do we go from here? *AI Magazine*, 1982, *2*.

Duda, R., Gaschnig, J., & Hart, P.E.: Model design in the PROSPECTOR consultant system for mineral exploration. In: D. Michie (ed.): *Expert systems in the micro-electronic age*. Edinburgh: Edinburgh University Press, 1979, 153-167.

Elam, J.J., & Henderson, J.C.: Knowledge engineering concepts for decision support system design and implementation. *Information & Management*, 1983, *6*, 109-114.

Fischhoff, B., & Johnson, S.: The possibility of distributed decision making. Unpublished manuscript, 1985.

Ford, F.N.: Decision support systems and expert systems: A comparison. *Information & Management*, 1985, *8*, 21-26.

Fox, M.S.: The intelligent management system: An overview. In: H.G. Sol (ed.): *Processes and tools for decision support*. Amsterdam: North-Holland, 1983, 105-130.

Fox, M.S.: Knowledge representation for decision support. In: L.B. Methlie & R.H. Sprague (eds.): *Knowledge Representation for decision support systems*. Amsterdam: North-Holland, 1985, 3-26.

Fuglseth, A.M., & Stabell, C.B.: Capture, representation, and diagnosis of user information perception. In: L.B. Methlie, & R.H. Sprague Jr. (eds.): *Knowledge representation for decision support systems*. Amsterdam, North-Holland, 1985, 191-210.

Hart, P.E.: Directions for AI in the eighties. *SIGART Newsletter, 79*, 1982, 11-16.

Hayes-Roth, F., Waterman, D.A., & Lenat, D.B.: *Building expert systems*. Reading, Mass.: Addison-Wesely, 1983.

Lindsay, R., Buchanan, B.C., Feigenbaum, E.A., & Lederberg, J.: *Applications of artificial intelligence for chemical inference: The DENDRAL project*. New York: McGraw-Hill, 1980.

Keen, P.G.: Adaptive design for decision support systems. *Database*, 1980, *12*, 15-25.

Keen, P.G. & Morton, M.S.: *Decision Support Systems: An organizational perspective*. Reading, Mass.: Addison-Wesely, 1978.

McDermott, J.: R1: A rule-based configurer of computer systems. *Artificial Intelligence*, 1982, *19*, 39-88.

Newell, A., Simon, H.A.: *Human problem solving*. Englewood Cliffs, N.J.: Prentice-Hall, 1972.

Pfeifer, R., & Nicholas, D.W.: Toward computational models of emotion. In: L. Steels & J.A. Campbell (eds.): *Progress in Artificial Intelligence*. New York: Ellis Horwood, 1985, 184-192.

ople, H.E. Jr.: Heuristic methods for imposing structure on ill-structured problems: The structuring of medical diagnostics. In: P. Szolovits (ed.): *Artificial Intelligence in medicine*. Boulder, CO: Westview Press, 1982.

Shortliffe, E.H.: *MYCIN: Computer-based medical consultations*. New York: Elsevier, 1976.

Simon, H.A.: *The new science of management decision*. New York: Harper & Row, 1960.

Sol, H.G.: Processes and tools for decision support. Inferences for future development. In: H.G. Sol (ed.): *Processes and tools for decision support*. Amsterdam: North-Holland, 1983, 1-6.

prague, R.H.: A framework for research on Decision Support Systems. In: G. Fick, & R.H. Sprague (eds.): *Decision Support Systems: Issues and challenges*. Oxford: Pergamon Press, 1980.

Sprague, R.H., & Carlson, E.D.: *Building effective decision support systems*. Englewood Cliffs, N.J.: Prentice-Hall, 1982.

Stamper, R.: Management epistemology: Garbage in, garbage out (and what about deontology and axiology?). In: L.B. Methlie, & R.H. Sprague (eds.): *Knowledge representation for Decision Support Systems*. Amsterdam: North-Holland, 1985, 55-77.

teels, L., & Van de Velde, W.: Learning in second generation expert systems. A.I. Memo code 3/M1, Artificial Intelligence Laboratory, Vrije Universiteit Brussels, 1985.

Watson, H.J., & Christy, D.P.: University support programs offered by vendors of DSS generators. *Communications of the ACM*, 1983, *26*, 1098-1099.

Responsive Decision Support Systems:
A Broad View Illustrates When to Include Expert Systems

Harold A. Kurstedt, Jr.
Management Systems Laboratories
Department of Industrial Engineering & Operations Research
Virginia Polytechnic Institute and State University
Blacksburg, Virginia 24061

ABSTRACT. We help managers most by providing tools to support
decision making. A management system model, used as an internal
framework, looks at management tools and their relationships with
the manager and his or her operation. To realize its full
potential, view a decision support system top-down, from the
manager's perspective. The model gives us a broad view so that we
can compare decision support systems (DSS), management information
systems (MIS), expert systems (ES), and other popular tools when
considering the shape of automation for molding management tools.
The computer is not a requisite for any such tools. Ultimately,
success for management tools depends on distinguishing between means
(management tools) and ends (operations tools) and on the
relationship between management tools and their user. When building
intelligence into management tools, responsiveness is the first
order of business, and expert replication is a lower order. Expert
replication leads to automation. The preeminent tool is the
decision support system; all other management tools are part of the
decision support system.

ACCREDITATION. The ideas presented in this paper represent the
cumulative work of more than a hundred people over eight years at
Virginia Tech's Management Systems Laboratories. Professional
managers from business and industry and faculty, graduate students,
and undergraduates from a wide variety of engineering and other
disciplines have participated in the research and development of the
management tools and techniques described in this paper. The
conceptual models have evolved from empirical evidence gained in
real-world laboratories which consist of applying the tools and
techniques in the work places of the Laboratories' contract sponsors.

MANAGERS USE TOOLS TO HELP MAKE DECISIONS--A SUMMARY.

(This section condenses the paper's content and could stand

53

H. G. Sol et al. (eds.), Expert Systems and Artificial Intelligence in Decision Support Systems, 53–77.
© 1987 by D. Reidel Publishing Company.

alone for the hurried reader. I encourage the reader seeking more
depth to continue reading after the summary to expand and support
these ideas.)

Decision making is synonymous with managing. Simon begins with
this premise for describing the decision process[1] and for
comparing repetitive, routine decisions to those requiring judgment
dependent on experience, insight, and intuition.[2] Forrester uses
this premise when constructing his model for information flow and
feedback within a business system.[3] Simon in 1960 and Forrester
in 1961 began a two-decade search involving many scholars to
understand a manager's domain of responsibility. A domain of
responsibility is a connected, identifiable object of authority for
which a person is accountable. Everyone has one or more domains of
responsibility; and, using Drucker's idea of an executive[4], each
such person uses information to make decisions resulting in actions
affecting what is managed within that domain.

The focal point of the search for understanding domains of
responsibility is decision making. I believe the one consistent,
irreducible object of the search is tools for helping make
decisions. Simon and others give us frameworks to place a domain of
responsibility in context; to view it externally, drawing
comparisons with other domains. Forrester and others give us
frameworks to view the internal or mechanical workings of a domain
of responsibility. Contextual frameworks show the cause-and-effect
matches between categories of management tools and categories of
domains. Mechanical frameworks show the relationships among
management tools, between the tools and their users, and between
users and their decisions.

I use the Management System Model (MSM) as a mechanical
framework to study management tools, their relationships, their
success, and reasons for their success.[5] The MSM comprises three
essential components: "who manages," "what is managed," and "what is
used to manage." You are "who manages." "What is managed" is the
physical, tangible things you are responsible for, including your
operations tools. "What is used to manage" is all management tools
including plans, structures, models, corporate culture,
communications, and the data-to-information chain. I separate
management tools from operations tools using the MSM.

This conceptual model embodies the manager's perspective and
characterizes management tools from that perspective. The manager
looks to management tools for support in making decisions affecting
"what is managed." Popular management tools like management
information systems (MIS), decision support systems (DSS), and
expert systems (ES) are defined and compared using the MSM. This
broad view helps us see both the shape of automation for molding
management tools and the relative merits of all management tools for
setting priorities in acquisition and use.

Although management tools are information-based, the
definitions, designs, and developments of these tools don't require
a computer. The need for more rapidly changing information is the
forcing function for the age of information. The computer only

relieves the technical constraint on getting the data to produce that information.

We limit the management tools with the most potential by requiring the computer as part of their definition. These tools include MIS, DSS, and ES. Computer-integrated manufacturing (CIM) has been confined to operational management levels by requiring the computer in the acronym and thereby in our perception. Fortunately, operations research (OR) tools are seen as generic solutions, and the computer is applied after hand solutions are understood.

To get all our management tools to work together for us, we must focus on our ends--what is managed. We manage physical things, representations of physical things, and our operations tools. What we manage is physical and measurable. We manage with our means--our management tools. We must distinguish between our means and ends from a management perspective. The user of our management tools includes both the manager and the operation being managed. To be successful, the tools must fit both.

The MSM gives us the framework to define success for our management tools. They must be used to manage by the manager and managed by someone else. A successful management system balances the essential "who manages," "what is managed," and "what is used to manage" MSM components by attention to their interfaces. With an idea of what success is, we can see how to get successful management tools.

The management tools of the "what is used to manage" component through their interrelatedness constitute a DSS. A taxonomy of these tools includes 1) relationships and structures, 2) methods, 3) guides and rules, 4) precedence, and 5) the data-to-information chain (the MIS). Quantitative models, heuristics, paperwork, and ES constitute the methods classification. Operations research tools are part of the methods classification. Guides include policies, plans, procedures, and instructions used for strategic-, tactical-, operational-, and clerical-level endeavors, respectively. You should produce a plan, an organization structure, an MIS, and other tools all working together by causing the goals and objectives of the domain of responsibility to influence their design. Then the strength of their interrelatedness would support decision making.

The MSM with other internal and external frameworks helps us choose combinations of tools from alternatives by seeing our domain of responsibility both "from the inside" and "from the outside." Based on the characteristics and components of the domain, we can determine the value, use, and mechanization of ES, MIS, and OR tools in a DSS package. Using the taxonomy for management tools, ES and OR tools are alternate methods for suggesting solutions; the MIS provides the routine links of acquiring, storing, and retrieving data to make and portray information; and the DSS integrates all management tools for decision making.

Relatively speaking and based on my own definitions, ES and quantitative models are tools within the methods classification, and MIS is a classification. However, DSS is an interacting assemblage

of all management tools--the totality of what we use to manage. The
DSS relates the tools to each other and to the domain of
responsibility. Then a type of tool (e.g. ES or OR model) dominates
only for those domains in which it's suitable. The manager selects
tools from available alternatives to match characteristics of the
domain. The inability to tell which tool best fits which domain of
responsibility has led to high failure rates within ill-conceived
management systems. The MSM is used descriptively to define
relationships and prescriptively for choosing tools to improve
decision making.

As I define it, we would expect DSS to apply everywhere and be
our only option, where other, more limited tools don't apply.
Expert systems are best for closed systems with operational
endeavors and structured decisions. Replicating an expert captures
intelligence for a DSS; so does developing responsiveness in
management tools. Expert systems make important specific
contributions to well-defined, routine decision making. Expert
systems lead to automation. Responsive systems have a more
immediate and far-reaching effect on improved decision making.

A responsive DSS is the concept of choice for improving decision
support tools. Responsiveness includes 1) timeliness, 2) the
ability to observe and understand "who manages" and "what is
managed"--collectively, the user--and 3) the ability to interpret
the user and willingly carry out the user's wishes and needs. I
define four types of responsive systems: adaptive, adaptable,
flexible, and custom fit. Responsiveness is a key influence at two
MSM interfaces: information-perception-to-information-portrayal
and measurement-to-data. Responsiveness is evaluated at the third
interface, decision-to-action.

THE MANAGEMENT SYSTEM MODEL PUTS MANAGEMENT TOOLS IN PERSPECTIVE.

Clearly, we need a structured approach for understanding and
applying management tools. To be useful to managers, the approach
should be based on information processing. I offer a manager's
approach for describing any domain of responsibility. I call the
structured approach the Management System Model (MSM). The domain
is a system with structure, process, and environment.

The Management System Model balances its essential
components--"who manages," "what is managed," and "what is used to
manage." This balance is achieved by focusing on the interfaces
between MSM components shown in Figure 1.[5]

"Who manages" is <u>anyone</u> who uses information to make decisions
resulting in actions affecting "what is managed." In addition to
presidents, directors, and controllers, "who manages" includes
scientists and the secretary who uses information to decide who can
or can't talk with the boss. The "what is managed" component
includes the tangible physical things that are managed and includes
operations tools (not to be confused with management tools used to
manage). For example, in a hardware wholesale-warehousing business,

"what is managed" is not pick tickets or sales reports; rather, this
component includes hammers and chisels, storage bins, trucks, and
loading docks.

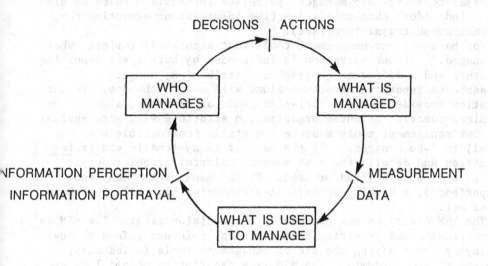

**Figure 1: A Successful Management System
Balances Three Essential Components.**

The "what is used to manage" component comprises the tools with
which we manage. This component is the link between the management
systems of different organizations. The link occurs through
communications (formal or informal, routine or non-routine), the
organization structure, an MIS, and other management tools. Routine
paperwork is also part of "what is used to manage," along with tools
like company policies and procedures and the data-to-information
chain used to manage the warehousing business in my example.

A manager who assumes that success will result from completing
paperwork, establishing a good organization structure, or developing
a computer-based MIS, will fail both in managing his or her
management system and in achieving the system objectives. A common
source of failure is the emphasis on "what is used to manage" as the
<u>end</u> rather than the <u>means</u>. The focal point of managerial concern
should be the physical things that constitute "what is managed."

We balance the three essential components by matching both sides
of each interface between the components. "Who manages" makes
decisions based on information that is useful or preferable. In his
fundamental work, <u>Industrial Dynamics</u>[6], Jay Forrester calls
management "the process of converting information into action."
Converting decisions to actions is the necessary end result of using
information (the decision-to-action interface). I say, "If you
don't know who does what to whom as a result of information, then
you don't need the information." Through measurements to assess

performance, data are generated which represent characteristics of
"what is managed" (the measurement/data interface). Information
results from biasing data[5] and is portrayed in one of four
portrayal formats; "who manages" perceives information based on his
or her individual characteristics (the information-perception-to-
information-portrayal interface).

For balance, our management tools must accurately reflect "what
is managed." If our operation is influenced by both a set reporting
structure and a different geographic distribution, budget
spreadsheets reporting structure alone will not do the job. If our
operation provides customer-oriented goods or services, a
technical-function-oriented organization structure will work against
us. Our management tools must be acceptable (comfortable and
useful) to "who manages." If the manager is systematic and prefers
definition and detail, the most modern, colorful graphics output
package will not be liked or used. If the manager is young and
inexperienced, a highly sophisticated financial plan will overwhelm
him or her.

The MSM describes the process of the decision maker. The MSM is
a conceptual model resulting from empirical evidence gained through
developing and studying the use of management tools in industry,
government, and academia. The MSM is a descriptive model; I am now
developing instruments for measuring characteristics of the
components and their interfaces and applying those instruments in
industry, government, and academia. Then, the MSM can be used as a
prescriptive model for relating the measured characteristics.
Ultimately, equations can be developed, and the prescriptive model
can be empirically applied to the domain of responsibility. I
expect to use effective descriptions to generate efficient
prescriptions. The MSM models decision making or, in other words,
managing.

The MSM is an internal or mechanical framework for understanding
a domain of responsibility. There are other internal frameworks. I
will briefly discuss other internal frameworks after I review four
external frameworks. The external frameworks help in characterizing
and comparing domains.

LOOK AT YOUR DOMAIN FROM DIFFERENT ANGLES, TO KNOW IT.

How can you characterize or specifically describe your domain of
responsibility (management system)? How is your domain like those
of others? What tools work well for domains like yours and may or
may not work for you? Why? How do you tell the difference?

I will describe four external frameworks for classifying what
you do and putting your domain of responsibility in context. The
first and fourth frameworks are mine, and the middle two are adapted
from Anthony[7] and Simon.[8] These frameworks will help you answer
questions like: I know I have a critical path, but why can't I
determine slack time? Why can't I control my operation? Why won't
my management tools work as well for me as they did for the manager
who recommended them to me?

Sometimes You Know Where You Are Going, and Sometimes You Don't.

In the first framework, I classify uncertainty (or lack of definition) in your domain of responsibility. I use Jay Galbraith's definition of uncertainty as the difference between information possessed and information required to complete a task.[9]

I classify the major broad efforts that you manage in your domain of responsibility into what I call pursuits.[10] Each pursuit fits one of the following classifications; perplexity, problem, program, project, or process.[5] In a perplexity, you possess almost none of the needed information because it is unknown. In a process, you possess almost all of the needed information. "As work-related uncertainty increases, so does the need for increased amounts of information, and thus, the need for increased information processing capacity."[11]

In a perplexity, you know neither the end nor the start of the pursuit. In emergency preparedness, for example, you must manage the preparation for any contingency. You do know the start of a problem but not the end. In emergency response, for example, you manage the incident within the constraints of occurrences beyond your control. A program has a definite starting point but only a qualitative fix on the end. A typical research and development program is an example. For a project, you have specifications for the end and know the beginning. A construction project is an example. When you are responsible for a pursuit that routinely and repeatedly achieves the same known end, that is a process; making bottles is such a pursuit.

Government agencies deal more with perplexities, problems, and programs than do industrial organizations. For these pursuits, the end isn't known, and traditional management techniques such as CPM and resource loading don't work. Greater amounts of information must be obtained, verified, and updated on a timely basis to support managers of these pursuits. Entirely new techniques based on the same requirements (resource loading, for example) must be developed. The system that supports decisions for these pursuits must be more flexible and more repeatable then for other pursuits.

For the more certain pursuits, we can concentrate on management tools for productivity and efficiency, which Peter Drucker[12] says means doing things right. For the more uncertain pursuits, we must attend to performance or effectiveness, which Drucker says means doing the right things.

As you think about the different pursuits, you will realize that you really have some of all (or almost all) of them in your domain of responsibility. You have a spectrum of responsibilities across the classifications of the framework. Therefore, you need many management tools so you can use the right tool for the right thing. You will also realize that to a greater or lesser extent, one of the classifications dominates and should influence your priorities in obtaining and improving your management tools.

One fundamental issue in artificial intelligence is inference under uncertainty. Perhaps this concept of uncertainty deals more with changing conditions then directly with Galbraith's definition. However, the concepts of uncertainty are not far apart. My question is whether in the reasonably near future artificial intelligence is going to support decision making more at the perplexity end of the spectrum or at the process end. The answer orients managers toward priorities in developing management tools for their domains of responsibility.

A Broad Effort Extends Your Effect and Limits Your Support.

The second framework is adapted from the work of R.N. Anthony.[13] I classify the things you do in your domain of responsibility as levels of endeavors. (I save the word "activity" for another meaning and another purpose.) I define endeavors as your serious, determined efforts directed toward a result. These endeavors are performed at sequentially greater levels of broadness of perspective, generality in direction, and responsibility (answerability). The four levels of endeavors in sequence toward greater broadness and generality are clerical, operational, tactical, and strategic. In this framework, you have a spectrum of endeavors, for which one predominates.

Anthony's framework, intended for thinking about management planning and control systems, categorizes organizational activities as strategic planning, management control, and operational control. His interest was in the purpose of management activities. Most information system and decision support problems have occurred when managers try to be successful at the strategic planning level based on successes at the operational control level. Expert systems will follow this phenomenon for the same reasons. I have adapted Anthony's framework to include strategic, tactical, operational, and clerical endeavors.

Your strategic-level endeavors are of greater importance within your integrated efforts; they embrace all considerations, entail greater risks and consequences, and are global in nature. Be careful not to confuse strategic-level endeavors with strategic-level managers. The corporate president is a strategic-level manager who has endeavors at the strategic as well as the tactical, operational, and even the clerical levels.

Of the four levels of endeavors, strategic, tactical, and operational are management levels. Tactical-level endeavors are aimed at controlling your operation. The operational level is the lowest level of management. This level assures that specific tasks are carried out effectively and efficiently. The fourth level, clerical, is a "doing" endeavor rather than a managing one.

On a production line in a manufacturing plant, the operator does mostly clerical-level tasks, as does a secretary. However, these people do have operational-level endeavors involving staffing, scheduling, and procurement. From time to time, they may plan procurement or measure performance—tactical-level endeavors. The

foreman on the same production line is concerned with scheduling
maintenance and keeping the line at peak performance; he has mostly
operational-level endeavors. The shift supervisor has production
goals and considers product changeover and other mostly
tactical-level endeavors. The plant manager is concerned with
profitability and long-range planning; these endeavors are strategic.

Which Decisions Are Based on Definite Procedures?

The third framework is adapted from the work of H. A. Simon [14]
and Gorry and Scott Morton [15]. As managers, we all must make
decisions, and these should result in actions that affect "what is
managed." For different domains of responsibility, different types
of decisions predominate.

Originally, H. A. Simon distinguished two polar types of
decisions: programmed decisions and unprogrammed decisions—those
which are made based on a definite procedure and those for which
there are no specific procedures. Gorry and Scott Morton used "the
terms structured and unstructured for programmed and unprogrammed
because they imply less dependence on the computer and more
dependence on the basic character of the problem-solving activity in
question."[16]

In the structured situation, all of Simon's phases of the
decision-making process—intelligence, design, and choice—can be
automated. In the unstructured situation, the human decision maker
must provide judgment, evaluation, and insights into the decision.
Gorry and Scott Morton [15] added a semi-structured classification
for those unstructured decisions just below a hypothetical dividing
line between structured and unstructured decisions. As our ability
to automate improves, the semi-structured decisions will become
structured. (This point is important later when I consider the
evolution of expert systems.) I classify unstructured,
semi-structured, and structured decisions as the decision-making
types in my third framework.

Gorry and Scott Morton coined the term Decision Support Systems
(DSS) to include management tools managers use to support their
semi-structured and unstructured decisions. Management tools for
structured decisions include "...an area that has had almost nothing
to do with real managers or information but has been largely routine
data processing."[17]

The mix of decision types regularly required within a domain of
responsibility at a given level indicates the parts of that domain
to be delegated to various subordinate personnel and machines to
effectively accomplish the manager's needs. In other words, these
frameworks help answer the question, "Who decides what and with what
kind of information?" The ideal is to free as much highest-level
managerial time as possible from making the least-structured
decisions. A manager's responsibility is, in short, to address his
or her endeavors and to provide structure and systematic guidance
for subordinate personnel—incorporating the human element into the
scientific approaches first suggested by Frederick Taylor.[18] The

manager does so by configuring the people, the information tools,
and the interfaces between people and tools so that 1) every element
of the domain works efficiently in his, her, and its
subresponsibility, and 2) all work together effectively as a system.

Your Management System Matures through Three Sequential Stages.

The fourth framework deals with the maturity of your management
system. Your management system, your operation, and your management
tools must mature sequentially through three maturity stages. To
try to skip a stage is to fail. The driving force for maturity is
"who manages" and requires that the three essential components of
the MSM be in balance for a preceding stage before the succeeding
stage can be attempted.

For success, the MSM components must be in balance. If an MIS
provides accurate and timely, but too sophisticated, information for
the decision maker, the components are not in balance and the
management system fails. The interfaces keep the components in
balance. This is an impedance matching problem; someday we will
model it mathematically to observe cause-and-effect relationships
and conduct sensitivity analyses.

When the components are in balance, the manager is happy and
successful; then, he wants more. Then the manager's manager wants
more. This series of demands induces a dynamic, always-maturing
system.

The stages through which managers mature with a successful
management system can be defined. They first gain visibility of
their physical operation. They learn how to control their domain by
being able to reduce the number of changes that occur and hold the
operation constant. Finally, they optimize their domain to get the
most out of the operation that they can. A management system
matures through the stages of visibility, control, and optimization.

Visibility is gained by effective presentation of key
information based on complete, comprehensive, coordinated, accurate,
and timely data. Key information varies throughout the life of an
organization. Without effective visibility, management action is
not completely informed.

An operation is stable when it can be held to steady-state, and
decisions do not have to be made based on unpredictable variations.
Even if the throughput is held constant--not necessarily at the best
throughput experienced--the stability provides improved
performance. Control means taking corrective action if performance
deviates too far from plans and standards and, thus, integrates
activities by keeping them all within established bounds.

Only after visibility can the manager move to control--the
"prescription" stage in which he or she moves the system back on
track through direction and curbing. Finally, the manager optimizes
the system to get the most out of the pursuit that he or she can.

Optimization is the accomplishment of maximum effectiveness,
efficiency, and/or usefulness. Optimization is accomplished by
varying plans and standards as a result of experience, and

controlling to the new plans and standards. (Some managers might be happy with satisficing after achieving control.)

The models or frameworks that describe the context or externals of your domain complement the mechanics or internals of your domain. The contextual and mechanical frameworks reinforce one another; together, they provide a full and accurate description of any manager's domain of responsibility. Let's now examine these mechanics or internals.

LOOK AT THE COMPONENTS OF YOUR DOMAIN TO PLACE YOUR TOOLS.

To supplement the MSM, look at other internal frameworks. I will briefly describe three frameworks reviewed from the literature.

Information for Decisions Should Lead to Actions.

Forrester[3] defines management as the process of converting information into action; that is, decision making. He structures the relationships between information, decisions, and actions in a feedback system where "Information is the input to a decision-making point that controls actions yielding new information."[19] In short, if you don't know who does what to whom as a result of information, you don't need the information.

The manager is an information converter who chooses those information sources to take seriously and those to ignore. The manager also chooses what use is made of the chosen information. Decision making is a response to the gap between the organization's objectives and its progress toward these objectives as indicated by the information system.

Forrester develops this very simple conceptual framework into a complex non-linear, closed-loop, feedback system. His industrial dynamics approach considers the "what is used to managed" component (as information) and the decision-to-action interface of the MSM. He also builds in time delays, amplification, and information distortion, and writes equations for groups of information-decision-action combinations.

A Complex Model is Hard to Use.

Blumenthal[20] synthesizes the works of Anthony, Simon, and Forrester. His framework was conceived specifically for planning and developing management information systems. It divides the organization into domains of responsibility, grouped by function, and considers how each type of organizational unit is linked through various subsystems. An MIS captures data about "what is managed" and generates information used in domains of responsibility throughout the organization for making decisions leading to actions.

This framework includes all components and interfaces of the MSM except how information is portrayed or how it is perceived by managers. As opposed to Forrester's framework, Blumenthal's framework is quite complex. A large number of definitions and relationships must be known to understand the framework.

Does the Management Tool Suit the Manager and the Operation?

Macintosh[21] explicitly considers the characteristics of the decision maker, along with those of the task and management tools. His framework is based on the premise that accounting and information systems should be congruent with the organizational context in which they are used. The context is determined by two variables--personal decision style and organizational technology. Organizational technology is based on whether task variety is low or high and whether the existing body of task knowledge leads to "analyzable" or "non-analyzable" searches for solutions. Organization structures should match decision style and technology. Decision style is based on how much information the manager needs to determine whether the data have single or multiple interpretations.
    Macintosh deals with the manager-to-management-tool interface, although not in terms of information portrayal formats or human perception. He also recognizies that the "what is managed" component should affect management tools.

YOU USE MANAGEMENT TOOLS TO MANAGE WITH.

    As a manager, you make decisions to affect your operation. Models and frameworks to describe your domain of responsibility help identify which tools will help you manage best.
    You manage some tools; you manage with others.[22] If you manage a factory, you are responsible for manufacturing process lines, trucks, and hammers--which I call operations tools; you manage these tools. In an office, you may manage reports, proposals, and analyses as well as people and machines. Your operations tools, and other things you manage, contact or become part of your product or service.
    You have other tools you use to manage; these are your management tools. Your management tools are information-based. You conceivably could potentially keep most, if not all, your management tools in your head. For example, you put a budget, an organization structure, a plan, or a management information system on paper because there is too much to keep in your head, and you also want to disseminate the tools: But, you could keep them in your head and still do your job. Some managers even try to do this. However, you cannot do your job with a truck or a hammer in your head.
    Take a moment and separate your means and ends. You manage physical things like people, materials, and machines; representations of physical things like reports, airline tickets, and positions; and your operations tools; these are your ends. Without them, you couldn't deliver your product or service. Through his or her senses, the user of your product or service expects to experience the results of what you manage. Our management tools

help us manage. They should work for us, not against us. Also, they should work together, not at odds with each other.

An important exception to all of this in the age of information is the manager whose business is developing or delivering management tools--a computer hardware or software business, for example. Separating ends and means is more difficult because you physically manage management tools and use management tools to manage with. You might even use your own product.

You have a system of tools which comprises all your decision support tools ("what is used to manage") and their degree of interrelatedness. I classify this system of tools into five functional groups.[5] The methods, guides and rules, precedence, and data-to-information chain (four of the groups) are tied together within your domain of responsibility and between your domain and the domains of others through relationships and structures (the fifth group).

Note that you don't manage your organization structure (one of the structures in the fifth group of management tools); you use it to manage with. Therefore, to help you, your organization structure must suit you and fit "what is managed" rather than vice versa.

Whether the method (one of the five groups) you use to manage is a quantitative model, paperwork, rule of thumb, or expert system, you look for a suggested solution based on the assumptions and limitations inherent in the method. As managers, we compare our solutions and judgment to the method and either agree with the method's solution, adjust our solution, or question the method by adjusting constraints or quizzing alternatives.

Your domain of responsibility has an attendant history and culture. I include history and culture[23,24] with concepts like socialization[25] in the group of tools called precedence. Waterman and Peters in In Search of Excellence[26] highlight the importance of corporate culture in success.

We use policies, plans, and other guides as formulation tools to support our goals and objectives at different levels of endeavor. Correlations can be drawn between our guides, what we accomplish, and our levels of endeavors.[5]

The data-to-information chain is what is commonly called MIS. The MIS is best understood using the MSM and comparing it to DSS.

THE MSM DEFINES MIS, DSS, AND ES FROM THE MANAGER'S PERSPECTIVE.

MIS and DSS are easily defined in terms of the Management System Model (MSM).[5] An MIS is one of the tools used to manage; it comprises the data-to-information chain. The word "chain" implies links in a process of acquiring, storing, retrieving, and manipulating data to generate and portray information. Output of the data-to-information chain can instantaneously feed heuristics and historically feed plans and procedures. In Figure 1, the MIS is the portion of the chain linking the measurement-to-data interface with the information-portrayal-to-information-perception interface.

The information-perception-to-information-portrayal interface is important here because <u>all information is biased</u>. Information can be portrayed in several formats, including tables. "Sensing" people prefer tables, which have the least bias and the most systematic presentation. Spreadsheets are a good example--they are a favorite for anyone dealing with financial data, especially government managers.

The MIS describes "what is managed" based on measurements and supports "who manages" based on information perception. Manual or automated, the regular and continuing process of making information from data is separate from other management tools such as policies, plans, procedures, and heuristics.

A DSS is more comprehensive than an MIS; it includes <u>all</u> the tools within the "what is used to manage" component, and it addresses their interrelatedness. The DSS focuses on the totality of the information portrayed to support decisions. The DSS includes the MIS and more--it also includes policies, plans, and procedures; formal and informal communications; heuristics, quantitative models, and experts; the organization structure; and many other tools. According to my definition, DSS includes not only MIS (for response), but also these last items for planning and preparing for (anticipating) change.[27]

Clearly MIS and DSS are tools or groups of tools within a management system. Hence, DSS is not a discipline. Only the MSM includes all the components and interfaces to close the loop. Thus, if a discipline is in question here, the management system is it, and DSS is a subdiscipline. As subdisciplines, OR models and DSS are in the discipline, bringing a wide range of tools together to focus on a specific domain of responsibility--the management system.

Unfortunately, almost all definitions in the literature of MIS and DSS specify that the tools be computer-based. But the foregoing discussion should help us see that the computer is obviously not a requisite for either MIS or DSS. From the management system perspective, any tool, whether manual or automated, formal or informal, routine or non-routine, is included in the concepts of MIS and DSS.

An expert system (ES) is one of the methods tools. The standard definition places the ES within the body of a computer; I do not. An ES includes the replication of an expert's knowledge of facts and rules for generating new facts or hypotheses from what is known. These facts and rules are applied to a very limited, well-defined domain of responsibility. The ES is structured in such a way that it can lead a machine or clerical person toward intelligent advice or an intelligent decision about the process of that domain of responsibility. Further, the ES allows the user to repeat and identify the line of reasoning by which the advice or decision was reached.

A deterministic logic chart is an ES I frequently use to capture an emergency manager's line of reasoning and action in responding to an unusual occurrence. The logic chart details the flow of response actions that the emergency plan elaborates. By documenting the step-by-step progression, I enhance training, employ intelligent automation, and clarify the place each tool occupies within the emergency management system. Each logic chart is designed to identify potential gaps and overlaps in emergency responsibilities and response actions.

A SUCCESSFUL DSS HELPS BALANCE THE MANAGEMENT SYSTEM MODEL COMPONENTS.

The industrial engineer's systems approach states that subsystems are successful only if they contribute to the success of the overall system of interest. MIS, ES, or DSS success therefore depends on management system success.

An examination of a successful MIS reveals three commonly used development stratgies that balance the MSM components. A fourth strategy to balance the components is dangerous, because it loses sight of management system objectives.[28]

First, a computer-based MIS can be implemented by merely automating an existing manual system. Second, a manager can get so excited about MIS development that he or she devotes inordinate amounts of time and energy to ensure a custom fit between the MIS and his or her needs. Third, for some common specific needs involving structured decisions, a range of computer-based MIS packages has been developed. These packages have broad application and markets. Often, a package can be found which fits the manager's specific need well enough that the management system components are nearly balanced.

Sometimes, in an effort to get aboard the computer bandwagon or to shore up management inadequacies, some managers will force the components of their management system to fit an improperly developed MIS or an off-the-shelf MIS package. The new management system, forced to fit the MIS, may appear to be balanced, giving an illusion of success. However, because of the forced fit, the new management system probably no longer addresses the original system goals and objectives. The computer-based MIS may appear successful while the entire management system fails. Such an illusory success portends dire long-term consequences for real MIS success.

Other management tools within the DSS exhibit similar development stratgies for balancing MSM components. Based on the "what is managed" component and the domain's environment, the manager will have many or few interactions with the environment. In addition to the manager's capability, experience, cognitive style, and personality traits, the uncertainty of pursuit, comprehensiveness of endeavor level, structure and routineness of decisions, and management system maturity will affect the choice of management tool. As we consider management tools, we focus on their characteristics and select tools based on suitability, not just on features.

Together, the external and internal frameworks fully describe the domain of responsibility. Externally, what domain characteristics indicate a plan, an organization structure, an ES, or an MIS as part of a successful DSS? Internally, does the manager prefer information to support problem formulation and decisions, or does the manager want suggested solutions from replicated experts? How can we best mechanize a guide, an expert, or a database for this domain of responsibility? How can we best automate strategy, decision making, action taking, or information portrayal?

The management problem must be defined before the solution can be determined. First, delimit the domain of responsibility. Describe that domain's characteristics using external frameworks and components using internal frameworks. Iterate as needed between the three considerations: delimiting the domain, describing its characteristics, and determining its components. A greater understanding of one consideration promotes understanding of the other two. Now consider the tools to balance the known components of a known domain with known characteristics. Assemble the consistent set of management tools to work interactively as a DSS to keep the MSM components in balance.

AN ES IS A METHODS TOOL IN DSS.

In my taxonomy, an expert system (ES) is one of the methods' classification of tools, and MIS is the data-to-information chain. With other tools and other classifications of tools, ES and MIS can work together to provide a DSS. The manager selects the best combination of management tools from available alternatives to make up a DSS.

The ES is different from the other methods in that it replicates an "expert" and can regurgitate its inferences and line of reasoning; thus, it includes and is the natural extension of automation techniques developed since the beginning of the century. Note that a speller and a manufacturing line operator is expert at more operational-level endeavors than a physician and crisis manager is at tactical- or strategic-level endeavors. However, all of these examples develop their expertise through learning, experience, and habit learned through repetition. They also all apply that expertise using intuition and judgment. The ES not only includes a problem-solving ability, which achieves high-levels of performance on problems that normally require years of special education and training for human beings to solve, but it also has the ability to adapt to the situation.

ES may or may not employ reasoning based on probability. Without probability, the chain of reasoning has the force of logic. With probability, we cannot guarantee that the conclusions are repeatable or are necessarily true.

Within the methods category of the "what is used to manage" component of the MSM, I include (in sequence of decreasing definition and repeatability and increasing requirement for the manager's judgment) quantitative models, ES, and heuristics. If any algorithmic solution will work, ES is inappropriate.

The broader categorization of artificial intelligence (AI), includes, among other things, robotics and ES. Robotics and ES are tools: the first, part of "what is managed;" the second, one of the methods of "what is used to manage."

Expert systems are now being called "knowledge-based systems," and the specialists in ES are calling themselves "knowledge engineers" and their work "knowledge engineering." Whether knowledge is power or knowledge goes hand-in-hand with power, the importance of knowledge does not automatically imply the importance of knowledge-based systems or ES. We must deal with the human element--"who manages."

Expertise involves both public knowledge and private knowledge contained in the judgment and insight of the expert. It has been suggested that if reasoning ". . . is not codifiable, then perhaps we may feel that it is not logical and therefore does not merit attention."[29] ES researchers emphasize knowledge because 1) difficult and interesting problems do not have algorithmic solutions (since complex social or physical implications defy precise description and rigorous analysis), 2) human experts perform because they are knowledgeable, and 3) knowledge is a scarce resource whose refinement and reproduction creates wealth.[30]

YESTERDAY'S HUMAN EXPERT IS TODAY'S ES AND TOMORROW'S AUTOMATION.

The ES bridges the gap between quantitative models and heuristics. Once the line of reasoning can be structured and automated, the knowledge engineers feel the system no longer is classed as ES. Thus, what is called ES is continually changing, and describing what constitutes ES is difficult.

I choose to believe that the automation line in the local plant certainly was and probably still is an ES. Forsyth says that "(ES) . . . actually works. It does a job that takes a human years of training."[31] I note the word "training" instead of "education" and think of all the jobs that have been automated that took years of training to learn in years past. The automation system, or ES, became the "who manages" in that very limited, well-defined management system.

Describing automation is as difficult as describing ES. Notice the similarity between the following definitions of automation and ES. "A scientific definition of the place of automation in the development of technology can not refrain from taking into account, on the one hand, the inseparable bond connecting automation with the entire history of the gradual strengthening and extension of the power of man over the forces of nature, and on the other, the qualitatively novel features which distinguish automation from the preceding stages of technological development. ...Therefore, the conversion to automation completes the liberation of man from the immediate participation in the industrial process and changes abruptly the entire character of human labor. Up to now, the machine replaced the hands and the muscles of man; at present, it

begins to replace, within certain limits, his brain and nervous
system."[32]   James Bright indicates that some authors equate
automation with "decision-making machinery."[33]   He emphasizes that
"Automation has a way of shifting with time. Yesterday's
'automated' plant is surpassed today, but how else except by
something 'more automatic'?"[34]   Bright suggests this definition:
"...automation simply means something significantly more automatic
than previously existed in that plant, industry, or location."[35]

At one time, even today's best defined, most routine, and very
likely highly-automated domain of responsibility needed an expert to
manage it. By expert, I mean someone with years of training who has
made intelligent decisions based on facts and inferences related to
their limited domain. By following the same facts and inferences,
the expert would repeat the same decisions. We couldn't immediately
replicate the expert because we couldn't quantify and measure the
expert's experience, judgment, and insight. We considered the
decisions of the expert largely unstructured or non-programmable, or
at least semi-structured.

I have many times experienced a sequence of events in
replicating an expert, and will share one such experience for
illustration. In the leading part of a cigarette factory, the
tobacco is moistened, dried, and blended to just the right
consistency for compaction. In the following part of the factory,
the infinite cigarette rod is compacted and cut into proper
lengths. In this leading part, an old man of many years experience
would sift the tobacco blend through his fingers close to his face
and decide if the tobacco was "ready" for compaction in a cigarette
rod. Did he taste the tobacco? Look at it? Feel it? Smell it?
He couldn't tell you what he did; but, he did it everyday. He was
making unstructured decisions because the variables were undefined,
and he couldn't identify any information as the basis for his
decisions. With much data logging, many wrong guesses and studying
cause-and-effect relationships between variables (gaining
visibility), we found he was measuring moisture history of the blend.

We replicated that expert, used sensors and computers, and
consistently reported the variables compared to reference points for
decision making. We made an expert system. Then we used the
reported information to make repeatable decisions, to control
actuators, and to debug and maintain the process by repeating the
facts and inferences leading to decisions. The ES could not only
report things based on the expert's knowledge, but could do things
based on the expert's knowledge. We automated the whole thing and
have progressed to the point where what we once considered expert is
now only automation. The decisions are now all structured or
programmable.

Whether we have an expert system or automation depends on where
we stand in perspective and maturity. Gorry and Scott Morton point
out that perspective and maturity affect whether a decision is
unstructured, semi-structured, or structured. They realized
decisions would evolve from unstructured toward structured as the
facts and inferences used by the decision maker were defined and

structured. So will go ES. As the expert's facts and inferences became known and replaced intuition and experience, we produced an ES.

The old man in the cigarette factor saw his domain of responsibility evolve from where he just maintained visibility of his operation. Now, through measurement and understanding, we not only have controlled but optimized the old man's expertise; we call this computer optimization or automation. The expert system led to automation. In any new problem, it starts out fuzzy, but when we understand it--turn intuition into information, facts, and inference rules--it seems so simple.

From the systems perspective, the leading part of the cigarette factory is a relatively closed system which, together with the rest of the factory, forms a larger, relatively open system with many complex social, economic, and legal implications of the world outside the factory. From the systems approach, we see each domain as part of a larger domain. Therefore, the automation of a simple domain shifts our attention to a larger, less-defined domain with more unstructured decisions and another opportunity for ES.

Which expert shall we replicate for the management ES, for example? Whose bias do we want? The one that best fits the software/hardware package? The one with the best defined line of logic? The one whose premises we like the most? Anthony Stevens asks, "Does anyone these days admire anyone who can dig a hole or paint a car quickly? We shall soon feel the same dullness about brain work."[36] Is there no brainwork in painting a car? Have you tried it? How about determining if the blended tobacco is ready to go to the compaction process in a cigarette factory? For years, we could not figure out what the worker who decided the right blend was doing or measuring. Nevertheless, the process is now automated.

Are we talking about "professional expertise" here or just "expertise?" We have automated much of what people were trained to do and what people were trained to report. ES are focusing on what people are trained to advise: law, medicine, and accounting. They are moving from blue-collar to white-collar activities. We will still have these counselors, because we pay most for their judgment and insight--and also their experience (a characteristic future ES are supposed to accomplish through learning). In my opinion, in regard to judgment, above the advisors are the teachers, managers, and perhaps the clairvoyants. To learn from teachers, managers, and clairvoyants, we must first develop a global scheme to ask questions to represent, if not capture, their intuition and judgment in a structured package. The bottom line: experts are specialists--they know more and more about less and less--and managers are generalists.

The domain of responsibility can be considered relatively either a closed or open system wherein the closed system has little or no interaction with its surroundings (environment). Expert systems are not appropriate for open systems and should not be applied where models work. Quantitative models bridge the closed-system/open-system gap, and heuristics are most valuable in open systems. Heuristics are redundant to more precise methods in closed systems.

RESPONSIVE SYSTEMS ARE INTELLIGENT TOO.

The greatest advantage of ES to today's managers is the
"fallout" that occurs when researching any new technology. For
example, error messages in computer systems are now suggestions
rather than vague criticism. The technical problems are opaque
explanations, combinatorial explosion, and casting human reasoning
into the form that an ES shell expects.[37]

Automation implies artificial intelligence, in that automation
is different from mechanization. A responsive system is an
intelligent system, although not expert. Responsiveness includes
three characteristics: 1) timeliness--computer-based systems have
shown this characteristic for years, 2) the ability to observe and
understand "who manages" and/or "what is managed"--the manager and
the operation collectively constituting the user, and 3) the ability
to interpret the user and willingly carry out the user's wishes.

I define four types of responsive systems: 1) adaptive systems
are self-molding and inherently adjust to the user without being
told, 2) adaptable systems adjust to the user when and as they are
told, 3) flexible systems offer a series of fixed alternatives from
which the user can choose, and 4) custom-fit systems are designed to
match the user, and any change in the user impairs the match.

We aren't close to an adaptive system. A machine or procedure
that can "read our pulse" and tell us we prefer graphics, need help
routines, or like menus is beyond our technical capability. A
system that can do these things can present different interfaces to
different users. Then we will do much better than our present poor
success rate for developing MIS or DSS.

Before we can build systems to inherently adapt to the user, we
will build systems capable of adapting once they are told how to
adapt. We will input preferences, and the system will adjust
precisely. I built a microcomputer-based simulation model that is
capable of adapting to the preferred simulation speed. By touching
the greater-than or less-than keys, the user tells the system
exactly what speed he or she wants. This is an adaptable
feature--not an adaptable system. We aren't close to an adaptable
system either.

While we wait for technolgy to progress toward adaptive and
adaptable systems, we will enjoy flexible ones. Windowing and other
features allowing the user to choose from several subsystems while
seeing several subsystems together are flexible features. Today's
office automation systems exhibit flexibility. Note that our
choices are specific and limited. Thus, not all users are
satisfied. Satisfaction is achieved through custom-tailored systems.

Responsiveness implies reasoning power and the ability to
monitor and interpret; that is a measure of artificial
intelligence. The characteristic we call "user friendly" is the
facade of responsiveness. The user sees "user friendly" but

experiences responsiveness. Not only should people be responsive but the decision support tools we use should be responsive to both "who manages" and "what is managed."

NO TOOL IS BETTER; IT MAY JUST FIT BETTER.

Expert systems are best for closed systems, inappropriate for open systems, and should not be applied where quantitative models work. ES finds more use moving from strategic toward operational activities and from non-programmed toward programmed decisions. ES is good for dealing with change that is planned and evolutionary.[27] Conversely, responsive DSS are more necessary in the opposite directions. ES and MIS are found in specialist-oriented organizations; DSS is desperately needed to stimulate broader vertical integration, which is now isolated at the top of the management structure.[38] DSS are found in generalist-oriented organizations; ES is needed to support many horizontal integration activities, which are now isolated in pockets at the bottom of the management structure.

ES, OR models, plans, organization structures, and MIS are all management tools working under the DSS umbrella, each with their own strengths and weaknessess. We must learn their differences to direct their use and apply them incisively to the domain of responsibility in question.

Debating the relative merits of a management tool is productive only when referring to a delimited domain of responsibility. Only after delimiting the domain and characterizing it through external and internal frameworks can the best tools be chosen.

Of the terms MIS, DSS, ES, OR and CIM, only DSS directly recognizes the concept of support. You will never replace the manager. We must accept the partnership between machine, model, or document and the manager. The human decision maker will always be an essential component in the management system. In the end, we must focus on the relationships between the management tools (machines, if the tools are mechanized) and the human. The human decision maker is supported by his or her management tools.

Responsive systems direct our efforts toward the relationship between the manager and his or her management tools. The human is always more intuitive than the machine. Humans provide the "I'll know it when I see it" type of intelligence based on intuition and experience. Thus, for perplexities and problems, strategic endeavors, unstructured and semi-structured decisions, and the visibility level of maturity, expect a DSS short on mechanization or automation and long on supporting information. My definitions of DSS and the management tools within DSS give the manager's broad view and stress their organizational validity.[39] The manager's perspective is the place to start; he or she will most want responsiveness.

In summary, responsiveness keys on two of the interfaces in the MSM: information portrayal/information perception and

measurement/data. Responsiveness is evaluated through the third
interface: decision/action. ES and MIS are tools, part of certain
DSS's, that are necessary in certain domains of responsibility and
not so useful in others. The inability to tell the difference has
led to high failure rates with both.

ACKNOWLEDGMENTS

The author thanks the professional managers, staff, faculty,
graduate students, and undergraduates at Virginia Tech's Management
Systems Laboratories for their good work. The pronoun I is used
throughout to separate all of us using management systems (we) from
the author (I). However, please recognize that "I" is more than one
contributor to this work.
The preparation of this paper is funded by U.S. Department of
Energy Special Research Contract No. DE AS05-83DP48013. Management
Systems Laboratories thanks the Department of Energy's Office of
Nuclear Materials for providing us a real-world laboratory for the
research, development, and testing of state-of-the-art management
tools and the frameworks for understanding how to make them
successful.

REFERENCES

1. Simon, Herbert A., The New Science of Management Decision,
    Harper & Brothers, New York, 1960, pp. 1-3.

2. Ibid., pp. 5-11.

3. Forrester, Jay W., Industrial Dynamics, The MIT Press, Cambridge
    MA, 1961, pp. 93-95.

4. Drucker, Peter, The Effective Executive, New York, Harper and
    Row, 1967, p. 5.

5. Kurstedt, Harold A., Jr., et al., a series of articles
    describing the Management System Model scheduled for publication
    in Industrial Engineering, 1986.

6. Forrester, Jay W., Industrial Dynamics, The MIT Press, Cambridge
    MA, 1961, p. 93.

7. Anthony, Robert N., Planning and Control Systems: A Framework
    for Analysis, Harvard, 1965, pp. 67, 93.

8. Simon, Herbert A., The New Science of Management Decision,
    Harper & Brothers, New York, 1960, p. 8.

9. Galbraith, Jay, Designing Complex Organizations, Addison-Wesley Publishing Company, 1973, p. 5.

10. Kurstedt, Harold A., Jr., R. Martin Jones, and Louis I. Middleman, "A DSS Model Applied to Government Organizations Functioning as Information Processors," Proceedings of the Sixth Annual Meeting, American Society for Engineering Management, September 1985, pp. 61-68.

11. Tushman, M. L., and D. A. Nadler, "Information Processing as an Integrating Concept in Organizational Design," Academy of Management Review, July 1978, pp. 613-624.

12. Drucker, Peter, The Effective Executive, New York, Harper and Row, 1967, p. 2.

13. Anthony, Robert N., Planning and Control Systems: A Framework for Analysis, Harvard, 1965, pp. 15-19.

14. Simon, Herbert A., The New Science of Management Decision, Harper and Brothers, New York, 1960, pp. 5-8.

15. Gorry, G. Anthony, and Michael S. Scott Morton, "A Framework for Management Information Systems," Sloan Management Review, Vol. 13, (Fall 1971), pp. 55-70.

16. Ibid., p. 60.

17. Ibid., p. 61.

18. Taylor, Frederick, W., The Principles of Scientific Management, W. W. Horton and Co., Inc., New York, 1967.

19. Forrester, Jay W., Industrial Dynamics, The MIT Press, Cambridge MA, 1961, p. 94.

20. Blumenthal, Sherman C., Management and Information Systems--A Framework for Planning and Development, Prentice-Hall, 1969, p. 24.

21. Macintosh, N. B., "A Contextual Model of Information Systems," Accounting, Organizations and Society, England, Vol. 6, No. 1, 1981, pp. 39-52.

22. Jones, R. Martin, Harold A. Kurstedt, Jr., J. Andrew Walker, and Roderick J. Reasor, "We Should Not Manage Our Own Management Tools," Proceedings of the 21st Annual Meeting, Southeastern Chapter of the Institute of Management Sciences, October 1985, in press.

23. Deal, T. E., and Kennedy, A. A., Corporate Cultures, Addison-Wesley, Reading, MA, 1982.

24. Schein, Edgar H., Organizational Culture and Leadership, Jossey-Bass Publishers, 1985.

25. Pascale, Richard, "The Paradox of 'Corporate Culture': Reconciling Ourselves to Socialization," California Management Review, Vol. 27, No. 2, Winter 1985, pp. 26-41.

26. Peters, Thomas J., and Robert H. Waterman, Jr., In Search of Excellence, Warner Books, 1984, pp. 103-106.

27. Kurstedt, Harold A., Jr., J. Andrew Walker, Eugene J. Gardner, and Richard E. DeBusk, "Supporting Management to Anticipate Change: Decision Support Systems Versus Expert Systems," Proceedings of the Sixth Annual Meeting, American Society for Engineering Management, September 1985, pp. 137-143.

28. Kurstedt, Harold A., Jr., R. Martin Jones, and Amod Singhal, "The Industrial Engineer's Approach and Computer-Based MIS/DSS/MSS Success," Proceedings of the 7th Annual Conference on Computers and Industrial Engineering, March 1985, pp. 526-531.

29. Forsyth, Richard, Expert Systems: Principles and Case Studies, Chapman and Hall, Ltd., 1984, p. 37.

30. Hayes-Roth, Frederick, Donald A. Waterman, and Douglas B. Lenat, Building Expert Systems, Addison-Wesley Publishing Company, Inc., 1983.

31. Forsyth, Richard, Expert Systems: Principles and Case Studies, Chapman and Hall, Ltd., 1984, p. 7.

32. Averham, Jan, Automation and Society, Moscow, USSR, 1960, U.S. Joint Publications Research Service, Washington DC, July 1961, p. 2.

33. Bright, James R., Automation and Management, Division of Research, Graduate School of Business Administration, Harvard University, Boston, 1958, p. 4.

34. Ibid., p. 7.

35. Ibid., p. 6.

36. Forsyth, Richard, Expert Systems: Principles and Case Studies, Chapman and Hall, Ltd., 1984, p. 39.

37. Forsyth, Richard, Expert Systems: Principles and Case Studies, Chapman and Hall, Ltd., 1984, p. 37.

38. Walker, J. Andrew, R. Martin Jones, Harold A. Kurstedt, Jr., and Richard E. DeBusk, "In High-Tech, We End up with Horizontal Answers to Vertical Questions," Proceedings of the 21st Annual Meeting, Southeastern Chapter of the Institute of Management Sciences, October 1985, in press.

39. Markus, M. Lynne, and Daniel Robey, "The Organizational Validity of Management Information Systems," Human Relations, Vol. 36, No. 3, 1983, pp. 203-226.

A LOGIC PROGRAMMING APPROACH TO BUILDING PLANNING AND SIMULATION MODELS

Ronald M. Lee
Information Systems Group
Graduate School of Business, CBA 5.202
University of Texas
Austin, TX 78712 USA

ABSTRACT: Logic programming, including languages like Prolog and its variants, is becoming popular for AI applications such as natural language processing and expert systems. These tools may also benefit more traditional management science applications such as planning and simulation. A framework is proposed for describing the problem domain ('model base') of planning and simulation problems in logical form, separate from the inferencing mechanisms applied to them. Applications are to dynamic programming, decision trees, PERT networks, and discrete event simulation.

KEYWORDS: Logic programming; planning; simulation; dynamic programming; decision trees; PERT; Petri Nets.

1. INTRODUCTION

For nearly twenty years, Artificial Intelligence (AI) has concerned itself with the exotic problems of building computational models of human cognition. To do this, AI programming techniques and tools sacrificed practical efficiency for high-level flexibility and modeling power. Thus, until relatively recently, most AI systems showed unusal cleverness, but only for very limited, 'toy' situations. However, during this same period, there have been incredible advances in hardware speed and economy, making computational power orders of magnitude faster and cheaper. Indeed, much of the current commercial success of AI is perhaps not due so much to subsequent breakthroughs in AI itself, but rather to the coincident advances in hardware technology (Brown, 1984). The thesis here is that the high-level, flexible tools used in AI are now becoming practical alternatives for more traditional types of management science applications as well. Here we focus on a particular AI tool, logic programming, illustrating its applicability to familiar management science applications such as dynamic programming, decision trees, PERT and simulation.

By logic programming, we refer to a class of programming languages based on the predicate calculus as a representational form (Davis, 1985). These languages are 'declarative' in that one specifies what is to be done rather than how to do it. The control structure is thus

W. G. Sol et al. (eds.), Expert Systems and Artificial Intelligence in Decision Support Systems, 79–111.
© 1987 by D. Reidel Publishing Company.

problem independent (Kowalski, 1979a). This is a potentially
controversial point for it suggests that a general purpose search
algorithm be applied to all problems. We take a different view: that
logic programming enables a separation of problem modeling/specification
from algorithm design. These are quite distinct talents that are
presently inter-mixed when using conventional procedural languages.
There is an analogue here to database management systems, which enable
the separation of logical data description from physical storage design.
Similarly, in logic programming, the choice of algorithms is separated
from applications programming and made part of compiler design. The
future evolution of these languages will involve recognizing problem
structures where more efficient algorithms can be exploited, and
applying these automatically. A case in point: some compilers can
recognize recursive specifications that are essentially iterative, thus
generating iterative code that does not accumulate stack space, etc.

There is an additional, more fundamental advantage. Most
procedural programming presupposes a sequential processor. However,
with the enormous decline in the cost of chips, highly parallel
architectures are now feasible. However, a procedural program can only
exploit one of these processors at a time. A logic program, by
specifying only goals rather than means, offers the opportunity for
parallel optimization. This has been a basic premise of the Japanese
Fifth Generation project (Warren, 1982).

Of course, these various optimization efforts are only warranted if
logic programming proves to be convenient and useful from an
applications standpoint. This is our basic focus here.

Like all tools, logic programming has advantages and disadvantages.
Its basic advantage is for applications that involve symbolic reasoning,
i.e. reasoning about qualitative descriptions. By contrast, it is
especially weak for heavily quantitative applications, e.g. matrix
operations. In this respect, it is complementary to existing management
science tools.

Another advantage of logic programs arises from their essentially
relational structure, specifying relations between data values, without
indicating which are to be supplied as arguments and which are derived
results. In a sense, this means that logic programs can be run either
'forward or backward'; e.g. you supply argument A and get back B, or
you can supply B and get back A. Another related benefit of this
relational structure of logic programming is that, representationally,
relational database structures are included as a special case. This
provides a useful conceptual integration for database inferencing
applications (Lee, 1985).

One other relative advantage of logic programming -- indeed for AI
in general -- is for applications that involve search through a large
number of alternatives. This feature is especially well suited for
applications that can be modeled as graph search problems. This is the

basis for our approach to planning and simulation models using logic programming.

Planning and simulation models share the characteristic that they involve reasoning about hypothetical sequences of activities. Activities take time -- they have a temporal duration -- and they transform the world from one state to another. In doing so, they may consume resources, e.g. incur costs, require the usage of a machine or labor, etc.

A simple form of planning model might therefore be described as a state transition diagram, with transitions corresponding to activities. The output of the model is a sequence of states (or activities) from a given start state to a certain goal state.

A simulation model may also be described as a state transition diagram, again with activities corresponding to states. In a simulation, however, there is a transition back from the goal state to the start state, so that the processing of the model may cycle through repeated iterations.

More sophisticated planning and simulation models differ from this basic structure in several ways:

a. Choice of activities. A planning model may be directed to simply find a sequence of activities to reach the desired goal. This is a satisficing model. Alternatively, if activities are marked with some metric of performance, e.g. cost, the model can find an optimum (least cost) plan.

b. Concurrency. In many situations, activities may be undertaken concurrently. Examples of models that reflect this characteristic are PERT and discrete event simulations. In this case, the nodes of the diagram are re-interpreted as transitions between sets of activities. A PERT diagram is a partial ordering of activities.

c. Choice and concurrency combined. A representation that includes both choice and concurrency is a Petri net (e.g. Peterson, 1981). Two types of nodes are involved: choice nodes, which indicate an exclusive choice between activities, and 'transition' nodes, which mark the termination and beginning of concurrent activities.

d. Role of probability.

i. Probability on choices. In some situations, certain choices are determined exogenously, e.g. the behavior of a competitor, or the reaction of the marketplace. This may be indicated by marking the transitions from a choice node with the estimated probability that it will be taken. Decision trees are examples of state transition diagrams including probabilistic choice.

ii. Stochastic aspects of activities. Generally, the motivation for modeling a situation using simulation is that the characteristics of the activities themselves are uncertain. Most commonly, the duration of the activity is taken to be a random variable, e.g. drawn from an exponential distribution.

These various aspects are consolidated in the table shown in the following diagram. While the model in each box might be either a planning or a simulation model, planning models seem more appropriate where choice is the dominant characteristic, whereas simulation seems more appropriate when stochastic concurrency dominates.

CONCURRENCY

CHOICE	none	deterministic duration	probabilistic duration
none	linear sequence	PERT	discrete event simulation
deterministic	state transition diagram	Petri net	simulation with choice
probabilistic	decision tree	and/or decision tree	simulation with probabilistic choice

2. LOGIC PROGRAMMING AND PROLOG

Logic programming is generally regarded as an ideal that current implementations only approximate (Davis, 1985). As noted earlier, much of the effort here focuses on the exploitation of parallel architectures (Shapiro, 1983). Nonetheless, existing dialects, namely Prolog and its variants, are sufficiently advanced to support useful management decision aiding applications. Here we make use of the Prolog syntax as described in Clocksin and Mellish (1985). In this notation, constants are denoted as lower case alphabetic terms or as numbers. Variable names are in upper case; also, "_" can be used to indicate an 'anonymous' variable name. Basic facts are indicated as predicates with constant arguments, e.g.

mother(eve, cain).

father(adam, cain).

indicates that Eve is mother to Cain and Adam is father to Cain. Derived predicates are defined by 'rules' of the form:

```
P0 :- P1, P2, ..., Pn.
```

read that to prove P0 it is sufficient to prove P1 and P2 and ... and
Pn. (In conventional predicate calculus notation, ":-" is reverse
implication, i.e. "<--", and the commas are interpreted as
conjunctions.) For example,

```
parent(X,Y) :- mother(X,Y).
```

```
parent(X,Y) :- father(X,Y).
```

indicate two alternatives to prove parenthood. These rules may in turn
appear in other rules, e.g.

```
grand_parent(X,Z) :- parent(X,Y), parent(Y,Z).
```

This says that to prove X is a parent of Z, it is sufficient to show
that X is parent of some Y, and that Y is parent of Z. Rules may also
be recursive, e.g.

```
ancestor(X,Z) :- parent(X,Z).
```

```
ancestor(X,Z) :- parent(X,Y), ancestor(Y,Z).
```

That is, to prove X is an ancestor of Z, it is sufficient to prove that
X is a parent of Z; or, it is also sufficient to prove that X is a
parent of some Y and that Y is an ancestor of Z.

The reasoning process is invoked by a <u>query</u>, denoted as a predicate
preceded by "?-". For instance,

```
?- ancestor(X,Y).
```

```
⟩ X = eve   Y = cain;
```

```
⟩ X = adam  Y = cain;   etc.
```

These examples are typical of predicate calculus in that predicates are
applied to (names of) individuals. However, much of the pattern
matching power in logic programming derives from the ability to specify
more complex 'structures' as arguments. These take the form of embedded
predicates (functors and arguments). For example,

```
likes(eve, adam).
```

```
likes(eve, eating(apples)).
```

```
?- likes(eve,X).
```

```
X = adam;
```

> X = eating(apples).

?- likes(eve, eating(X)).

> X = apples

The first query simply asks what Eve likes; the second query asks specifically what Eve likes to eat.

A more flexible kind of structure is a list, which may have a variable number of elements. The notation is:

[X|Y]

where X is the first element (head) and Y is the rest (tail) of the list. Lists are typically processed in recursive fashion. For example, a specification of list membership is as follows:

member(X, [X|_]).

member(X, [_|L]) :- member(X,L).

That is, X is a member of a list if it matches the head or if it is a member of the tail.

3. SEARCHING A STATE TRANSITION GRAPH -- EXAMPLE

A farmer needs to ferry a goat, a (very large) cabbage and his pet wolf across a river. The only available boat holds only the farmer and one passenger (the cabbage counts as a passenger). The goat cannot be left alone with the cabbage, and the wolf cannot be left alone with the goat. The problem is to devise a plan for transporting all four across the river. (Kowalski, 1979b.) This is a simple planning problem that can be easily modeled as a sequence of states and transitions. A state might be described by four binary variables, e.g.

s(F,G,C,W).

indicating whether each of the individuals is on the near side (0) or far side (1). There are thus 16 possible states. However, some states are not allowed. We indicate this in the form of explicit infeasibility assertions:

        /* goat alone with cabbage */
        infeasible(s(1,0,0,_)).
        infeasible(s(0,1,1,_)).

```
/* goat alone with wolf    */
infeasible(s(1,0,_,0)).
infeasible(s(0,1,_,1)).

/* possible transitions between states */

trans(s(0,G,C,W),s(1,G,C,W), 'farmer goes alone').
trans(s(0,0,C,W),s(1,1,C,W), 'farmer takes goat').
trans(s(0,G,O,W),s(1,G,1,W), 'farmer takes cabbage').
trans(s(0,G,C,O),s(1,G,C,1), 'farmer takes wolf').
```

These transitions are bi-directional, i.e. one can go from the first state to the second state or vice versa. The corresponding state-transition diagram is shown in the following figure:

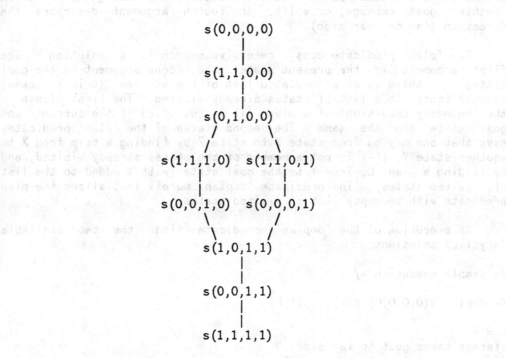

The above assertions constitute the 'model base' for this problem. The essence of this problem type is that it involves a search through a state space, with <u>choices</u> available as to which transition to take. A solution amounts to finding a sequence (list) of states with no repetitions (a state is never re-visited), and not traversing any infeasible states. The additional Prolog rules needed to do this are as follows:

```
/* logic program */

trip(X,Y,Action,'to far side')  :- trans(X,Y,Action), not(infeasible(Y)).
trip(Y,X,Action,'to near side') :- trans(X,Y,Action), not(infeasible(X)).

doplan(X,Z,L) :- plan(X,Z,L,[X]).

plan(X,X,[],_).
plan(X,Z,[(Act,Dir)|L],Q) :- trip(X,Y,Act,Dir), not(member(Y,Q)),
    plan(Y,Z,L,[Y|Q]).
```

This is a complete logic program. The first predicate, 'trip', is
satisfied by a transition in either direction (X to Y or Y to X), as
long as it does not arrive in a state that is infeasible. The third
argument is a description of the transition, indicating what is taken
(nothing, goat, cabbage, or wolf); the fourth argument describes the
direction (far or near side).

   The 'plan' predicate does a recursive search for a solution. The
first argument is the present state; the second argument is the goal
state; the third is an accumulated list of the actions (trips) taken;
and the fourth is a list of states already visited. The first clause is
the 'boundary condition' of a plan: it is satisfied if the current and
goal state are the same. The second clause of the 'plan' predicates
says that one may go from state X to state Z by finding a trip from X to
another state Y, if Y is not a member of the states already visited, and
by finding a plan, L, from Y to the goal state (with Y added to the list
of visited states). The predicate 'doplan' merely initializes the plan
predicate with an empty list of visited states.

   An execution of the 'doplan' predicate finds the two available
(acyclic) solutions:

```
/* sample execution */

?- doplan(s(0,0,0,0),s(1,1,1,1),L).

L = [
(farmer takes goat,to far side),
(farmer goes alone,to near side),
(farmer takes cabbage,to far side),
(farmer takes goat,to near side),
(farmer takes wolf,to far side),
(farmer goes alone,to near side),
(farmer takes goat,to far side)] ;
```

```
L = [
(farmer takes goat,to far side),
(farmer goes alone,to near side),
(farmer takes wolf,to far side),
(farmer takes goat,to near side),
(farmer takes cabbage,to far side),
(farmer goes alone,to near side),
(farmer takes goat,to far side)] ;
```

4. DYNAMIC PROGRAMMING

In the above example, there was no metric of goodness for a particular solution. Any solution would do. By adding a numeric weighting to the transitions, e.g. a cost, duration or distance, the problem becomes a candidate for optimization, e.g. by a dynamic programming algorithm. For example, suppose the state space is given by the following (directed) graph:

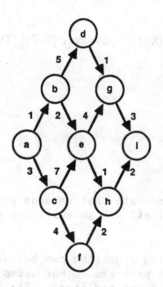

This state transition diagram is represented by the following assertions:

```
/* model base */

trans(a,b,1).
trans(a,c,3).
trans(b,d,3).
trans(b,e,2).
trans(c,e,7).
trans(c,f,4).
trans(d,g,1).
trans(e,g,4).
trans(e,h,1).
trans(f,h,2).
trans(g,i,3).
trans(h,i,2).
```

A dynamic programming type of recursive search through such a state space is as follows:

```
/* logic program */

dynamic(X,X,[X],0).

dynamic(X,Z,LL,TC) :-
    setof((K,[Y|L]), (Y,C,CC)^(trans(X,Y,C),dynamic(Y,Z,L,CC),K is C+CC),SS),
    minof(SS,(TC,LL)).
```

```
/* sample execution */

?- dynamic(a,i,L,C).

L = [a,b,e,h,i]

C = 6
```

Comments: 'setof' is a built-in predicate that returns a list of tuples selected from the database; 'minof' is an auxiliary predicate that finds the minimum element in a list.

The preceding dynamic programming algorithm can be easily adapted to other types of graph search problems. For example, consider a database listing flights, departure times and fares. For simplicity, we assume that flights all occur in a single day, and that times are recorded in minutes past midnight. A sample database might be:

```
/* flight(ID, SOURCE, DESTINATION, DEPARTURE, ARRIVAL, COST). */

flight(18, london,    amsterdam,  900, 1000, 200).
flight(97, london,    paris,     1000, 1130, 400).
flight(26, amsterdam, zurich,     930, 1100, 500).
flight(52, amsterdam, brussels,  1015, 1045, 100).
flight(83, brussels,  zurich,    1100, 1230, 300).
flight(35, brussels,  paris,     1100, 1200, 200).
flight(62, paris,     zurich,    1100, 1400, 350).
```

The logic to find the minimum cost sequence of flights between any two points follows the basic pattern of the foregoing dynamic program, but with the additional constraint that any connecting flight must depart after the arrival of the incoming flight. The logic program is, as follows:

```
/* logic program */

flightplan(X,Z,C,L) :- flightplanx(X,Z,C,L,DEP,[X]).

flightplanx(X,X,0,[],9999,_).

flightplanx(X,Z,TC,LL,DEP,Q) :-
    setof((C,L,D), path(X,Z,C,L,D,Q), S),
    minof(S, (TC, LL, DEP)).

path(X,Z,C,[ID|L],DEP,Q) :-
    flight(ID, X, Y, DEP, ARR, CO),
    not(member(Y,Q)),
    flightplanx(Y,Z,C1,L,D,[Y|Q]),
    D > ARR,
    C is CO+C1.

/* sample executions */

?- flightplan(london,zurich,C,L).

L = [18,52,83],
C = 600

?- flightplan(london,paris,C,L).

L = [97],
C = 400

?- flightplan(amsterdam,paris,C,L).

L = [52,35],
C = 300
```

Several differences are noteworthy. First, whereas the 'dynamic' predicate recorded the nodes (e.g. cities) visited, here only the identification (ID) of flights is recorded. Also, since there is the possibility of cycles, an extra list, Q, is carried along to prevent going back to previously visited cities. Further, each stage of the dynamic program carries its departure time, D, for comparison to the arrival time of the preceding flight. This illustrates how peculiar constraints in the problem domain can be incorporated into the dynammic programming search.

5. DECISION TREES

A decision tree is another form of state space search solvable in dynamic programming fashion. In this case, there are two types of nodes: choice nodes (drawn as circles) and 'outcome' nodes (drawn as diamonds). Choice nodes indicate choices to be made by the decision maker or planning algorithm; each arc emerging from a choice node has an associated cost for that alternative. Outcome nodes indicate choices made external to the model, represented as probabilities on the transitions. A simple decision tree (graph) is shown on the previous page. The logic programming representation is as follows:

```
/* model base */

/* transitions from choice nodes */

xtrans(a,b,20).
xtrans(a,c,40).
xtrans(d,g,10).
xtrans(d,h,30).
xtrans(e,h,25).
xtrans(e,i,50).
xtrans(f,i,25).
xtrans(f,j,15).

/* transitions from outcome nodes */

ptrans(b,d,.5).
ptrans(b,e,.5).
ptrans(c,e,.3).
ptrans(c,f,.7).
ptrans(g,k,.2).
ptrans(g,l,.8).
ptrans(h,l,.1).
ptrans(h,m,.9).
ptrans(i,m,.4).
ptrans(i,n,.6).
ptrans(j,n,.5).
ptrans(j,o,.5).

/* values of final 'result' nodes */

result(k,100).
result(l,200).
result(m,300).
result(n,250).
result(o,150).
```

The expected value of a given node can be found by the following recursive predicate:

```
/* logic program */

val(X,V) :- result(X,V).

val(X,V) :-
    bagof(M, (Y,P,K)^(ptrans(X,Y,P), val(Y,K), M is K*P),L),
    sumof(L,V).

val(X,V) :- bestchoice(X,Z,V).

bestchoice(X,Z,V) :-
    bagof((M,Y), choice(X,Y,M), L),
    maxof(L, (V,Z)).

choice(X,Y,M) :- xtrans(X,Y,C), val(Y,K), M is K - C.
```

Alternatives and their expected values at a give choice node are given by the predicate, 'choice', e.g.

```
/* sample execution */

?- choice(a,Y,M).

Y = b    M = 25;
Y = c    M = 23
```

The best alternative at a given choice node is given by 'bestchoice', e.g

```
?- bestchoice(a,Z,V).

Z = b    V = 25
```

6.   STATE SPACE SIMULATION

State transition diagrams may also provide the knowledge base for a simulation model.   In this case, the final state in the graph has a transition cycling back to the start state.   Such simulations are usually only interesting, however, when there are stochastic aspects involved, for instance, exponentially distributed activity times.

For example, consider a simple case where the system has only two states, s1 and s2, having two activities, (s0,s1) and (s1,s0), whose durations are exponentially distributed with means 10 and 20 respectively.   The system is diagrammed as follows:

This system is described by the following transition assertions:

```
/* model base */

trans(s0,s1,X) :- eran(X,10).

trans(s1,s0,X) :- eran(X,20).
```

Here, 'eran(X,M)' is a built-in predicate returning exponential variates, X, having a mean of M. The basic logic for a simulation of this system is as follows:

```
/* logic program */

cycle(T0,X) :-
    trans(X,Y,DT),
    T1 is T0+DT,
    cycle(T1,Y).
```

This program merely follows the state transition graph, updating the current time after each transition. Using the Prolog 'spy' for tracing, its behavior is as follows:

```
/* sample execution */

?- spy cycle.
Spy-point placed on cycle/2.

?- cycle(0,s0).

**   0 Call : cycle(0,s0) ?
**   1 Call : cycle(16,s1) ?
**   2 Call : cycle(22,s0) ?
**   3 Call : cycle(26,s1) ?
**   4 Call : cycle(48,s0) ?
**   5 Call : cycle(70,s1) ?
**   6 Call : cycle(103,s0) ?
**   7 Call : cycle(130,s1) ?
**   8 Call : cycle(136,s0) ?
**   9 Call : cycle(140,s1) ?
**  10 Call : cycle(200,s0) ? a
[ Execution aborted ]
```

Note that the 'cycle' predicate does not do any data collection, nor does it have a termination condition. A more sophisticated version with these features added is the following:

```
/* logic program */

go(L) :- sim(s0,100,0,[],L).

sim(X,Q,T,L,L) :- T>=Q,!.

sim(X,Q,T0,L,LL) :- trans(X,Y,DT),
    update(Y,DT,L,W),
    T1 is T0+DT,
    sim(Y,Q,T1,W,LL).

update(Y,DT,[(Y,T0)|L],[(Y,T1)|L]) :- T1 is T0+DT, !.

update(Y,DT,[],[(Y,DT)]) :- !.

update(Y,DT,[Z|L],[Z|W]) :- update(Y,DT,L,W).

/* sample execution */

?- go(L).

L = [(s1,34),(s0,66)] ;

?- go(L).

L = [(s1,31),(s0,103)] ;

?- go(L).

L = [(s1,65),(s0,51)]
```

An implementation consideration: doing the iterations of the simulation using recursive logic will eventually cause an overflow in the stack space using the Prolog interpreter. However, most compilers now support 'tail recursion optimization', which recognizes deterministic uses of recursion (where there are no backtracking alternatives) and does not accumulate stack space. Thus, in compiled form, the above logic programs run efficiently for an arbitrary number of iterations.

A slightly more elaborate situation might involve choice between the transitions to be taken, for instance the least cost activity. An example is the following state transition diagram:

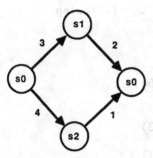

This is incorporated into the previous structure if we call the basic transitions e.g. 'xtrans', adding a cost parameter, and re-code the 'trans' assertions to pick the minimum cost alternative (assume all times are exponentially distributed with a mean of 10):

```
/* model base */

xtrans(s0,s1,3,X)  :- eran(X,10).
xtrans(s0,s2,4,X)  :- eran(X,10).
xtrans(s1,s0,2,X)  :- eran(X,10).
xtrans(s2,s0,1,X)  :- eran(X,10).

trans(X,YY,TT) :-
    setof((C,Y,T),xtrans(X,Y,C,T),L),
    minof(L, (CC,YY,TT)).
```

Elaborating the States.

In the farmer example earlier, states were not given individual names (s0,s1,...), but rather were identified in terms of more elementary components, e.g. the position of the farmer, the goat, etc.. The same approach can be applied to simulation modeling. For example, suppose a simple case of two machines in sequence, controlled by a single operator. Thus, each machine must wait while the other is processing. A sketch of the system is as follows:

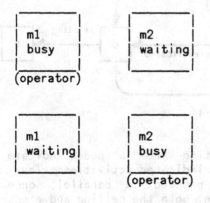

This is described in 'trans' assertions like the following:

```
/* model base */

trans(s([(m1,busy),(m2,wait)]),
      s([(m1,wait),(m2,busy)]), X)  :- eran(X,5).

trans(s([(m1,wait),(m2,busy)]),
      s([(m1,busy),(m2,wait)]), X)  :- eran(X,3).

go(L) :-  sim(s([(m1,busy),(m2,wait)]),100,0,[],L).

/* sample execution */

?- go(L).

L = [(s([(m1,wait),(m2,busy)]),66),(s([(m1,busy),(m2,wait)]),36)]

?- go(L).

L = [(s([(m1,wait),(m2,busy)]),67),(s([(m1,busy),(m2,wait)]),37)]

?- go(L).

L = [(s([(m1,wait),(m2,busy)]),64),(s([(m1,busy),(m2,wait)]),39)]
```

7. CONCURRENCY OF ACTIVITIES -- PERT

In many, indeed most, situations, activities occur concurrently. A planning model often used in these cases is a PERT diagram. A simple example is the following plan for building a house:

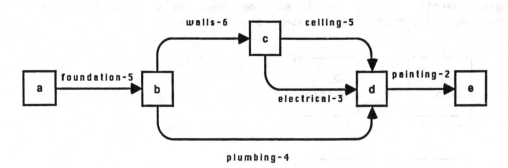

In a PERT diagram, multiple arcs emanating from a node indicate not choice but rather concurrency of the indicated activities. Thus, work on the walls and the plumbing can proceed in parallel, once the foundation has been laid. Likewise, both the ceiling and electrical work can be done in parallel once the walls are done. All these must be completed before painting can begin.

Note that the nodes in a PERT diagram no longer represent states of the entire system (e.g. the construction of the house). Rather, they represent 'sub-states', indicating a momentary status of only part of the system. More commonly, the nodes are viewed as instantaneous transitions between two or more activities. The total state of the system is therefore given as the set of activities that are currently being performed. The above diagram is described by the following Prolog assertions:

```
activity(a,b,foundation,5).
activity(b,c,walls,6).
activity(b,d,plumbing,4).
activity(c,d,ceiling,5).
activity(c,d,electrical,3).
activity(d,e,painting,2).
```

The critical path is found as the maximum length path of activities between two nodes:

```
critical(X,X,[],0).

critical(X,Z,Total_Time, Activity_List) :-
    setof((T,Y,[A|L]),
        (T1,T2)^(activity(X,Y,A,T1),critical(Y,Z,L,T2),T is T1+T2),SS),
    maxof(SS,(Total_Time,_,Activity_List)).
```

3. DISCRETE EVENT SIMULATION

Concurrency of activities is also an important feature of many simulation models. A discrete event simulation may be characterized as a PERT diagram having cycles, that is, where sequences of activities repeat. For example, consider the following PERT diagram:

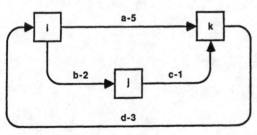

As with other PERT diagrams, we note that the nodes in this graph no longer represent states. Rather, a state in this system is given by the

set of activities currently active. Thus, it is the nodes, rather than
the arcs, that mark transitions in the system. (PERT diagrams, more
generally called 'marked graphs', are sometimes regarded as the
graphical dual of state transition diagrams -- see e.g. Peterson, 1981,
p. 204.)

Representing the set of currently active activites as a list of
pairs giving the activity and its scheduled completion time, the 'trans'
assertions are as follows:

```
/* model base */

start([(_,0,d)]).

/* node i */

trans(T,[(T,_,d)],[(Ta,T,a),(Tb,T,b)]) :- Ta is T+5, Tb is T+2.

/* node j */

trans(T,[(T,_,b)], [(Tc,T,c)]) :- Tc is T+1.

/* node k */

trans(T,[(T,_,a),(T,_,c)],[(Td,T,d)]) :- Td is T+3.
```

A logic program that performs the simulation iterations is as follows:

```
/* logic program */

go :- start(L), bump(0,L).

bump(T0,L0) :-
    transit(T0,L0,T1,L1),
    bump(T1,L1).

transit(T,L0,T,L1) :-
    trans(T,WW,AA),
    remove(WW,L0,MM),
    append(AA,MM,L1).

transit(T0,L0,T1,[(_,T,A)|LL]) :-
    qsort(L0,[(T1,T,A)|LL]).


/* sample execution */

?- spy bump.
Spy-point placed on bump/2.

?- go.
```

```
**   1 Call : bump(0,[(_44,0,d)]) ?
**   2 Call : bump(0,[(5,0,a),(2,0,b)]) ?
**   3 Call : bump(2,[(_206,0,b),(5,0,a)]) ?
**   4 Call : bump(2,[(3,2,c),(5,0,a)]) ?
**   5 Call : bump(3,[(_556,2,c),(5,0,a)]) ?
**   6 Call : bump(5,[(_683,0,a),(_556,2,c)]) ?
**   7 Call : bump(5,[(8,5,d)]) ?
**   8 Call : bump(8,[(_1071,5,d)]) ?
**   9 Call : bump(8,[(13,8,a),(10,8,b)]) ?
**  10 Call : bump(10,[(_1082,8,b),(13,8,a)]) ?
**  11 Call : bump(10,[(11,10,c),(13,8,a)]) ? a
[ Execution aborted ]
```

The addition of concurrency into the simulation introduces the
problem of waiting: among concurrent activities, some will finish
earlier, hence must wait for the others to complete. In the above
program, when an activity is waiting, its scheduled completion time is
left as an uninstantiated variable (noted in the spy trace as an
underscore followed by an integer). Thus, there are actually two types
of transitions ('transit') of the system -- those given by the 'trans'
assertions, and the completion of the next scheduled activity. (Note:
'qsort' orders the activity list from earliest to latest, with waiting
activities sorted last.)

In the above example, waiting was represented implicitly as the
time between the completion of one activity and the start of the next.
However, often we would like to represent waiting explicitly, as a
distinct arc type. A revised form of the program to do this is as
follows:

```
/* logic program */

go :- start(L), bump(0,L).

bump(T0,L0) :-
    transit(T0,L0,T1,L1),
    bump(T1,L1).

transit(T,L0,T,L1) :-
    atrans(T,WW,AA),
    remove(WW,L0,MM),!,
    append(AA,MM,L1).

transit(T,L0,T1,L1) :-
    qsort(L0,[(T1,T0,A)|LL]),
    xtrans(T,[(T1,T0,A)],AA),
    append(LL,AA,L1).
```

Note that this version recognizes two types of transitions, 'atrans' and 'xtrans'. An 'atrans' describes the node transitions between substates. An 'xtrans' permits the representation of waiting times as explicit activities. Here we assume that certain types of activities are 'busy', i.e. involving a definite action and with a scheduled completion time. Other activities are 'waiting', and their completion time is left as an uninstantiated variable. An 'atrans', corresponding to the previous 'trans' assertions, marks a transition from waiting to busy, whereas an 'xtrans' marks the completion of a busy activity, and the beginning of waiting. (Actually, the two are distinguished by their pre-conditions only: 'atrans' marks the end of waiting; 'xtrans' marks the end of busy. The post-conditions can be anything.)

The following example serves to illustrate. Again there are two machines, m1 and m2, that operate in sequence. However, m2 can now operate concurrently with m1. As before, m1 is fed continuously, and m2 unloads its job with no delay. However, m2 must wait to be fed by the output of m1. The activities of m1 are thus busy or waiting to unload. The activities of m2 are busy and waiting to load. The configuration of the system is sketched as follows:

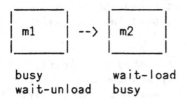

busy   wait-load
wait-unload   busy

This can be described by the following PERT diagram:

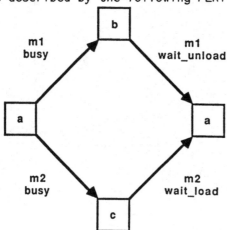

This system is described by the following model base:

```
model base */
art([[(_,0,act(m1,wu)), (_,0,act(m2,wl))]]).

node a */
rans(T, [(_,_,act(m1,wu)),(_,_,act(m2,wl))],
        [(T1,T,act(m1,b)),(T2,T,act(m2,b))]) :- eran(X1,5), eran(X2,3),
                                                 T1 is X1+T, T2 is X2+T.

node b */
rans(T, [(_,_,act(m1,b))], [(_,T,act(m1,wu))]).

node c */
rans(T, [(_,_,act(m2,b))], [(_,T,act(m2,wl))]).
```

ing the Prolog 'spy', the execution behavior of this system is as follows:

```
spy bump.
y-point placed on bump/2.

go.
 1 Call : bump(0,[(_44,0,act(m1,wu)),(_45,0,act(m2,wl))]) ?
 2 Call : bump(0,[(8,0,act(m1,b)),(0,0,act(m2,b))]) ?
 3 Call : bump(0,[(8,0,act(m1,b)),(_558,0,act(m2,wl))]) ?
 4 Call : bump(8,[(_558,0,act(m2,wl)),(_719,0,act(m1,wu))]) ?
 5 Call : bump(8,[(21,8,act(m1,b)),(9,8,act(m2,b))]) ?
 6 Call : bump(9,[(21,8,act(m1,b)),(_1260,8,act(m2,wl))]) ?
 7 Call : bump(21,[(_643,8,act(m2,wl)),(_804,9,act(m1,wu))]) ?
 8 Call : bump(21,[(25,21,act(m1,b)),(22,21,act(m2,b))]) ?
 9 Call : bump(22,[(25,21,act(m1,b)),(_1345,21,act(m2,wl))]) ?
10 Call : bump(25,[(_1345,21,act(m2,wl)),(_1506,22,act(m1,wu))]) ?
11 Call : bump(25,[(44,25,act(m1,b)),(31,25,act(m2,b))]) ? a
Execution aborted ]
```

PETRI NETS

A PERT diagram conveys concurrency of activities, but does not
dicate choice between alternative courses of action. A state
ansition diagram, by contrast, indicates choice, but not concurrency.
Petri net is a combination of these two. Two types of node are

included: choice nodes (drawn as circles), analogous to the nodes in
S-T graphs;   and transition nodes (drawn as boxes), analogous to nodes
in PERT graphs.

In drawing a Petri net diagram, activities are indicated as labels
on choice nodes (circles). As before, transition nodes (boxes)
represent an instantaneous transition between activities. The previous
PERT diagram is re-drawn in Petri net notation as follows:

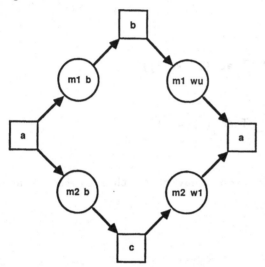

To exemplify the modeling of choice in a Petri net, consider the
following elaboration of the machine shop example. Assume there are now
three machines, m1, m2 and m3.   Again there are two phases to the
processing: the first phase is done by machine m1; the second phase is
done by either m2 or m3, depending on which is available first.   Assume
that processing times are exponentially distributed with means of 10, 30
and 15, respectively. The configuration of the system and activities of
each machine is sketched as follows:

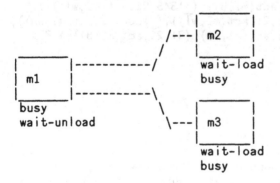

A Petri net diagram of the processing is as follows:

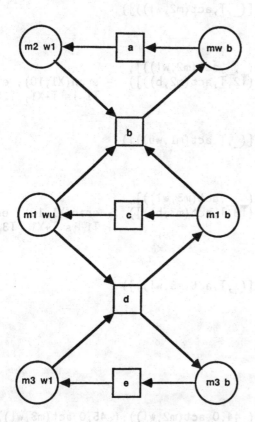

The flow of processing in a Petri net is described by means of 'tokens' that flow through the network. Tokens may reside at choice nodes, also called 'places'. A transition node 'fires' by removing a token from each of its input places and depositing a (new) token on each of its output places. The state of the system is given by the location of tokens at each of the various places. (We assume that a place can have at most one token; this assumption is sometimes relaxed.)

The previous simulation program remains essentially the same for simulating Petri nets. Transition nodes in the Petri net become 'trans' assertions in the logic program. As before, 'atrans' is used where the pre-conditions (here, input places) are waiting activities; 'xtrans' is used where the pre-conditions are busy activities. The above system is thus programmed as follows:

/* model base */

start([(0,0,act(m1,b)), (_,0,act(m2,wl)), (_,0,act(m3,wl))]).

```
/* node a */

xtrans(T, [(_,_,act(m2,b))], [(_,T,act(m2,wl))]).

/* node b */

atrans(T, [(_,_,act(m1,wu)), (_,_,act(m2,wl))],
          [(T1,T,act(m1,b)), (T2,T,act(m2,b))]) :- eran(X1,10), eran(X2,30)
                                                   T1 is T+X1, T2 is T+X2.
/* node c */

xtrans(T, [(_,_,act(m1,b))], [(_,T,act(m1,wu))]).

/* node d */

atrans(T, [(_,_,act(m1,wu)), (_,_,act(m3,wl))],
          [(T1,T,act(m1,b)), (T3,T,act(m3,b))]) :- eran(X1,10), eran(X3,15)
                                                   T1 is T+X1, T3 is T+X3.

/* node e */

xtrans(T, [(_,_,act(m3,b))], [(_,T,act(m3,wl))]).
/* sample execution */

?- spy bump.
Spy-point placed on bump/2.

?- go.

** 1 Call : bump(0,
            [(0,0,act(m1,b)),(_44,0,act(m2,wl)),(_45,0,act(m3,wl))]) ?
** 2 Call : bump(0,
            [(_44,0,act(m2,wl)),(_45,0,act(m3,wl)),(_251,0,act(m1,wu))]) ?
** 3 Call : bump(0,
            [(22,0,act(m1,b)),(50,0,act(m2,b)),(_45,0,act(m3,wl))]) ?
** 4 Call : bump(22,
            [(50,0,act(m2,b)),(_45,0,act(m3,wl)),(_789,0,act(m1,wu))]) ?
** 5 Call : bump(22,
            [(31,22,act(m1,b)),(31,22,act(m3,b)),(50,0,act(m2,b))]) ?
** 6 Call : bump(31,
            [(31,22,act(m3,b)),(50,0,act(m2,b)),(_805,22,act(m1,wu))]) ?
** 7 Call : bump(31,
            [(50,0,act(m2,b)),(_805,22,act(m1,wu)),(_1044,31,act(m3,wl))])
** 8 Call : bump(31,
            [(41,31,act(m1,b)),(60,31,act(m3,b)),(50,0,act(m2,b))]) ?
** 9 Call : bump(41,
            [(50,0,act(m2,b)),(60,31,act(m3,b)),(_1687,31,act(m1,wu))]) ?
** 10 Call : bump(50,
            [(60,31,act(m3,b)),(_1687,31,act(m1,wu)),(_1926,41,act(m2,wl))]
** 11 Call : bump(50,
            [(82,50,act(m1,b)),(72,50,act(m2,b)),(60,31,act(m3,b))]) ? a
```

xecution aborted]

this example, if both m2 and m3 are waiting, the choice defaults to
by the ordering of the rules.

   A refinement of this example is to consider that there are multiple
es of jobs, e.g. 'standard' and 'custom', and the choice between m2
m3 is based on job type: m2 for standard jobs, and m3 for custom.
model base in this case is as follows:

```
model base */

rt([[(0,0,act(m1,b(standard))), (_,0,act(m2,wl)), (_,0,act(m3,wl))]]).

node a */

ans(T, [(_,_,act(m2,b))], [(_,T,act(m2,wl))]).

node b */

ans(T, [(_,_,act(m1,wu(standard))), (_,_,act(m2,wl))],
       [(T1,T,act(m1,b(X))), (T2,T,act(m2,b))]) :- eran(X1,10), eran(X2,30)
                                                   T1 is T+X1, T2 is T+X2,
                                                   draw(X,[standard,custom]).

node c */

ans(T, [(_,_,act(m1,b(X)))], [(_,T,act(m1,wu(X)))]).

node d */

ans(T, [(_,_,act(m1,wu(custom))), (_,_,act(m3,wl))],
       [(T1,T,act(m1,b(X))), (T3,T,act(m3,b))]) :- eran(X1,10), eran(X3,15)
                                                   T1 is T+X1, T3 is T+X3,
                                                   draw(X,[standard,custom]).

node e */

ans(T, [(_,_,act(m3,b))], [(_,T,act(m3,wl))]).
```

transitions in this case differ only in the description of machine
s activities, which must now record the type of job. (The predicate
aw' returns a random element from the list.)

```
/* sample execution */

?- spy bump.
Spy-point placed on bump/2.

?- go.

**   1 Call : bump(0,
[(0,0,act(m1,b(standard))),(_44,0,act(m2,wl)),(_45,0,act(m3,wl))]) ?
**   2 Call : bump(0,
[(_44,0,act(m2,wl)),(_45,0,act(m3,wl)),(_252,0,act(m1,wu(standard)))]) ?
**   3 Call : bump(0,
[(22,0,act(m1,b(standard))),(50,0,act(m2,b)),(_45,0,act(m3,wl))]) ?
**   4 Call : bump(22,
[(50,0,act(m2,b)),(_45,0,act(m3,wl)),(_861,0,act(m1,wu(standard)))]) ?
**   5 Call : bump(50,
[(_45,0,act(m3,wl)),(_861,0,act(m1,wu(standard))),(_1100,22,act(m2,wl))]) ?
**   6 Call : bump(50,
[(51,50,act(m1,b(custom))),(76,50,act(m2,b)),(_33,0,act(m3,wl))]) ?
**   7 Call : bump(51,
[(76,50,act(m2,b)),(_33,0,act(m3,wl)),(_1287,50,act(m1,wu(custom)))]) ?
**   8 Call : bump(51,
[(63,51,act(m1,b(custom))),(76,51,act(m3,b)),(76,50,act(m2,b))]) ?
**   9 Call : bump(63,
[(76,50,act(m2,b)),(76,51,act(m3,b)),(_2133,51,act(m1,wu(custom)))]) ?
**  10 Call : bump(76,
[(76,51,act(m3,b)),(_2133,51,act(m1,wu(custom))),(_2372,63,act(m2,wl))]) ?
**  11 Call : bump(76,
[(_2133,51,act(m1,wu(custom))),(_2372,63,act(m2,wl)),(_2611,76,act(m3,wl))]
**  12 Call : bump(76,
[(81,76,act(m1,b(custom))),(80,76,act(m3,b)),(_2372,63,act(m2,wl))]) ?
**  13 Call : bump(80,
[(81,76,act(m1,b(custom))),(_2372,63,act(m2,wl)),(_3307,76,act(m3,wl))]) ?
[ Execution aborted ]
```

The simulation logic here only shows the minimum needed for each iteration. An extended program that includes a boundary condition and collects data on the time spent in each activity is as follows:

```
/* logic program */

go(Quit,History) :- start(L), bump(Quit,0,L,[],History).

bump(Q,T,L,H,H) :- T>=Q, !.

bump(Q,T0,L0,H0,HH) :-
    transit(T0,L0,T1,L1), !,
    DT is T1-T0,
    update(DT,L0,H0,H1),
    bump(Q,T1,L1,H1,HH).

update(0,_,H,H) :- !.

update(_,[],H,H) :- !.

update(DT,[(_,_,A)|L],H,[(TT,A)|HH]) :-
    delete((T,A),H,H1), !,
    TT is T+DT,
    update(DT,L,H1,HH).

update(DT,[(_,_,A)|L],H,[(DT,A)|HH]) :-
    update(DT,L,H,HH).

transit(T,L0,T,L1) :-
    atrans(T,WW,AA),
    remove(WW,L0,MM),!,
    append(AA,MM,L1).

transit(T,L0,T1,L1) :-
    qsort(L0,[(T1,T0,A)|LL]),
    xtrans(T,[(T1,T0,A)],AA),
    append(LL,AA,L1).
```

Using the previous model base, a sample execution is as follows:

```
/* sample execution */

?- go(1000,History).

History = [(748,act(m2,b)),
(641,act(m3,wl)),
(411,act(m1,wu(standard))),
(170,act(m1,b(standard))),
(366,act(m3,b)),
(116,act(m1,wu(custom))),
(310,act(m1,b(custom))),
(259,act(m2,wl))]

?- go(1000,History).

History = [(810,act(m2,b)),
(676,act(m3,wl)),
(406,act(m1,wu(standard))),
(225,act(m1,b(standard))),
(219,act(m2,wl)),
(353,act(m3,b)),
(243,act(m1,b(custom))),
(155,act(m1,wu(custom)))]

?- go(1000,History).

History = [(757,act(m2,b)),
(583,act(m3,wl)),
(439,act(m1,wu(standard))),
(190,act(m1,b(standard))),
(281,act(m2,wl)),
(455,act(m3,b)),
(213,act(m1,wu(custom))),
(196,act(m1,b(custom)))]
```

ACKNOWLEDGEMENTS

We thank William Maxwell and Louis (Kip) Miller for many interesting discussions about modeling automated factories, and to Kip in particular for the collaborative work on logic and simulation. We also gratefully acknowledge the Department of Decision Sciences, Wharton School, University of Pennsylvania, which provided the setting for the initial phases of this work.

BIBLIOGRAPHY

Brown, John Seely, 1984. "The Low Road, the Middle Road, and the High Road", in Winston and Prendergast (eds), The AI Business, The MIT Press, pp. 81-90.

Coelho, H., Cotta, J.C., and Periera, L.M., 1980. How to Solve it in Prolog, 2nd Ed., Laboratorio Nacional de Engenharia Civil, Lisbon, Portugal.

Clark, K.L., and McCabe, F.G., 1984. Micro-Prolog: Programming in Logic, Prentice Hall International.

Clocksin, W.F., and Mellish, C.S., 1985. Programming in Prolog, 2nd Ed., Springer-Verlag.

Davis, R.E., 1985. "Logic Programming and Prolog: A Tutorial", IEEE Software, September, pp. 53-62.

Kowalski, R.A. 1979a. "Algorithm = Logic + Control", Communications of the ACM, Vol. 22, No.. 7, July, pp. 424-431.

Kowalski, R.A., 1979b. Logic for Problem Solving. Elsevier-North Holland.

Lee, R.M., 1985. "Database Inferencing for Decision Support", Decision Support Systems, Elsevier-North Holland.

Peterson, J.L., 1981. Petri Net Theory and the Modeling of Systems, Prentice-Hall.

Shapiro, E.Y. 1983. A Subset of Concurrent Prolog and Its Interpreter, Technical Report, Weizmann Institute of Science.

Warren, D.H.D., 1982. "A View of the Fifth Generation and Its Impact", The AI Magazine, Fall, pp. 34-39.

APPENDIX -- AUXILIARY PREDICATES

```
/* miscellaneous predicates */

not(P) :- \+ P.

member(X,[X|_]).
member(X,[_|L]) :- member(X,L).

append([],L,L).
append([X|L1],L2,[X|L3]) :- append(L1,L2,L3).

permute([],[]).
permute(X,[Y|YY]) :- delete(Y,X,Z), permute(Z,YY).

delete(X,L,LL) :-
    append(L1,[X|L2],L), /* X is intermediate element of L */
    append(L1,L2,LL). /* LL is append of front, back */

remove([],M,M).
remove([X|L],M,MM) :- delete(X,M,M1), remove(L,M1,MM).

split(H,[A|X],[A|Y],Z) :- order(A,H),!, split(H,X,Y,Z).
split(H,[A|X],Y,[A|Z]) :- split(H,X,Y,Z),!.
split(_,[],[],[]).

qsort([],[]).
qsort([H|T],S) :-
    split(H,T,A,B),
    qsort(A,A1),
    qsort(B,B1),
    append(A1, [H|B1],S).

order(X,Y) :- var(X),!,fail.
order(X,Y) :- var(Y),!.
order(X,Y) :- atomic(X),!, X@<Y.
order(X,Y) :- X=..XX,Y=..YY, compare(XX,YY).

compare([],_):- !.
compare([X|L],[Y|LL]) :- X==Y, compare(L,LL),!.
compare([X|_],[Y|_]) :- order(X,Y).

minof([X],X) :- !.
minof([X|L],Y) :- minof(L,Y),Y@<X,!.
minof([X|L],X).

maxof([X],X) :- !.
maxof([X|L],Y) :- maxof(L,Y),Y@>X,!.
maxof([X|L],X).

random(R,N) :-
```

```
    retract(seed(S)),
    N is (S mod R)+1,
    NewSeed is (125*S+1) mod 4423,
    asserta(seed(NewSeed)), !.

nth(1,[X|_],X) :- !.
nth(N,[_|L],X) :- M is N-1, nth(M,L,X).

draw(X,L) :- length(L,N), random(N,R), nth(R,L,X).
```

KNOWLEDGE-BASED FORMULATION OF LINEAR PLANNING MODELS

Meral Binbasioglu and Matthias Jarke
Graduate School of Business Administration
New York University
90 Trinity Place, New York, N.Y. 10006, USA

ABSTRACT. As decision support systems (DSS) move towards more strategic application domains, there is a growing need for the capability of aiding the decision maker in modelling unanticipated planning problems efficiently without the support of scarce operations research specialists. A major contribution towards the development of model formation subsystems in DSS is expected from the use of Artificial Intelligence (AI) techniques. However, it is claimed in this paper that under current AI technology, model formation subsystems cannot be made fully general and user-friendly at the same time. Instead, a problem-solving approach to model formation is proposed that combines the use of knowledge-based classification techniques as employed in many expert systems, with interactive construction of specialized submodels based on structural knowledge about an operations research technique and domain-specific knowledge about the requirements of an application area. The problem-solving approach is illustrated by a largely implemented system that assists decision makers in the formation of linear planning (LP) models for the application domain of production planning.

1. INTRODUCTION

In comparison to other issues such as model evaluation, database management, or dialog management, the problem of forming appropriate decision models has received little attention from DSS researchers. As shown in surveys by Bonczek et al. [1984] and Hwang [1985], current model management systems -- where they exist at all -- support at best the correct coupling of existing models by the user [Blanning, 1982, 1985].

H. G. Sol et al. (eds.), Expert Systems and Artificial Intelligence in Decision Support Systems, 113–136.
© 1987 by D. Reidel Publishing Company.

Much of the scarce literature in the field has expressed some hope that artificial intelligence may improve on this situation. A few knowledge representation schemes for models have been developed [Dolk and Konsynski, 1984] and automatic model formation strategies based on the composition of existing models have been implemented [Sivasankaran and Jarke, 1985]. However, in many domains, there is no reasonably complete set of models to build on. Only model "prototypes" can be identified which provide some guidance to those model builders who are aware of them; the remaining formulation tasks must be handled based on the model builder's knowledge about the application and the mathematical tools he or she is using.

The question of how general (i.e., application-independent) a tool for model formulation with semantic and syntactic capabilities can and should be made is open. For the present we hypothesize that, under the current AI technology, an automatic model building system cannot be made fully general and user-friendly at the same time. In order to provide sufficient guidance -- semantic capabilities -- to a naive user, expert systems for model formulation have to specialize. Therefore, our approach to model formulation makes use of the structural knowledge of model construction in a particular type of mathematical model along with the application-specific knowledge about a particular domain.

We are currently building a demonstration prototype that supports the formulation of linear programming (LP) models in production applications. The system approaches the problem of model formulation in three hierarchical levels: context identification, problem formulation and model building. Only the problem formulation step will be of interest here; for a description of the other components, see [Binbasioglu and Jarke, 1986]. Throughout model formulation, the system utilizes the structural knowledge about LP models as well as the application specific knowledge about a particular domain of interest (in our case: production).

Certain model types, such as product-mix, blending, or transportation constitute the backbone of LP. These models could be sufficient to model a problem if circumstances warrant or they could be somehow integrated to model a complex problem. The main theme of this paper is to investigate the possibilities to view the model formulation task as problem decomposition to well-known LP model types and discuss the strategies to integrate the resulting submodels. The rationale for this two-phased approach will be presented from the standpoint of both artificial intelligence and management science.

2. A PROBLEM-SOLVING APPROACH TO MODEL FORMATION

2.1. PROBLEM-SOLVING STRATEGIES

The attempts to categorize heuristic programs (expert systems) based on application-oriented descriptions like "diagnosis" or representational terms like "rule-based" are found to be too general to provide a useful framework while handling AI applications.   Rather, the focus is on the way the problem solving is carried out, that is, whether the solution is reached by systematically relating data to a pre-enumerated set of alternative solutions or the solution is constructed with the help of structural and behavioral domain knowledge [Clancey, 1984]. The prior, "classification" problem solving, has the capability to relate the problem description to a pre-enumerated solution set by data abstraction, heuristic association and refinement. An application, say "medical diagnosis", can be conceived of as a classification problem [MYCIN, Shortliffe, 1976] if the program's job is to select one of a fixed list of disease entities that best matches the facts of the case, or as a non-classification problem when there are multiple, interacting diseases so that it is not practical to enumerate all of the possible disease combinations a priori [Pople, 1982].

2.2. APPLICATION TO MODEL FORMATION

Mathematical models are general purpose tools applicable to many situations for various purposes. This makes it impossible to enumerate all possible solution models a priori.   Hence, it is not possible to match a given problem description to one of a fixed set of alternative models. Therefore, the solution model has to be constructed. This is similar to R1, an expert system which configures VAX computers [McDermott, 1982]. However, we defer the ultimate construction task as late as possible and first try to decompose the initial problem into subproblems of standard (proto-)types by taking advantage of the well-structured classification method.   Thus, model formation is conceived both as a classification and a non-classification problem at various stages of problem solving.

At the initial stages, model formation is viewed as a classification problem.   The problem is partitioned into independently workable subproblems using attention focusing heuristics. The subproblems are LP problem types that have certain distinguishing elements, like product-mix, blending, etc. (cf. section 3).   These generic problem types provide general model construction knowledge to be specialized later when the formulation issues unique to the given problem are addressed. At later stages of model formation the problem solver switches to a "construction" strategy that applies structural and behavioral knowledge about Linear Programming and about the production domain to come up with the specialized solution. The solution is an integration of the initially diagnosed subproblems such that a customized model for the specific problem is attained.

To be able to decompose the problem into LP model types the problem solver employs a hypothesis generator to delineate the applicable models. The user's statement of the problem is associated with model types based on necessary and sufficient conditions associated with each model type. That is, the finding about the delineating conditions must be sufficient to select the associated model type. The classification by model types works the same way the "constrictor" concept is used in medical diagnosis -to warrant the conclusion of the disease associated with the constrictor [Pople, 1977]. However, in medicine the constrictors come with varying degrees of certainty making it necessary to view the diagnosis process as conjectural, and have provision for retreating from any multiple problem hypothesis if future findings suggest so. In our domain, once hypotheses are identified using the constrictors they remain valid throughout the rest of the formulation.

The decomposition into subproblems and their classification are decided using a hypothesis-test strategy as part of the classification problem. Successive hypotheses are generated as the initial problem is progressively accounted for. Each hypothesis is marked true if there is sufficient reason to believe it without making any assumptions. That is, all the crucial information is selectively gathered by searching the knowledge base and/or interacting with the user.

At this stage, attention focusing heuristics provide the necessary knowledge required to discriminate among competing hypotheses. Whenever a hypothesis is marked as explaining part of the problem description, it will never be retracted again. To avoid making assumptions, data found to be weakly associated with one or more hypotheses will not be marked as part of a certain hypothesis but rather will be considered as part of "float" which is considered during the integration stage along with the identified subproblems. This way the system will avoid assumptions and make critical decisions as late as possible.

At this stage of model formation the problem solver is employing the match method [Newell, 1969]. The match method is applicable if it is possible to order a set of decisions in such a way that no decision has to be made until information sufficient for committing to it is available [McDermott, 1982]. This is in contrast to problem solving methods such as constraint propagation and dependency-directed backtracking where the system is making assumptions about missing data to come up with a hypothesis which forces the system to undo all the dependent steps when the hypothesis is retracted at a later stage [Pople, 1982; Dhar, 1984].

Knowledge stored with model types provides the core of the final model to be constructed. Structural and behavioral knowledge about subproblem types provide guidelines for further model construction. In addition, some integration rules are required. Note that, since the subproblem representations carry formulation information that must and/or might be part of that problem definition, the generic formulation knowledge about LP model types is available as a consequence of the classification stage.

A knowledge base maintains information about the form of equations and the way they can be instantiated in a given situation. This enables the system to construct the equations from the given problem context. The knowledge-based approach to equation construction provides the flexibility to accomodate various problem contexts where the activities, resources, and policies vary, and where it is not practical to enumerate all possible models.

To recapitulate, the problem solver employs the hypothesis generation method till the set of relevant hypotheses are decided. Then, it exploits knowledge of its task domain to construct a single acceptable solution by integrating the hypothesized problem types.

This two-phased problem solving strategy has certain advantages. First, it is expected that rapid convergence to a final solution model is more likely than in the case of starting model construction immediately. Second, as Clancey [1984] points out, classification as a method is supported by cognitive studies and provides a high-level structure for decomposing problems. Finally, the attention focusing heuristics used during problem decomposition serve to investigate the given problem thoroughly before making a hasty decision. It employs stored knowledge and, when necessary, gathers missing information from the user to test the hypotheses. This way, the problem solver is more or less simulating the thought process of an operations researcher: it processes sufficient data to make a decision rather than being confined within the boundaries of the initial problem statement. The need for determining missing data during the process of classification is pointed out by Ackoff:

The operations research worker, like the medical doctor, is usually presented with symptoms, rather than diagnosis. Ordinarily he must look for additional symptoms before he can diagnose correctly [1968, page 23].

2.3. PROBLEM SOLVING STEPS IN PRACTICE

In order to test the feasibility of the concepts presented in this paper, a model formation prototype system has been designed and partially implemented. This system contains structural knowledge about the model types and mathematical structures of Linear Programming, and domain knowledge about business entities, policies, and processes required for production planning.

The system views the task of model construction as hierarchical problem solving where the findings at any level determine and coordinate the activities in the next level. At each step, the interactions among the components are taken into consideration so that any subpart will not be optimized at the expense of the whole. Model formation is divided into three subtasks: context identification, problem formulation and model building.   While this paper concentrates on problem formulation issues, the other two steps are equally important to have a complete system.

In the context identification step, the complete set of problem components are gathered by relating the problem to its immediate environment.   The objects in the user's problem description are disambiguated and incompleteness in problem description is detected. The importance of this step within problem solving is stressed [Ackoff, 1962, p.68]:

... the environment of the problem contains many forces which can affect the kinds of choice which can be made and the kinds of outcome they will yield. It is generally necessary, therefore, to determine first how the environment and the context are related to the problem under consideration. By so doing, the various components of the problem can be identified and a foundation can be laid for subsequently establishing the relationship between these components.

While context identification defines the environment in which to formulate a problem, model building uses the results of the problem formulation step in order to select and access (or compute) the parameters that go with the constraints and the objective function.

LP model formulation itself is conceived to have two dimensions, a semantic and a syntactic one. The semantic difficulties are encountered while deciding what constraints are relevant in a given problem situation, whereas the syntax of formulation refers to the formal representation of equations, e.g., how to formulate constraints consistent with the rules of LP.

Technically, the problem formulation step classifies the LP subproblems and determines the ways to integrate them so as to come up with the appropriate decision and index variables, the form of the constraining equations and the objective function, using dummy parameter values. In the remainder of this paper, these tasks will be illustrated in some more detail.

3. CLASSIFICATION OF LP SUBMODELS

3.1. Brief Review of Linear Programming

Mathematical models are symbolic representations which incorporate the essential features of actual problems. Mathematical programming refers to techniques for solving a general class of optimization problems dealing with the interaction of many variables, subject to set of restraining conditions. Such problems are called allocation problems when activities and resources have to be combined in such a way so as to maximize the overall effectiveness [Arnoff and Sengupta, 1961, p.109]. We are interested in static (single time period) and dynamic (multi period) allocation problems and their formulation in linear programming. Linear programming (LP), a subclass of mathematical programming, is used to minimize or maximize a linear function in the presence of linear constraints. It can be represented mathematically [Bazaraa and Jarvis, 1977; Charnes and Cooper, 1967] as:

Maximize/minimize:

$$\sum_j c_j X_j$$

Subject to:

$$\sum_j a_{i,j} X_j <= b_i \text{ for each } i$$

$$X_j >= 0 \text{ for each } j$$

where: $j = 1, \ldots, n, \quad i = 1, \ldots, m$

The decision variables, or activity levels, to be determined are represented by X_1, X_2, ..., X_n. c_1, c_2, ..., c_n represent the cost or return coefficients associated with these variables. The $a_{i,j}$ are called technological coefficients.

Mathematically speaking, the problem of model formulation is the problem of determining the index sets i and j, the decision variables, and the coefficient values. There are many ways to formulate such models. As Charnes and Cooper [1967] point out it is possible for models to be inadequate, to overlook essentials, or to incorporate extraneous features and thereby misrepresent the situation. It is the task of a model formation support tool to reduce these risks.

3.2. A Review of Problem Types

LP is a management science tool applicable to a wide variety of problems which may arise in quite different contexts. Analogous mathematical structures can be associated with problems in diverse areas. However, in each application area there are a number of LP problem types that frequently occur by themselves or as part of a larger allocation problem. In this section, we review LP problem types common to production applications, with an emphasis on what knowledge should be represented and how it will be used during problem solving.

3.2.1. Product-mix Problem

Product-mix models seek to determine the profit-maximal levels for a number of production activities. The possible constraints could be on machine, material and employee availability. A limitation on any of these resources is sufficient to label a subproblem as product mix. The objective function maximizes the total profit contributions of all the production activities. The decision variables X_j represent the production level of product j. The standard product-mix problem has the following structure:

Maximize: $\sum_j$ contr-margin$_j$ X_j

(or Minimize: $\sum_j$ cost$_j$ X_j)

Subject to:

$\sum_j$ resource-usage$_{i,j}$ X_j < resource$_i$

where i ε {machine, material, and employee}.

To compute the contribution margin the system uses only those resource costs that are not explicitly accounted for in the constraining equations. Hence, a formulation tool cannot use a fixed formula but has to adjust the computation depending on the requirements of the problem.

If each process varies in its input requirements and the profitabilities of the processes differ (even for processes producing the same product) then we have to consider explicitly the level of the products processed in different processes by adding another index variable, say, k. The decision variables become $X_{j,k}$, and the contribution margins will be calculated accordingly. An extra index must also be added to the standard model when it is possible to produce the products in more than one process and if we want to determine the level of the product produced in each process.

Further, the above standard product-mix model can be augmented by taking into consideration market feasibility conditions such as not producing more than the demand, or producing at least a certain minimum amount; the latter is called a service-level constraint. These constraints might have the following structures:

Demand constraint:

$X_j \leq Demand_j$ or $\Sigma_j X_j \leq Demand$

Service-level constraint:

$X_j \geq Demand_j$ or $\Sigma_j X_j \geq Demand$

3.2.2. Feed-Mix Problem

This problem type determines the cost-minimal mixture of raw material so that the mix will satisfy certain nutritional requirements. Decision variables X_i represent the level of raw material i to be used in a mixture. The coefficient $a_{i,j}$ represents the level of nutritional ingredient j in raw-material i. The coefficient, c_i, represents the cost per unit weight of raw-material i. The typical feed-mix problem has the following mathematical structure:

Minimize:
$\Sigma_i c_i X_i$

Subject to:

$$\Sigma_i \ a_{i,j} X_i \ \geq \ \text{Required level of ingredient } j \text{ in the mix}$$

This core representation of a feed-mix model can be augmented with constraints defined on the availability levels or the minimum usage levels of certain raw materials if the problem description requires so.

3.2.3. Blending Problem

Blending is a variant of the feed-mix model in which the aim is to determine the proportion of raw material i to be used in the blend of product j, denoted by the decision variable $X_{i,j}$. The basic characteristics of this model are the following constraints where the existence of one is sufficient to label the problem type as blending.

Mixture constraint:

$$\frac{\Sigma_i \ \text{proportion}_{i,k} \ X_{i,j}}{\Sigma_i \ X_{i,j}} \ \begin{matrix} > \\ = \\ < \end{matrix} \ \text{desired proportion of k in product j}$$

where k denotes the desired constituent.

The minimal/maximal ratio to be observed between the inputs in the blends are formulated using Ratio Constraints such as:

$$\frac{X_{f,j}}{X_{g,j}} \ \begin{matrix} > \\ = \\ < \end{matrix} \ \text{desired ratio of f to g in blend j}$$

where f and g correspond to different inputs in the blend of product j.

The typical objective function of a blending problem is as follows:

$$\text{Maximize: } \Sigma_i \ \Sigma_j \ P_{i,j} \ X_{i,j}$$

where $P_{i,j}$ is the profit associated with a unit of activity $X_{i,j}$.

Blending problems can be augmented with some other constraints such as availability of inputs, demand requirements for the products and capacity constraints on the processes.

Availability constraint:

$\Sigma_j \ X_{i,j}$ <= Availability input i

Demand constraint (assuming no volumetric loss):

$\Sigma_i \ X_{i,j}$ >= Demand product j

Capacity constraint:

$\Sigma_j \ u_{i,j} \ X_{i,j}$ <= total processing capacity for input i

where $u_{i,j}$ is the amount of processing capacity input i used while blending product j.

3.2.4. Transportation / Distribution Problem

The transportation problem can be conceived of as that of minimizing the cost of distributing a product from several suppliers to a number of customers such that the customer requirements will be met while not exceeding the capacity of any supplier. In the standard interpretation of the model [Wagner, 1975], there are m supply points with items available to be shipped to n demand points such that Plant i can ship at most S_i items, and Demand Point j requires at least D_j items. The cost of shipping each unit from Plant i to Demand Point j is $c_{i,j}$ and the decision variable $X_{i,j}$ represents the amount of goods shipped from Plant i to Demand Point j. The mathematical description is as follows:

Minimize: $\Sigma_i \ \Sigma_j \ c_{i,j} \ X_{i,j}$

Subject to:

$\Sigma_j \ X_{i,j}$ <= S_i for i = 1,2,...,m (supply)

$\Sigma_i \ X_{i,j}$ >= D_j for j = 1,2,...,n (demand)

Limits to the flow from a source to a sink extend the model to a capacitated transportation problem. The linear programming formulation of transportation problem can accomodate lower and upper bounds on the variables as follows:

0 <= lower-bound$_{i,j}$ <= $X_{i,j}$ <= upper-bound$_{i,j}$

Another extension which is mathematically equivalent but different from a modelling point of view is the generalization to network models which allow intermediate points in the transportation flow.

3.2.5. Warehouse Problem

Warehouse problems search for the optimal pattern of purchasing (or production), storage and sales (or usage) of a certain product or raw material. The items are subject to known seasonal price and cost variations, the warehouse has a fixed capacity and the initial stock of an item is known. The firm maximizes the difference of total revenues from sales minus total cost of purchasing (or production) of goods throughout the planning period. This objective function is subject to Selling Constraints where the total sales should not exceed the goods available, and to Buying Constraints which limit the amount of storage to the available warehouse capacity, denoted by H. Mathematically, the warehouse problem can be stated as follows [Charnes and Cooper, 1967]:

Maximize:

$$\Sigma_{t=1 \text{ to } n} \text{ price}_t \text{ Sales}_t - \Sigma_{t=1 \text{ to } n} \text{ cost}_t \text{ Purchase}_t$$

Subject to:

Selling constraints:

$$\Sigma_{t=1 \text{ to } i} \text{ Sales}_t < = \text{Inventory}_{\text{initial}} + \Sigma_{t=1 \text{ to } i-1} \text{ Purchase}_t$$

$$(i=1,2,\ldots,n)$$

Buying constraints:

$$\Sigma_{t=1 \text{ to } i} \text{ Purchase}_t < = H - \text{Inventory}_{\text{initial}} + \Sigma_{t=1 \text{ to } i} \text{ Sales}_t$$

$$(i=1,2,\ldots,n)$$

The single-product warehousing problem can be extended to a multiple product and multiple warehouse problem. Another extension is to augment it by money considerations ("warehouse-funds-flow-model"). Then, the following constraints relating funds inflow to funds outflow and to cash level have to be added.

$$\Sigma_{t=1 \text{ to } i} \text{ cost}_j \text{ Purchase}_j - \Sigma_{t=1 \text{ to } i-1} \text{ price}_j \text{ Sales}_j < = \text{Cash}_{\text{initial}} - \text{Cash}_{\text{desired balance}}$$

Further limitations that can be part of this model are availability of machine hours, employee hours or number of employees, desired level of overtime etc. If the problem domain is expanded, in addition to adding new constraints we might need some revisions in the existing objective function and constraints, too. For instance, while constructing the above cash equation the added activities that change the cash balance should be taken into consideration.

3.2.6. Inventory Model

This is a variation of the warehouse model where the amount of inventory at any time period is taken into consideration explicitly. As a result, holding costs are taken into account while determining the production (and/or purchase) schedule. Another difference is that in the warehouse model, the sales level at each period is a decision variable, whereas in inventory models sales might be determined implicitly, too. The costs to be minimized depend on the production quantity, the resources utilized during the process of production (or purchase), the inventory level and possibly on the time period.

Since inventory levels at each period are taken into consideration explicitly, balance flow equations relate the purchase (or production) and sales (or usage) of goods:

$$\text{Inventory}_t = \text{Inventory}_{t-1} + \text{Purchase}_t - \text{Sales}_t \text{ (for each period)}$$

When inventory at any time period is explicitly accounted for, we can accomodate other constraints on the level of inventory such as:

Do not maintain more than a certain fraction of the estimated sales for the current period and the next z periods:

$$\text{Inventory}_{j,t} \ <= \ \Sigma_{i=t \text{ to } t+z} \text{ fraction}_j \text{ Demand}_{j,i}$$

Space Constraint:

$$\Sigma_j \text{ space-required}_j \text{ Inventory}_{j,t} \ <= \ \text{Total space available}$$

The objective function in this model will be as in the warehouse model, maximizing the difference between sales revenues and costs incurred to produce (acquire) the goods. In addition, the costs incurred due to holding inventory have to be minimized:

Maximize:

$$\Sigma_t \, [\Sigma_j \, (\text{contribution}_j \, \text{Sales}_{j, \, t} - \text{holdcost}_j \, \text{Inventory}_{j, \, t})]$$

As in the case of the warehouse model, constraints on workforce or machine capacity, working capital, can be optionally added to the problem formulation. If any of them appear in the objective function, we exclude the corresponding cost from the contribution margin. Finally, service level or other demand constraints can be set.

3.3. Knowledge Representation for Problem Types

The association of subproblems with the model types presented in the previous subsection is greatly facilitated if an appropriate knowledge representation is chosen for both. Such a knowledge representation should emphasize the prototypical nature of model types, i.e., allow for a large amount of diversity within each model type while preserving the essential properties.

In the LP model formulation tool being developed by us, knowledge about LP submodel types is represented as 'frames' [Minsky, 1975]. All the facts about a given model type are attached to slots provided by the frame structure. Some of these slots are used to describe the constraint types that must be part of the problem to belong to a certain model type. Among these, some may be sufficient by themselves to commit to a model type.

For instance, product-mix models must have availability constraints on some types of resources such as employees, machines, and raw-materials. However, an availability constraint on any of these is sufficient to conclude that a product-mix submodel is needed (in the application context selected for the system). Also, for each model type, the type of constraints that may be part of a model are stored. This way, the system has semantic knowledge about the constraint types that can (as contrasted to "must") go with a problem.

The knowledge about the constraints that must or may be part of a problem type are stored in two specialized slots called the 'must-be' and 'may-be' slots. The information stored in the 'must-be' slot is used while the problem solver is determining whether the necessary and sufficient conditions of a model type are met. The 'may-be' slots are used later on to assign remaining "float" (cf. section 2). For example, a product-mix frame looks roughly as follows:

Name: Product-mix

Is_a: Model type

Obj-Fun: Σ_j cont-margin $_j$ Product $_j$

Must-be: (availability, raw-material) OR
              (availability, employee) OR
              (capacity, machine)

May-be: (service-level, product),
              (market_limitation, product)

The form of the equations can also be largely inferred by the system. This is accomplished by storing detailed information about the structure of equations along with some other properties (e.g., what type of objects could be part of the same equation simultaneously) in equation frames. Some additional rules help the user customize the form of the constraints, e.g., deciding the index variables or instantiating the generic equation components.

The model type and equation frames represent knowledge about object types in a business setting at the most generic level. This will reduce conceptual and storage redundancies while retaining the flexibility to use the system in various production problems.   The knowledge representation relates different levels of object description using an is-a hierarchy. Only after this abstraction, the model type and equation type frames provide formulation information.

4. THE RELATIONSHIP BETWEEN CLASSIFICATION AND CONSTRUCTION

Model formulation can be approached at two levels, semantics and syntactics of formulation. Semantic difficulties are encountered while deciding what equations are relevant in a given problem description. Equation construction leads to syntactic difficulties; here, the main issue is how to construct an equation knowing its type, consequently its form and the problem components that go with it.

The rationale for matching the given problem data to prototype model types is to alleviate the semantic difficulties of equation construction. The information stored in the frame representation of model types makes the system justify the appropriateness of certain equation types and the ways to instantiate them. However, as discussed already, the chances that a given problem description will match a prototype model is low. Usually, formulations use more than one model type to model the given problem. Even if only one model type is sufficient to formulate the given problem, we still need to adjust the generic formulation to come up with a tailored solution.

To recapitulate, the semantics of equation formulation has two stages, the first associating the constraints to model types, classification stage, the second adjusting the formal representation of constraints. We now illustrate this process by a lengthy example. (Other aspects of the same example are discussed in [Binbasioglu and Jarke, 1986].)

Consider the production process in a bakery shop. The baker initially has a vague idea that some planning is needed in the area of cookies production, and the purchasing of associated raw materials. Moreover, he suspects that there are constraints on sales, the minimum required service level, the availability of his mixer, and raw material budgets. The initial problem statement would look as follows:

```
?- problem([production,cookies], [purchase,sugar]),
   constraints(mixer, sugar, [service_level,cookies],
               [sales_limits,cookies]).
```

The initial problem statement is interactively analyzed and refined during the context identification step. Depending on the level of initial knowledge the user can express, the interaction alternates between user-driven and system-driven dialog, so that all the objects and the relationships among them are identified. Therefore, the function of the context identification step is to locate the relevant area of the knowledge base from which a more detailed analysis of the formulation problem at hand can be initiated.

To do this, the system tries to associate the information given to it with certain nodes and arcs in a business knowledge base which is organized as a semantic network of frame-like structures, similar to that described above for model types. For details, see [Binbasioglu and Jarke, 1986]; here, we just state the findings.

The final products which can be classified as cookie-types are searched to determine the items relevant to the problem. The missing constraint types for mixer and sugar in the initial statement are decided to be availability. Since at this step the system also reminds the user of the other aspects that can be part of a problem, the problem domain is expanded to consider the storage of final goods and raw materials. The possibilities to purchase raw material before using it for production, or to produce final products for future demand, lead to a multi-period problem. The set of relevant constraints identified during the context identification step can be summarized as follows:

Machine availability constraint for a machine called mixer

Raw-material availability constraint for a raw material called sugar

Market limitation constraint (Demand) for a class of products called cookies

Service level constraint for a class of products called cookies

Balance equation among storage, purchase and usage for a raw material called sugar

Balance equation among storage, production, and sales for a class of products called cookies

4.1. An Example of Problem Decomposition

After identifying the boundaries of the problem context, the system proceeds to assist the user in determining the necessary equations, and in specifying the format of these constraints and of the objective function. The first step in this process is the choice of a suitable problem decomposition that relates the problem via classification to a set of applicable submodel types.

To be able to justify the existence of a model type, the problem solver matches the constraints with the constraint list stored in the must-have slots of model frames. Where no clear match can be found, constraints are retained in the "float" rather than committing to premature decisions. If constraints are left unassociated with any model type, the system looks at the may-have slots of the accounted model type frames to associate the constraints with those model types. Balance

equations are considered last so that the system can get a simple view
of the problem before introducing the complications of multi-period
formulation.

The keyword, production, in the problem statement in conjunction with
the availability constraints on sugar and mixer are matched with the
must-have slot of the Product-mix model where it is stated that it is
neccessary to have an availability constraint on machines or employees
or raw materials and any of these is sufficient to decide on the model
type.

The major remaining problem component, related to purchase of sugar, is
hypothesized to be a cost minimization model. The must-have slots of
such a model type identify the constraint stating the minimum service
level for the decision variables that are part of the objective function
(here: the level of sugar to be purchased). The user is asked if such a
constraint is applicable. The confirmation leads to the problem type,
the cost minimization problem subject to a newly identified service
level constraint.

The service-level equation and the market limitation equation are not
yet associated with a model type and rather left as float. At this
stage, the system tries to associate them as part of the identified
model types and it finds by looking at the may-have slots of product-mix
model that they can be viewed as part of it. The multi-period feature of
the formulation is deferred to model integration. Before that, the
product-mix problem (problem-I) and the raw material purchasing problem
(problem-II) are elaborated.

Since the constraint types and the basic decision variables are known,
the remaining tasks are mostly at the syntactic level. Syntactic
difficulties arise when determining the form of the constraining
equations, that is, designing the right equations and objective
function, given the decision variables and the type of the constraints.
The form of the relevant constraints is retrieved from the knowledge
base using the 'form' slot of the equation frames. Further, the system
has to decide the coefficients of the decision variables and their units
of measure, as well as select the necessary index sets.

To illustrate this process, we demonstrate equation construction for the
identified model types: product-mix (Problem-I) and raw material
purchasing (Problem-II). We consider the following constraints for
problem-I.

(I.1) Machine availability constraint
(I.2) Raw material availability constraint
(I.3) Market limitation (Demand)
(I.4) Service level
(I.5) Objective function.

A major problem in LP formulation is the choice of the decision variables and their index sets. Rules are associated with the model type frames to guide this process. The following rule can be used to determine the decision variables: "IF the aim is to determine the production level of final products THEN the decision variable P is the level of final product to be produced." Another rule says that "IF the problem type is product-mix THEN an index for product (say i) is needed." This leads to the following set of equations for subproblem I.

(I.1) Machine Availability Constraint:

The stored form of this constraint, specialized from general resource availability as presented in the previous section looks as follows:

$$\Sigma_i \text{ capusage}_{i,j} P_i <= \text{capacity}_j$$

where:
$\text{capusage}_{i,j}$ = Units of time each unit of product i requires on machine j.

Using the knowledge acquired during the Context Identification Step, this standard form can be specialized. Since the problem is product mix, the index i is required and takes the values defined in the set "cookies", e.g., "PEANUT_BUTTER_COOKIE, DANISH_BUTTER_COOKIE, CHOCOLATE_CHIP_COOKIE". On the other hand, the system knows that there is only one machine which could be a bottleneck, namely the "MIXER". Therefore, the index j can be dropped. Thus, we get the specialized constraint:

$$\Sigma_{i \in \text{COOKIES}} \text{capusage}_{i,\text{MIXER}} P_i <= \text{Capacity}_{\text{MIXER}}$$

In a similar way, the other constraints can be specialized:

(I.2) Raw Material Availability Constraint:

$$\Sigma_{i \in COOKIES} \; rawusage_{i,SUGAR} P_i <= Availability_{SUGAR}$$

(I.3) Market Limitation (Demand)

$$P_i <= Demand_i$$

(I.4) Service Level Equations

$$P_i >= MinimumSales_i$$

(I.5) Objective Function

Maximize: $\Sigma_{i \in COOKIES} \; P_i Contribution_i$

In equal fashion, we determine constraints and objective function in problem-II:

(II.1) Meet the Internal Demand:

$$Purchase_{SUGAR} \; > = \; \Sigma_{i \in COOKIES} \; rawusage_{i,SUGAR} P_i$$

(II.2) Objective Function:

$$Minimize \; cost_{SUGAR} Purchase_{SUGAR}$$

Note that in (II.2) the Σ sign has been removed from a standard formula since there is only one summand.

4.2. Integration of Subproblems

For the subsequent model integration step, it is important to observe that both problems are coupled only via the raw material variables. However, when the system combines the two subproblems, it cannot simply use the existing equations. While equations I.1, I.3, and I.4 will be used as they are, equation I.2 will be merged with II.1:

$$Availability_{SUGAR} + Purchase_{SUGAR} >= \Sigma_{i \in COOKIES} \; rawusage_{i,SUGAR} P_i$$

The global objective function includes components from both subproblems. A new contribution margin which excludes sugar costs is computed for the products, because the combined model takes care of raw material cost explicitly.

The combination of the subproblems must also take into account that the problem is multi-period. As stated earlier, we can pre-purchase raw materials or pre-produce final products. IF the problem is a multi-period problem THEN it is necessary to distinguish the quantities of each raw material bought, used and stored and the quantities of each final product produced, sold and stored at each time period. Moreover, there is a rule that "IF a problem is multiperiod THEN add an index t to all variables". (There are also additional, more complex rules which are skipped here for simplicity of exposition.)

All the previous equations should be indexed by t. Equation I.3. must also reflect the fact that Sales for any period -instead of production-must be less than the Demand for the period. The objective function has to be modified and balance flow equations have to be added.

(I.3') $Sales_{i,t} \leq Demand_{i,t}$

We assume here (realistic in a bakery) that all demand not satisfied in the period is lost. If backorders are allowed sales will be a function of current demand and previously unfilled demand. In addition, another rule states that multi-period problems require balance flow equations:

$$Storage_{SUGAR,\,t-1} + Purchase_{SUGAR,\,t} = Usage_{SUGAR,\,t} + Storage_{SUGAR,\,t}$$

$$Storage_{i,\,t-1} + P_{i,\,t} = Sales_{i,\,t} + Storage_{i,\,t}$$

where $i \epsilon COOKIES$.

The new objective function will use the sales level instead of the production level, and will accomodate the minimization of storage costs. The final version has the following form:

Maximize:

$$\Sigma_t\, \Sigma_i\, (Sales_{i,t} NewContribution_{i,t} - Storage_{i,t} StorCost_{i,t})$$

$$- (\Sigma_t (Purchase_{SUGAR,t} Cost_{SUGAR,t} + Storage_{SUGAR,t} StorCost_{SUGAR,t}))$$

We have now completed the problem formulation step. In the model formation tool developed by us, the next step requires the instantiation of right-hand sides and coefficients which will usually be done either interactively or -- better -- by retrieval from a database followed by the necessary computations (e.g., of contribution margins). The final model is then submitted to a matrix generator.

5. CONCLUSION

The example has demonstrated the utility of combining a problem classification step which provides a high-level structure to a problem to be formulated as an LP model, with a knowledge-aided construction step that employs business and operations research knowledge to adapt and integrate generic submodel types as to model a complex problem situation faithfully. As in medical "differential diagnosis", the classification subproblem is complicated by the fact that multiple submodels may be needed in combination, although the "symptoms" tend to be clearer than in medicine. Therefore, some classification decisions must be delayed until -- maybe only at the model integration stage -- sufficient knowledge is available to justify a commitment.

For more sophisticated users who want to build very large models where little previous application experience is available, a similar support strategy can still be useful, although responsibility for semantic completeness is left to the user. Such a mostly syntactic support tool for the OR professional is being developed in a companion research effort at New York University [Murphy and Stohr, 1985]. Both systems are currently in an advanced stage of implementation, using the logic programming language Prolog for knowledge-based model formation and standard LP tools for matrix generation, optimization, and sensitivity studies. It is intended to combine the two modelling environments by attaching the system presented here as a "semantic front-end" to the syntactic tool and its associated LP packages. The ultimate goal is to offer a friendly DSS environment in which syntactically and semantically correct LP models of realistic size can be built by fairly OR-naive decision makers.

6. REFERENCES

Ackoff, R. L. (1962). Scientific Method, John Wiley & Sons.

Ackoff, R. L. and Sasieni, M. W. (1968). Fundamentals of Operations Research, John Wiley & Sons.

Arnoff, E. L. and Sengupta, Sankar S. (1961). Mathematical Programming, Progress in Operations Research, in Ackoff, R. L. (ed.), John Wiley & Sons.

Bazaraa, M., and Jarvis, J.J. (1977). Linear Programming and Network Flows, John Wiley and Sons.

Binbasioglu, M. and Jarke, M. (1986). Domain-specific DSS tools for knowledge-based model building, to appear in Decision Support Systems, also presented at 19th Hawaii International Conference on Systems Sciences, Honolulu.

Blanning, R. W. (1982). What is happening in DSS?, Interfaces, 13(5), pp. 71-80.

Blanning, R. W. (1985). A Relational Framework for Join Implementation in Model Management Systems, Decision Support Systems, Vol. 1, No. 1, pp. 69-82.

Bonczek, R.H., Holsapple, C.W., and Whinston, A.B. (1984). Developments in decision support systems, in Advances in Computers, Vol. 23, Academic Press, pp. 141-175.

Charnes, A., and Cooper, W.W. (1967). Management Models and Industrial Applications of Linear Programming, John Wiley & Sons.

Clancey, W. J. (1984). Classification problem solving, Proceedings National Conference on Artificial Intelligence, Austin, Tx, pp. 49-55.

Dhar, V. (1984). PLANET: an intelligent decision support system for the formulation and investigation of formal planning models, unpublished Ph.D. thesis, University of Pittsburgh, Pa.

Dolk, D., and Konsynski, B.R. (1984). Knowledge representation for model management, IEEE Transactions on Software Engineering, SE-10(6), pp.619-628.

Hwang, S. (1985). Automatic model building systems: a survey, DSS-85 Transactions, San Francisco, Ca., pp. 22-32.

McDermott, J. (1982). R1: a rule-based configurer of computer systems, Artificial Intelligence, 19(1), pp.39-88.

Murphy, F.H., and Stohr, E.A. (1985). An intelligent system for formulating linear programs, New York University Working Paper Series, CRIS #95, GBA 85-40 (CR).

Newell, A. (1969). Heuristic programming: ill-structured problems, in J. S. Aronofsky (ed.), Progress in Operations Research, John Wiley & Sons, New York, pp. 361-414.

Pople, H. E., Jr. (1977). The formation of composite hypotheses in diagnostic problem solving: an exercise in synthetic reasoning, Proceedings Fifth International Joint Conference on Artificial Intelligence, pp. 1030-1037, Pittsburg, Pa.

Pople, H. E., Jr. (1982). Heuristic methods for imposing structure on ill-structured problems: the structuring of medical diagnostics, in Szolovits, P. (ed.), Artificial Intelligence in Medicine, Westview Press, Boulder, CO.

Shortliffe, E. H. (1976). Computer-based Medical Consultations: MYCIN, Elsevier, New York.

Sivasankaran, T.R. and Jarke, M. (1985). Logic-based formula management strategies in an Actuarial Consulting System, to appear in Decision Support Systems.

Wagner, H. M. (1975). Principles of Management Science, Prentice-Hall.

LINGUISTIC EXPLORATORY ANALYSIS FOR DECISION SUPPORT

Dr. H. Koppelaar
Technical University Delft
Department of Mathematics & Informatics
P.O.Box 356, 2600 AJ Delft
Netherlands

ABSTRACT. This work aims to clarify the relationship between verbally formulated description of a system and experimentation with its properties via a computer. The computer software technique employed here stems from the use of fuzzy sets. This technique will be explained and an example of its application will be given: linguistic exploratory ('what if') analysis.

1. INTRODUCTION

With the need to make more and better decisions, and because of the time involved in scanning through relevant data, management obviously needs some way to reduce the burden of professional decision making. Decision Support Systems (DSS) provide a means of satisfying these needs, see Elam e.a. (1986) and Gorry & Scott Morton (1971). DSS describes a new class of information systems that are intended for traditional data access and to simplify decision making, speed up the process of choosing between alternatives and help ensure the accuracy of each decision.

Hussain e.a. (1981; ch. 20) distinguish three levels of decision making: operational, managerial and strategic. DSS's can be of great value at all three levels. Most operational-level decisions make up the majority of routine choices, they are usually standardized, they require detailed information, but the data is readily available and its conversion into decision making information is often subconscious or can be delegated. Managerial-level decisions require a broader context of information. The manager must rely on prior experience, training and educated guesses. Managerial-level decisions cannot be delegated, but they can be speed up. For instance, a manager cannot advise his board until all the data concerning a problem is in. Strategic-level decisions require a wide range of information. This

137

H. G. Sol et al. (eds.), Expert Systems and Artificial Intelligence in Decision Support Systems, 137–150.
© *1987 by D. Reidel Publishing Company.*

type of decision is usually made after longer periods of
thought and planning and they often require the generation
of new data. The majority of strategic decisions cannot be
standardized, canned, or delegated.

The computer software tools aiming at satisfying the
needs of managers have been Management Information Systems
(MIS). A MIS is a large data-gathering system. A DSS is a
refinement of the MIS to apply to individual's decision-
making needs. In the past, both MIS and DSS systems had to
be implemented on large computers. Today, most managers can
benefit from a microcomputer to reduce and standardize the
decision making. For a more detailed discussion of the side-
effects of introducing personal computing in this way, see
Sol (1985). The computer's ability to play 'what if' from
existent initial data or assumptions, yields the possibility
to experiment with various (sub)decisions summing up to
competing scenario's. One problem, however, remains:
numerical data for 'what if' analyses often are not
available.

This paper reports a DSS tool for non-numeric
('linguistic') exploratory ('what if') analysis. From a
different viewpoint one could describe the 'what if'
analysis to be a simulation method (Sol, 1982). The areas in
which the simulation method has been demonstrably and
spectacularly successful are characterised by the possibility of performing experiments, or making observations (at
random) whenever these are deemed necessary. Managerial
decision making usually has no access to 'experimental'
data.

In Operations Research it is traditionally assumed that
any doubts concerning a model can be resolved by further
experimentation and observation. This has resulted in a
neglect of explicit consideration of scientific methods
which hypothesize models and scenario's from pure non-
numerical data: non-experimental research. The books by
Blalock (1964, 1969) are the first methodological treatments
of the question: "How to play with ideas if none of the
relevant company-variables can be manipulated by the
manager". The approach in this paper is to fill in details
of such an Inquiry System (Bosman and Sol, 1985) with the
technique of Linguistic Reasoning. This is a technical
extension of the Logic Programming approach by Bots (1986)
and Lee (1985) and a counterpart of the statistically
oriented 'non-experimental' approach, depicted as Structural
Equation Models by Saris & Stronkhorst (1984).

2.   EXAMPLE OF A LINGUISTIC EXPLORATORY PROBLEM

Logic Programming is based on predicate calculus. The
advantage of Logic Programming as advocated by Bots (1986)
and Lee (1985) is to enable a manager to specify his
reasoning to a computer in a declarative manner, that is one
specifies what is the line of thought instead of how to do
the reasoning.

The format of Logic Programming, however, is confined
to binary logic and to the logical syntax of 'if ... then'
statements, without resort to the many valuedness and the
rich syntax of managers' reasoning in natural language. It
is the aim of this paper to show an utility for a DSS-user
interface to bridge the gap between the manager's own style
of reasoning and automated reasoning. The technique
advocated in this paper is to extend Automated Reasoning
with help of Logic Programming in two ways:

- Extending Automated Reasoning with many-valuedness;
- Extending Automated Reasoning with a generative grammar
      for a more natural language output.

In practice much of the managerial reasoning is stated in
simple covariate form. Where both X and Y are variables, the
statement of a covariance relationship would be of the form,
'the greater the X, the greater the Y', or 'the smaller X,
the smaller Y', or 'X's tend to be associated with Y's',
etc. These covariate statements may or may not be testable,
depending on whether each of the variables in the
proposition has been measured. The question Blalock (1969)
deals with, is that of how one goes about deducing one
covariate statement from another. How can one build deductions on the basis of such statements? He considers a
specific example of a theory about cooperation in a
professional task group. The theory is set-up to predict
solidarity in a task group from a.o. the (equal)
distribution of labor. The whole theory consists of ten
statements as follows:

1.   The greater the division of labor, the greater the
        consensus within the group.
2.   The greater the solidarity, the greater the number of
        associates per member.
3.   The greater the number of associates per member, the
        greater the consensus.
4.   The greater the consensus, the smaller the number of
        rejections of deviants.
5.   The greater the division of labor, the smaller the number
        of rejections of deviants.
6.   The greater the number of associates per member, the
        smaller the number of rejections of deviants.

7. The greater the division of labor, the greater the
    solidarity.
8. The greater the solidarity, the greater the consensus.
9. The greater the number of associates per member, the
    greater the division of labor.
10. The greater the solidarity, the smaller the number of
    rejections of deviants.

The question one could ask is: 'What' happens in this task
force 'if' conditions get changed? For instance: if a group
starts with a low division of labor and with a low number of
associates per group member, what does the theory predict
for this situation? In this paper a system is explained to
entry statements, such as the above, in a computer and to
have the computer to do the reasoning upon questions from
the user. And also to obtain answers in a natural language
format. Blalock (1964, 1969) in his time could not come to
such an exploratory machinery.

3. NUMERICAL VERSUS LINGUISTIC SIMULATION

For 'what if' or exploratory analysis one could resort to
the existing numerous simulation techniques, based upon
analogue computer techniques and upon digital computer
languages like SIMULA, CSMP, GASP, DYNAMO, LEANS, CELLSIM.
Recently for the same purpose the so called 'spread sheets'
computer software is also advocated: VISICALC, MULTIPLAN,
LOTUS 1-2-3, etc. A factor common to the packages is that
they are numerical, i.e. the variables assume probabilistic
and/or numerical values. The power of probabilistic/numeri-
cal methods, however, is seriously restricted because 'what
if' analysis requires all variables to be defined nume-
rically, hence they have to be accessible or estimated with
numerical precision. This is why Harbordt (1974) brings
about the following disadvantages of numerical models
against verbally stated models of reasoning:

- the danger of 'overstraining' the analysis to meet the
    requirement of numerical precision;
- the danger of 'over-interpreting' the numerical results of
    the analysis;
- the danger of 'overstraining' all kinds of vague
    relationships, by making them exact relationships,
    usually by means of simplification and approximation.

The main difficulty of 'what if analysis' is caused by the
requirement of numerical precision in attempting to model
the mechanisms behind complex decision making upon information embodying ill-defined concepts. If exploratory analysis, that is the 'what if' Inquiry (Bosman and Sol, 1985)

could only be done in a an automated natural language environment, much ease-of-use for a DSS would be gained. Since
natural language has a precision level which can efficiently
express the degree of inexactness of the reported information.

4. WHAT IS A LINGUISTIC EXPLORATORY MODEL?

Zadeh's concept of fuzzy sets (1965) had been the object of
increasing attention as a potential mathematical tool for
the exploratory analysis of complex systems of verbal statements. It has been suggested by Zadeh (1975) that it might
be possible to combine the virtues of both calculus and
natural language, by designing an auxiliary language which
resembles natural language with respect to vocabulary, syntax and semantics, and where the semantics is represented
mathematically as fuzzy sets.

In the mathematical sense, Zadeh's suggestion goes back
to Boole (1958) and Lukasiewicz (1966). The latter introduced many valued logics, while Zadeh's semantical representation by fuzzy sets can be regarded as an infinitely valued
logic. Fuzzy set theory is essentially a generalization of
Boolean algebra which was originally developed by
Boole (1958) as an instrument for the semantical analysis of
a certain class of propositions. Boolean algebra has as its
basis a semantical model of the meaning of the connectives
'or', 'and' and 'not'. This makes it possible to calculate
the truthvalues of propositions that are otherwise too complicated to infer by simple unaided reasoning. Zadeh's approach broadens the area to which these principles can be
applied. It becomes possible also to put forward semantic
definitions of several words which in natural language are
used to approximately characterize both magnitudes (Lakaff
1972, Zadeh 1972) and the casual relations between such
magnitudes as well. This opens up the possibility of
linguistic models of reasoning in a domain of knowledge.

Zadeh's suggestion could be traced back to
Carnap's (1946) attemps to construct an empirically anchored
auxiliary language for formulating physics. A first attempt
to computerize Carnap's ideas is from Lindenberg (1971).
Lindenberg's main question is, whether there exists a
transformation for every dynamical empirical scientific
theory, such that a computer can explore the theory. An
auxiliary language, with the properties required by
Lindenberg, is from Wenstøp (1976), designed in APL according to Zadeh's suggestions. The main requirements of a
linguistic reasoning language, functioning as an auxiliary
language for verbal reasoning according Wenstøp (1976), are:

- a precision level near that of natural language;
- easy to learn to use and to understand;
- it should be deductive;
- it should be implementable on a computer such that
      deductions are performed automatically;
- it should be versatile enough to give a fair description
      of a reasonably large class of knowledge domains.

The first two demands would be met if one uses a quasi-
natural language where the semantics are as close as
possible to natural English. The third demand is met by
using fuzzy set theory. The fourth can be solved by implementing the language in APL. The versatility of the
auxiliary language relates directly to the size of the
vocabulary and the syntactical freedom. The linguistic reasoning language is completely defined by a vocabulary, a
syntax and a semantics with a linguistic approximation
routine.

4.1. Vocabulary

LEXICAL CATEGORY	SYMBOL	MEMBERS
primary terms	T	high, low, medium, undefined, unknown
hedges	H	above, below, around, upper, lower, rather, moreorless, very, not, neither, possibly, truly indeed, fuzzily
connective	C	and, or, but, nor, plus, minus, to, except
trend mode	M	increasingly, decreasingly, linearly
trend direction	D	falling, climbing, growing
relative connect.	RC	then
pointer	W	with
truth evaluator	IS	is
conditionalizer	IF	if
names of variables	X	unrestricted, except for reserved keywords above

4.2. Syntax

S represents every assignment statement
V represents every linguistics value
R represents every linguistic relation
N represents truthvalues

THE GRAMMAR (using the symbols above) IS:

S => X <-- V
V => X, T, (H V), (V C V), (V IFN), (R W X)
N => (N C N), (X IS V)
R => (R RC R), D
D => (H D), (M D)

*(The right pointing arrow means that the symbol
on the left of the arrow can be rewritten by any
one of the compound symbols/expressions, separated by commas on the right. The parentheses
play essentially the same role as commas: they
divide the statement into sentence parts).*

4.3. Examples

It is easy to show that the following assignment statements
are syntactically correct:

y ((neither high nor (below medium))

X (below Y)

x (((moreorless high or (around Y)) if (y is (not high))))

X (X plus DX)

Y ((increasingly falling with Y2)

Previous exposition of vocabulary and syntax for linguistic
models enables us to state the concept of linguistic models
more precisely: we shall by a linguistic model understand
simply a list of verbal assignment statements which are
ordered so that all independent variables in a given
statement have been assigned values in statements preceding
it.

Given a verbal model, it is usually not intuitively
easy to predict its behavior. This is especially true when
feed-back loops are involved since these are difficult for
the human mind readily to assimilate. What we need,
therefore, is an automated system which understands the
meaning behind each assignment statement in the sense that
it can make intuitively acceptable inferences from them and
in addition can put this together and thereby calculate the
implied dynamic behavior of the total system. The meaning
behind each assignment statement is a matter of semantics.

4.4. Semantics

A necessary component of linguistic statements is an
internal machine representation, embodying the meaning
(semantic) of the statements. Such a component can be
realized by computerized semantics based on fuzzy set
theory. APL has been found by Wenstøp to be a computer
language remarkably suited for this purpose. The present
semantical system will therefore be described partly by use
of APL-symbols.

Variables are treated as linguistic variables in the
sense of Zadeh. For practical purposes, a fuzzy set will be
represented by a discrete collection of points from the
universe of discourse with their respective membership-
values. In the concrete language of APL, therefore, fuzzy
sets will be represented as arrays or (higher order)
matrices of membership-values, the structure depending on
the dimensionality of the actual fuzzy set. With respect to
the individual words in the vocabulary, it thus becomes
natural to interpret primary terms and elementary relations
in the form of constant fuzzy sets. The words from these two
lexical categories will accordingly be called fuzzy
constants. The syntactical rules ensure that hedges always
precede their arguments. The hedges may be referred to as
monadic semantic operators since they modify the meaning of
what is to follow in an expression. All other words are seen
to operate on the combined meaning of what is on each of
their sides. These words may correspondingly be referred to
as dyadic semantic operators.

The three syntactical categories, in which the
vocabulary can be split, are equivalent to the APL-
categories of constants, monadic functions and dyadic
functions. A semantic model may therefore be defined by

specifying each word from the vocabulary directly as
appropriate APL constants, monadic, or dyadic functions. If
this has been done, any verbal assignment statement will
also automatically be an APL statement.

4.4.1.   Semantics of some of the individual category
members. The meaning of the four primary terms are shown
below:

high   <--0 0 0 0 0 0 .1 .7 1.

low   <--1. .7 .1 0 0 0 0 0 0

undef.   <--0 0 0 0 0 0 0 0 0

unknown <-- 1 1 1 1 1 1 1 1 1

The semantics of the individual hedges has been defined by
Wenstøp according to the general principles and ideas set
forth in Zadeh (1972) and Lakoff (9). For simplicity, hedges
are assumed to operate only on membership-values, i.e. their
effect is independent of positions of the operand in the
universe of discourse. This is also true of the relation
hedges which act in a uniform manner on all elements in the
relation in question. Examples of the effects of some of the
hedges are:

high   <--0 0 0 0 0 0 .1 .7 1.

moreorless
   high   <--0 0 0 0 0 .2 .6 .9 1.

very high <--0 0 0 0 0 0 0 .2 1.

rather
   high   <--0 0 0 0 0 0 .2 1. .3

The connectives 'and' and 'or' are defined in the standard
fuzzy set-theoretical way.
        An example of the use of a trend direction is the
operation of the pointer 'with' on a linguistic variable AGE
with a value labelled VERY YOUNG.

We put in:

AGE <-   1   .8   .6   0   0   0   0   0   0

and ask for the value of AGE after operating with a trend
direction:

AGE GROWING WITH AGE

AGE ->   1   .8   .6   .25   .04   .01   0   0   0

From the above example it is clear that AGE has grown. An
example of its linguistic values, represented as fuzzy sets
(membership-values equal to zero are omitted) and a universe
of discourse limited to 45 years is in the picture below.

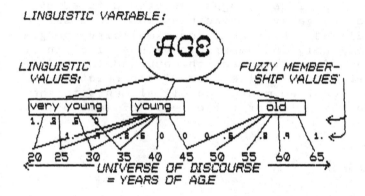

In summary of this section we conclude that 'meaning' of
linguistic values is represented as number arrays. The
positions on the array may be thought of as positions on a
scale where the leftmost position corresponds to the lowest
value and vica versa. The numbers are the degree of
membership to which a position is included in the label.
Hence the arrays are fuzzy sets (for a definition of fuzzy
sets see the Appendix).

4.4.2. Linguistic approximation. In order to complete the
semantical system, it is not enough to devise rules for
computation and representation of meaning. Wenstøp (1984)
also designed a function which goes the opposite way,
finding appropriate linguistic labels for a given meaning.
This process is known as linguistic approximation.

A meaning representation system is a function from the
set of grammatical linguistic values to the set of fuzzy
sets. A linguistic approximation routine is a mapping from
the set of fuzzy sets to a subset of linguistic values.
Linguistic approximation stems from Pattern Recognition
techniques. The function LABEL, which performs linguistic
approximation, considers two parameters of any fuzzy set to
be labelled, its imprecision and its location. The
imprecision of a fuzzy set is in this context defined as the
sum of membership-values whereas the location is the center
of gravity. 56 Linguistic values - or labels - were chosen
which lie approximately evenly spread out in a location -
imprecision coordinate system. The label with the shortest
distance to the fuzzy set to be labelled is chosen. It turns
out, however, that the two parameters location and
imprecision are insufficient criteria for satisfactory
liguistic approximation. As a further refinement other
characteristics of fuzzy sets were included as well:

- Non-normality: If none of the numbers in x exceeds 0.65, x
   will be normalized and its label preceded by POSSIBLY
   indicating reduced values of possibility.
- Multi-modality: All 56 standard labels have unimodel fuzzy
   sets. If a fuzzy set has more than one local maximum,
   the valleys will be separately labelled and EXCEPTed
   from the label of the least unimodal fuzzy set which
   includes the fuzzy set to be labelled. Thus the meaning
   of (RATHER LOW) OR RATHER HIGH would be labelled
   (RATHER LOW) TO (RATHER HIGH) EXCEPT MOREORLESS AROUND
   MEDIUM.
- Fuzziness: If many of the values of the unlabelled fuzzy
   set lie around 0.5, uncertainty with regard to which
   values are included by the unlabelled fuzzy set is
   present. This is taken care of by separating x in two
   parts, the label of the fuzzy part being preceded by
   POSSIBLY.
- Concentration and dilation: Two fuzzy sets with identical
   location and imprecision may have more or less sharp
   boundaries. If the boundary of x is sufficiently
   sharper than the selected label, the label will be
   preceded by INDEED indicating concentration of possibilities. In the opposite case, it will be preceded by
   FUZZILY indicating dilation.

The APL-function LABEL consists of about 20 statements,
exclusive of the names of the 56 labels which are stored
elsewhere. In spite of this, LABEL can produce a virtually
unlimited number of different labels. This is achieved by
using recursive function calls. Some times, of course, this
leads to labels which are not easily intelligible. One
example is the label of the meaning of HIGH OR MEDIUM OR LOW
which is UNKNOWN EXCEPT ((NEITHER HIGH NOR LOW) EXCEPT
(INDEED MEDIUM)). To understand this, one has to take
careful notice of the parentheses. Most often, LABEL returns
short, easily understandable labels.

5. RESULTS

By the original author of the theory (Zetterberg) from
section 2 in this paper, the last four statements are
selected as 'what if' statements and he claims that the
remainder can be deduced from this combination of four. He
does not, however, adequately discuss the crucial question
of why these particular four were selected. Translating
these ten propositions with help of syntactical rules and
plugging them as causal relations in the APL environment as
developed before yields a simple program. Running this
program with an appropriate input ('if'-parts) shows that
after three periods of exploration the output becomes
stable: all variables stay above medium in the long run.
This output means (assuming that the theory underlying the
model is correct) that in the long run a professional
situation becomes stable in a favorable sense. There is one
new and unexpected result: from every 'if'-state the
rejection of deviants and of deviant behavior is not low in
the long run. This result is not foreseen by Blalock. A
personnel manager, if having to decide about formation task
groups, should not forget this.

5.1. Acknowledgement

The author is indebted to professor Dr. H.G. Sol and to Drs.
P. Bots, both from Delft University of Technology, for their
stimulating criticism on a previous version of this paper.

6. APPENDIX: DEFINITION OF FUZZY SETS

Let X be a space of points (objects), with a generic element
of X denoted by x. A fuzzy set (class) A in X is
characterized by a membership (characteristic) function
fA(x) which associates with each point in X a real number in
the interval (0,1), with the value of fA(x) at x
representhing the 'grade of membership' of x in A. Thus, the
nearer the value of fA(x) to unity, the higher the grade of
membership of x in A. When A is a set in the ordinary sense
of the term, its membership function can take on only two
values 0 and 1, with fA(x) = 1 or 0 according as x does or
does not belong to A. Thus, in this case fA(x) reduces to
the familiar characteristic function of the set A.

7. REFERENCES

Blalock, H.M., _Causal Inferences in Non Experimental
Research_. Univ. of Carolina Press, Chapel Hill, 1964.

Blalock, H.M., _Theory Construction_. Prentice-Hall, Englewood
Cliffs, N.J., 1969.

Boole, G., _The Laws of Thought_. Dover, New York, 1958 (first
published by Macmillan, 1854).

Bosman, A. and H.G. Sol, 'Knowledge Representation and
Information Systems Design'. In: Methlei, L.B. and R.H.
Sprague Jr. (Eds.), _Knowledge Representation for Decision
Support Systems_, North-Holland, 1985, pp. 81-91.

Bots, P.W.G., 'Logic Programming Using a Constructive
Approach'. In: Duijvestijn, A.J.W. e.a. (Eds.), NGI-SION
SYMPOSIUM 4 PROCEEDINGS, April 1986, pp. 393-401.

Bunge, M., _Philosophy of Physics_. Reidel, Dordrecht,
Holland, 1973.

Carnap, R., _Introduction to Semantics_. Harvard Univ. Press,
Cambridge Mass., 1946.

Elam, J.J., G.P. Huber and M.E. Hurt, 'An Examination of the
DSS Literature'. In: _Decision Support Systems: a Decade in
Perspective_, McLean E.R. and H,G. Sol (Eds.), North-Holland,
Amsterdam, 1986.

Gorry, A. and M. Scott Morton, 'A Framework for Information
Systems'. _Sloan Management Review_, Fall, 1971.

Harbordt, S., _Computer Simulation in der
Sozialwissenschaften_. Rowohlt Verlag, Reinbek, 1974.

Hussain, D., Hussain, K., Information Processing Systems for Management. Richard D. Irwin Inc., Homewood, Ill., 1981.

Lakoff, G., 'Hedges: a study in meaning-criteria and the logic of fuzzy concepts'. In: Proc. 8th Regional Meeting of Chicago Ling. Soc., Univ. of Chicago Linguistic Dept., 1972.

Lee, R.M., 'A Logic Programming Approach to Building Planning and Simulation Models'. In: Methlei, L.B. and R.H. Sprague Jr. (Eds.), Knowledge Representation for Decision Support Systems, North-Holland, 1985, pp. 81-91.

Lindenberg, S., 'Simulation und Theoriebildung'. In: Sozialtheorie und soziale Praxis, Albert, H. (ed.), Mannheim, 1971.

Lukasiewicz, J., 'Philosophical remarks on many-valued systems of propositional logic'. In: Polish Logic 1920-1939, McCall, S. (ed.) Clarendon Press, Oxford, 1967.

Saris, W., Stronkhorst, H., Causal Modelling in Nonexperimental Research. Sociometric Research Foundation, Blauwburgwal 20, 1015 AT Amsterdam, 1984.

Sol, H.G., Simulation in Information Systems Development. Ph-D Thesis, University of Groningen, Groningen, Netherlands, 1982.

Sol, H.G., 'DSS: Buzzword or OR challenge?' European Journal of Operational Research, Vol. 22, 1985, pp. 1-8.

Wenstøp, F.E., 'Deductive verbal models of organizations'. Journal of Man-Machine Studies, 1976, pp. 293-304.

Wenstøp, F.E., 'Verbal formulation of fuzzy dynamic systems'. International Journal of Fuzzy Sets and Systems, 1984, North-Holland, Amsterdam.

Zadeh, L.A., 'Fuzzy Sets'. Information and Control, 8, 1965, pp. 338-353.
Zadeh, L.A., 'A fuzzy-set-theoretical interpretation of liguistic hedges'. Journal of Cybernetics, 5, 1972, pp. 4-34.

Zadeh, L.A., 'The concept of a linguistic variable and its application to approximate reasoning-II'. Information Science, 8, 1975, pp. 301-357.

MODELLING SUPPORT ENVIRONMENTS

Ulrike Maschtera
J.K.University of Linz
Department of Computer Science
Altenbergerstr.69,A-4040 Linz
Austria

ABSTRACT. Operations Research Algorithms are strictly coupled with the models to which they can be applied. If they should be incorporated during the decision process, a person is needed, who extracts the users' knowledge of the problem domain, decides on a suitable algorithm (if existent), designs a model and expresses the model in a form which is suitable for the chosen algorithm. In order to make users independant and willing to accept models and their solutions, these activities are combined within a modelling support environment. It contains a (natural language) interface to extract and a base to represent users' knowledge (this implies the definition of basic entity types (abstraction aids:generalization/specialization) and coupling operations (abstraction aids:aggregation/association)), expert knowledge with respect to model reformulation and applicability of algorithms and model (in)validation aids (these are based on axioms which have to be guaranteed for certain algorithms and on semantic relations between system entities).

1. INTRODUCTION

The uneasiness and complaints on the amount of time and effort needed for the development and maintenance of models shows the need of a tool for modelling support. In this paper, the shape and nature of such a tool will be derived. Thereby attention has to be focused on the model building process.

The first part of this paper describes the (conceptual) knowledge used by models and the (factual) knowledge represented by models. It is obtained by using the result of todays investigation in the field of abstraction. It results in common relational units which can be viewed as relaxation of concrete model components. Therefore, examples are interspersed among the text in order to illustrate the process of generalization by which the common semantics of models of different disciplines is obtained.

In the second part the components of a modelling support environment are derived. It is shown that distributed modelling requires the

H. G. Sol et al. (eds.), Expert Systems and Artificial Intelligence in Decision Support Systems, 151–173.

(factual) knowledge they represent. The result is a distributive
modelling support environment.

2.   MODELS AS (VALID) REPRESENTATIONS OF KNOWLEDGE

2.1.   Model Semantics

2.1.1. Factual knowledge represented by models. Greenberg (1981) views
a model *"as a collection of variables and relations among them"*. These
relations reflect the "semantic structure underlying the set of
variables" (Zeigler 1979). They define a "meaning convention" (Carnap
1960) which makes "legal those and only those assignments of values
to variables A (with range R_A) and B (with range R_B) which satisfy
the relation $(R \subseteq R_A x R_B)$." (Zeigler 1979)

ex1: In linear optimization (abbreviated LINOPT in the following) the
equation $x_1 + x_2 = 30$ defines a relation $R := \{(x_1, x_2) | x_1 + x_2 = 30; x_1, x_2 \epsilon R^+\}$
between the x_i (with range $R_i := \{x_i | x_i < 30; x_i \epsilon R^+\}$). It reflects the
underlying structure of a consumption process, which is a
specialization of a COMPETITIVE PROCESS.
ex2: (LINOPT) The equation $x_1 - x_2 = 30$ defines a supply process.
ex3: (disrete event simulation, abbreviated DES in the following)
Transactions and equipments within one transaction flow are
competitive with respect to the - per definitionem limited -
capacity of an equipment. While transactions have the wish
to occupy the equipment, the equipment aims at 'being idle'
(compare Frankowski/Franta(1980), Maschtera(1984))

By using less abstract model definitions, eg. Minsky's reality/observer
relationship(Minsky 1965) or Shannon's notion of representation
(Shannon 1975), it can be seen that the semantic structure of objects
is only observed and expressed by the modeller but is defined by the
objects themselves. Thus the modeller's range of view determines the
boundary of the universe (the variables representing objects, ideas,
entities); his point of view determines the sort of relations to be
observed; and a description of the observed objects - the model
provided by the modeller - is valid if and only if it reflects the
objects' semantic structure regardless of the form or notation of the
description (eg. equations or programs or English or German ....).

ex4: (LINOPT) If x_1 is the representation of the free capacity of machine
M and x_2 is the representation of the amount of products P produced
by M, then $x_1 + x_2 = 30$ describes a production process. (The
competitive nature of such a process is illustrated in Maschtera
(1984)).
Thus $x_1 + x_2 = 30$ is the generalization of a production process or a
specialization of the (linear) competition of two interdependant
elements (for "30 units of anything").
Like every competitive process it can also be described in the

following form

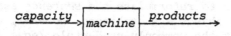

2.1.2. Conceptual knowledge used by models. As mentioned in Zeigler (1979) two variables are logically independant as long as no meaning convention has been declared by the modeller to bind them. Therefore uniting the variables within the range of view according to the point of view is achieved by observing and installing relationships among them. Then a complete description of a system – which is represented by a set of n variables – would need the (explicit) definition of $n(n-1)/2$ relationships per point of view (note that a complete description also includes relationships of type 'no influence').

ex5: *(LINOPT) If the definition of one relationship would take only one minute, the definition of the relationships of one linear constraint with 1000 variables would take 1000.999/2 minutes, that are approximately 4 man years.*

The reason why this number does not describe the true effort of modelling can be found in the conceptual knowledge which is intrinsic in any form/notation chosen for the description of the model (see ex6). This kind of knowledge is defined by the fact that every model is a representation of reality and that reality consists of communicating processes. It has been shown in Maschtera(1984) that this results in a partitioning of the elements into two disjunctive sets according to the role of the elements during communication. These sets are called r-dual, because any communication can be described by chosing the elements of any r-dual set as active (dominant) members. However, a concrete problem domain may have a preference for one r-dual set (see ex7).

ex6: *(LINOPT) The partitioning of the variables into basic and nonbasic ones makes it possible to define a model by relationships between one basic and one or more nonbasic variables. Applied to ex5, the definition of one restriction in 1000 variables will take at most 999 minutes, that is less than 17 hours of modelling time. This enormous reduction in the amount of necessary relationships is due to the (conceptual) knowledge inherent in a LINOPT-formulation, namely the fact that the pivot transformation can be used to derive relationships for any other partitioning of the variables where the resulting two disjunctive sets have the same cardinality as the sets of basic/nonbasic variables.*
(DES) The set of entities is partitioned into transactions and equipments. This allows us to describe the system in the form of transaction flows (eg. transaction oriented).
(natural language) Context sensitivity describes the fact that a text 'is more than a collection of words'.
ex7: *(natural language) Given a natural language sentence describing a communication between two elements, the subject is the active (dominant) member and the object is the passive (dependant) member*

*It is always possible to reformulate the sentence such that the
roles of subject and object are exchanged. However, the resulting
sentence may not suit the commonly used style (eg. English favours
an 'active style').*
*(DES) Choosing an active member for communication means choosing a
world view. Queueing models are said to favour the transaction-
oriented world view.*

Thus the (conceptual) knowledge inherent in the form of description
chosen for the model is the reason that the relations of a system can
be subdivided into basic relations and derived relations.

Basic relations are relations which exist between two directly
communicating elements, these are elements of two different r-dual sets.
These relations depend only on the components or - more precisely - on
the types of the components. Because of their generalized (type-oriented)
nature they remain fix throughout the component's life.

Derived relations are a consequence of the transitive nature of
relations: $R_a(x_1,x_2)$ & $R_b(x_1,x_3)$ ==> $R_{ab}(x_2,x_3)$. They are context
sensitive, where the context is given by the relations R_a, R_b and the
element x_1, which have been used or could be used for their derivation.
Therefore derived relations can change from aspect to aspect and - in
case the point of view combines more than one aspect - even within
one model. With respect to R_a, R_b their components (namely x_2, x_3) belong
to the same r-dual set. Thus these two components do not communicate
directly, but with the 'help of x_1'.

As a consequence, the set of relations which have to be observed
is reduced to the set of basic relations. They define the aspects
included in the model.

*ex8: The semantic structure of a basic production relation: (a product
uses up free capacity of a machine) is the same for every tuple
(product,machine) and is independant of the modeller or target
formulation. A derived relation could be the result of
R(product1,machine) & R(product2,machine) == R(product1,product2).
(LINOPT) For instance, such a derived relation R describes alternative production of the two products on the machine (resulting
in a mixed integer problem) or 'conjunctive' production, that means
sharing of the capacity of the machine by the two products.*

2.2. Model Composition

The procedures for obtaining derived relations are dependant on and have
to be consistent with the form of description of variables and basic
relations. Together with generalized representation units for basic
relations they form the conceptual knowledge needed for a concrete
modelling task.

They are called *coupling operations* because they are a generalization of Wymore's coupling scheme (Wymore(1982), Zeigler(1982)) such
that a coupling scheme - describing links between pairs of variables -
is viewed as a specialization of the semantics responsible for the link.

The general semantics for coupling has two components: definition of the individuals (Who?With whom?) and definition of the way/conditions of coupling (How?). Note that the coupling constraints mentioned in Zeigler(1982) pertain to the definition of individuals and not to the definition of the conditions of a link. Furthermore note that a modeller installs a coupling scheme to describe general coupling relations, whereas coupling operations are procedures for establishing concrete coupling relationships according to general rules.

ex9:(System Specification at Observation Frame Level, Zeigler 1982,p.207)
Given a link ($<p_1,r_1>\to<p_2,r_2>$) where p_i are variables with range set r_i, then equivalencing of p_1 and p_2 induces the requirement that range set r_1 is included within range set r_2. Thus (Who? With whom?) is answered by defining an equivalence relation between p_1 and p_2 and (How?) is answered by the inclusion of range set r_2 within range set r_1.

ex10:(LINOPT) The semantics responsible for a link are (BY_NAME and BY_MEASURE). BY_MEASURE is a consequence of the requirement that the terms of an equation must have equal measures. It has been shown in Maschtera/Schneider (1985a) at a mixing problem that these two requirements are needed for composing linear optimization models from a set of basic relationships.

ex11:(DES) The semantics responsible for a link are (BY_DATA_STRUCTURE and BY_CONDITION). Note that a data structure can contain the name (coupling constraint: BY_NAME) and/or type of the element (coupling constraint: BY_TYPE). Furthermore it usually contains information of the stage the unit is in. Striking illustration of the completeness of this requirement is C.Walter's specification of manufacturing processes (Telichevesky/Castilho/Walter(1984)). With respect to conditions consider also the conceptual set model in Kohel/Maschtera(1985), which contains one layer which provides means for (aggregative) description of conditions for an association relation.

2.3. Modelling Process

Thus modelling consists of
1) DECOMPOSING the user's factual knowledge into basic factual units,
2) MAPPING those units onto basic types of relations (by viewing them as specializations of general basic relations) and
3) applying COUPLING operations to the result of step 2 (see fig.1).

2.4. Model Validity

One consequence of the above considerations is that - as long as the semantics of the universe is described by basic factual units which have been mapped correctly onto basic types of relations - a model which is derived by the application of the coupling operations is a valid model.

The basic factual units are elementary. The possibility of forming groups of elements is desired from the point of view of hierarchic

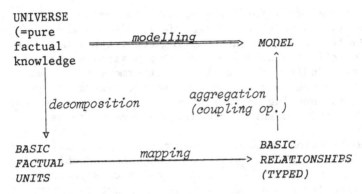

fig 1: steps of modelling from point of view of inherent
       knowledge (PURE FACTUAL KNOWLEDGE is transformed by the
       application of *pure conceptual knowledge* into a MODEL
       via components with CONCEPTUALLY PROCESSED FACTUAL
       KNOWLEDGE).

decomposition as well as from the point of view of reducing work (see
ex12). If the groups are formed according to the underlying semantic
structure, that means if the semantics of all relations concerning a
group is inherited by all group members, semantic model validity is
preserved. Therefore model validity will be injured only if groups
with inhomogeneous semantics are a)defined or b)obtained, when an aspect
having discriminating nature with respect to other model components
(see ex13) is introduced during the modelling process.
     The relations describing the discriminating nature of the new
aspect have to be defined explicitly. As long as they are missing, the
two points of view are logically independant parts of the model (see
ex13). These relations have the nature of specializations, which is
expressed by 'IS_A' in ex13. The fact that their generalized component
(bottle) is also a member of a set (set of bottles) implies a
decomposition of the set according to the new aspect and imposes the
requirement that specializations have to be defined for all states which
are discerned by the new aspect.

ex12: *elementary production relations: PRODUCES(machine,product) for all*
                  n products and all m machines (n*m times!)
      grouped input: PRODUCES(maschines,products)   (once) and
                  BELONGS_TO(machines,machine)   for all m machines,
                  BELONGS_TO(products,product)   for all n products.
ex13:*(LINOPT) Introducing the filling aspect of ex.B (fig.2) into ex.A*
      (fig.2) makes the semantics of group 'bottles' noninheritable,
      because the subgroups 'empty_bottles' and 'full_bottles' have
      different semantics within the filling aspect. This shows that
      filling is a discriminating aspect for the above subgroups. As a
      consequence the basic relations of ex.A (fig.2) {CONTAINS(store,
      bottle)| ∀bottle(s)} are no longer basic anymore and have to be
      replaced by the respective basic relations of ex.C (fig.2)
      {CONTAINS(store,full_bottle)| ∀full_bottle(s)} and {CONTAINS(store,

$\{CONTAINS(store,empty\_bottle)|\forall\ empty\_bottle(s)\}$. *Together with*
IS_A(full_bottle,bottle) and IS_A(empty_bottle,bottle) the basic
relations of ex.A (fig.2) are derived. These two IS_A-relations
describe the discriminating nature of the filling aspect with
respect to bottles.

This shows that the nature of an aspect always includes a
specialization. More concretely, an aspect describes a decomposition,
that is a partitioning of a (generalized) entity into a set of
(specialized) entities. This partitioning is exhaustive with respect to
the knowledge (the semantics) introduced by the aspect. Such a
knowledge can have both factual and conceptual nature (compare the
example of cointossing in Zeigler(1979)) or factual nature (ex13:
filling aspect) and it can have different levels of refinement (the
filling aspect is basic, whereas the description of the flying aspect
within cointossing could be further decomposed, eg. by isolating the
contribution of each variable or by isolating the knowledge per
experiment and the (repetitive) knowledge of experimentation).
The knowledge ("context") of the aspect also serves for an
organization (coupling) within the set of specialized entities. This
results in the requirement that all specialized entities represent
the same generalized entity within the observed aspect. This shows
that an aspect also has the nature of a derived relation and that
specialization is obtained by viewing the components of the derived
relation (namely x_2,x_3, eg. empty_bottle and full_bottle within the
filling aspect) as specializations of a more general component (eg.
bottle) (see fig. 3, ex14,15,16).
Expressed in another way, a specialization becomes a decomposition
if the modeller includes into his model an aspect describing the
coupling of the specialized components. Thus coupling is the knowledge
which makes it possible to view a set of specialized entities as a
decomposition of their generalized entity.

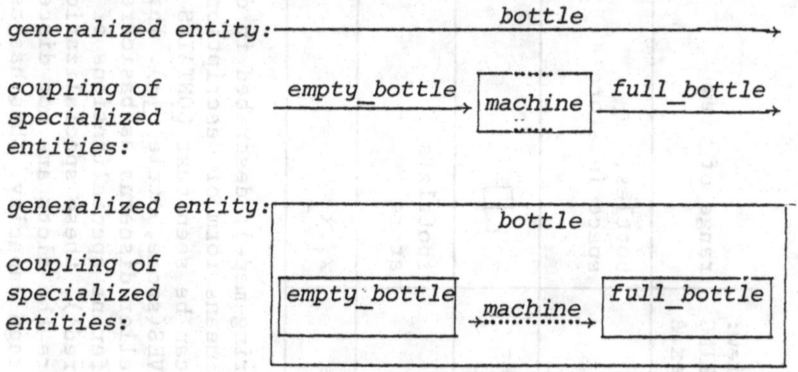

fig.3: the filling aspect in the two r-dual views;
       coupling is depicted by ˵˵˵˵˵ ; the active element is ☐;
       the passive element is →.

point of view: STORING ex.A FOD	range of view	relations B: basic relations D: derived relations	coupling operations
English	bottles, space in store	B: a bottle occupies space D: any two bottles are competitive with respect to space	coordinative ('and')
entity-block-diagram	→ , □	B: →□→ D: →□→↑	associating input/output
formal	{bottle(s)} store	B:{CONTAINS(store,bottle)|∀bottle(s)} D:{EITHER(bottle$_i$,bottle$_j$)|∀bottle(s)}	transitivity of relations
LINOPT	x_1, x_2	B: x_2 :$x_1 \leq M$	

fig.2A) storing model: described in different forms of description (LINOPT means linear optimization) FOD means form of description. If compared with the basic elements of fig.5 (chapter3.1.), it can be seen that CONTAINS can be further decomposed (into IS_PUT_ON(store,bottle) →⌐ and LEAVES(store,bottle) ⌐→). This shows that the degree of refinement is defined by what the modeller discerns as basic relations: 1) although the 'input-arcs' and the 'output-arcs' are different specializations of the entity bottle ('bottle_to_be_stored', 'bottle_which_has_been_stored'), these specializations are not discerned; 2) space describes a set of space_slots, where the slots are not discerned by the modeller explicitly. Note that this implies unlimited storage capacity. This has as a consequence, that in LINOPT (for example) there is only one basic relation and no derived relation! Note, that M in the LINOPT-formulation represents unlimited storage capacity.

point of view: FILLING ex.B / FOD	range of view	relations B: basic relations D: derived relations	coupling operations

English	empty bottles,
	full bottles
	machine
		B: machine fills empty bottles
		   machine emits full bottles
		D: empty bottles are transformed to
		   full bottles by the machine
			coordinative ('and')

entity-block-diagram	E→, F→, □	B: E→□ , □→F; D: E→□→F	combining input and output

formal	{empty_bottle(s)}
	{full_bottle(s)}
	machine
		B: IS FILLED(empty_bottle,machine)
		   HAS BEEN FILLED(full_bottle,machine)
		D: FILLING(empty_bottle,full_bottle)
		these relations hold $\bigwedge$empty_bottle(s)
		           and $\bigwedge$full_bottle(s)
			transitivity

LINOPT	x_{11}, x_{12}, x_3	B: x_3: $x_{11} \leq M$; x_3: $x_{12} \leq M$ D: x_3: $x_{12} \leq x_{11}$	expand (compare Maschtera/ Schneider(1985a))

fig.2B): filling model: described in different forms of description (LINOPT means linear optimization) FOD means form of description. As before, M represents unlimited (undefined) capacity.

point of views: FILLING AND STORING, ex.C FOD	range of views	relations B: basic relations D: derived relations	coupling operations
English	empty bottles, full bottles, space, machine	B: an empty bottle occupies space a full bottle occupies space machine fills an empty bottle machine emits a full bottle D: any two empty bottles are competitive with respect to space; any two full bottles are competitive with respect to space; each empty bottle diminishes the amount of space available for full bottles; empty bottles are transformed to full bottles by machine	coordinative ('and')
entity-block-diagram	$E\to$, $F\to$, $\boxed{S}$, $\boxed{M}$	B: $*E\to \boxed{S} \to E$, $F\to \boxed{S} \to F*$, $E\to \boxed{M}$, $\boxed{M}\to F$ D: $*E\to \boxed{S} \to E\dots E\to \boxed{M}\to F\to$ $F\to \to F*$	coupling S.output/M.input combining input/output(M) coupling M.output/S.input
formal	{empty_bottle(s)} {full_bottle(s)} store machine	B: CONTAINS(store,empty_bottle) CONTAINS(store,full_bottle) IS_FILLED(empty_bottle,machine) HAS_BEEN_FILLED(full_bottle,machine)	transitivity

fig.2C,part1) storing and filling model: described in different forms of description

point of views FILLING AND STORING, ex.C FOD	range of views	relations B: basic relations D: derived relations	coupling operations
formal (continued)	x_{11}, x_{12}, x_2, x_3	D: EITHER(empty_bottle$_i$,empty_bottle$_j$)	relations B1,B1
		EITHER(full_bottle$_i$,full_bottle$_j$)	relations B2,B2
		EITHER(full_bottle$_i$,empty_bottle$_j$)	relations B1,B2
		FILLING(empty_bottle$_i$,full_bottle$_i$)	relations B3,B4
		SENDS(store,machine)	relations B1,B3
		all relations hold $\bigvee$empty_bottle(ε) $\bigvee$full_bottle(s)	(compare Maschtera/ Schneider (1985a)) 'shared' } 'add' 'expand' }
LINOPT		B: $x_2:x_{11} \leq M$; $x_2:x_{12} \leq M$ $x_3:x_{11} \geq M*$; $x_3:x_{12} \leq M*$ D: $x_2:-x_{11}+x_{12} \leq M$ $x_3:-x_{11}+x_{12} \leq 0$	

fig.2C) storing and filling model: described in different forms of description (LINOPT means linear optimization) FOD means form of description. In the LINOPT-models M and M* denote unlimited (undefined) capacity and 'add' of LINOPT denotes in the entity-block-diagram all couplings depicted by $\rightarrow\cdots\rightarrow$. Note that *E_and_E* of LINOPT are different specializations of empty_bottles with respect to their stage ('to_be_stored', 'leaving store'$\equiv$'to_be_filled'). Analogously *F and F are different specializations of full_bottles. (compare chapter 3.1.2.1. axioms on model validity).

ex14: entity: bottle
      data structure: characteristic .. obtained by specialization
                        glas   ....material
                        1L   ....max_contents
                        green   ....colour
      specialization: current_contents

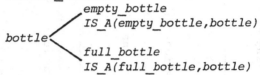

                            empty_bottle
                            IS_A(empty_bottle,bottle)
              bottle
                            full_bottle
                            IS_A(full_bottle,bottle)

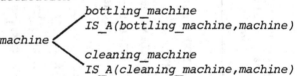

            with: empty_bottle   full_bottle
data structure: glas   ⎫   glas
                    1L   ⎬ inherited   1L
                    green   ⎭   green
                    empty   ⎫ introduced   full
                              ⎭

      aspect: filling
      knowledge: current contents changes from empty to full
          using: bottling_machine(context)
      basic relations (see fig.2,ex.B and fig.3)
      o n e object bottle changes from type empty_bottle to type
      full_bottle.
ex15: entity: machine
      specialization: dedication

                            bottling_machine
                            IS_A(bottling_machine,machine)
              machine
                            cleaning_machine
                            IS_A(cleaning_machine,machine)

      aspect: setting_up (b→c)
      knowledge: dedication changes from bottling to cleaning
          using: worker
      basic relations: IS_ADAPTED(bottling_machine,worker)
                       HAS_BEEN_ADAPTED(cleaning_machine,worker)
      coupling: ┌───┐
                │   machine   │
                │ ┌─────────┐   ┌─────────┐   │
                │ │bottling_│→....worker....→│cleaning_│   │
                │ │ machine │   │ machine │   │
                │ └─────────┘   └─────────┘   │
                └───┘

ex16: If both a filling aspect and a cleaning aspect are included into
      a model, where the reference of the context (entity bottling_
      machine or cleaning_machine respectively) points to the same
      entity (machine), then also   setting_up (b⤳c) aspects have to be
      included into the model. The default time_span for setting_up
      can be 0. However, the decision, whether this default holds or not
      has to be done by the modeller.

3. REQUIREMENTS FOR A MODELLING SUPPORT ENVIRONMENT

Recently, a large amount of work had to be invested in the development
of a model. This justified to view every model development separately
and had as a consequence the 'one-way-dedication' of models. The first
extension of that view has been done very soon and pertained to
numerical changes. The most recent extension contributes to acquisition
and maintenance of knowledge for modelling.

All those modelling supports have emanated from instantaneous needs.
That is why they contain support for exactly the problems which created
the demand for them. In this chapter, another procedure is adopted. The
requirements for modelling support environments are viewed as a
consequence of the definitions and objectives of models. Thus they will
be derived by applying the considerations of the last chapter.

Analogously to Minsky, a model has been viewed as a device to
answer questions. Any question is the outcome of a communication between
modeller and reality. Describing such a relationship by a 4-tupel
(range of view, point of view, form of description, time span), every
realisation of such a 4-tupel defines a model (see fig.4).

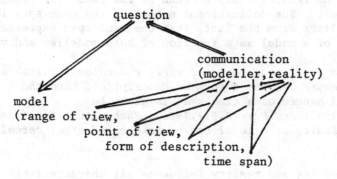

fig.4: a model as an outcome of a communication between
modeller and reality

The definitional nature of the first three components has already
been shown in the previous chapter (see fig.2). Here I would like to
point out their r-dual nature. The r-dual nature is a consequence of the
fact that each component expresses one characteristic of a communication
of modeller and reality. This means, that the 'value' of each component
is a function of the respective characteristics of the two r-dual
partners of the communication, namely of both modeller and reality. If
the characteristic of one of the r-dual partners is neglected,
assumptions on that characteristic are induced.

x17: *The variables forming the range of view are part of reality*
    (together with lots of other elements); they become part of the
    model only because the modeller chooses to discern them as part
    of 'his reality', that is that part of reality for which he
    constructs the model. Usually the influence of the modeller is not

*expressed explicitly. This induces the assumption that reality is
what the modeller discerns as reality.*
*Analogously, the relationships describing the point of view are
part of reality (together with lots of other relationships), but
they become part of the model only because the modeller includes
them into 'his reality'. Neglecting the influence of reality, it
would be aasumed that there exists only one (global) model in and
of this world. Neglecting the influence of the modeller, progress
of science - expressing itself in enhancement of knowledge -
would be ignored.*
*The form of description is chosen by the modeller; however, it has
to be chosen according to criterias defined by reality. If the
influence of the modeller on the form of description would be
neglected, it would be assumed that there is but one possible
way to describe reality. If the influence of reality would be
neglected, it would be assumed that all ways of description are
possible for 'every' reality.*

Just like the other three components, time span has a r-dual nature.
This means that the time span is a function of the time spans defined
by both modeller and reality. Both are/can be the cause for changes of
a model (over time).   The definitional nature of the time span is not
as obvious. It follows from the fact, that the time span expresses the
limit of validity of a model as a function of both modeller and reality.

*ex18: If R denotes a suitable range of view, P denotes a suitable
point of view, F denotes a form of description, then the
definitional nature of a time span is given by
M1:=(R,P,F,1985) and M2:=(R,P,F,1986). Such situations arise
when the validity of a model has to be checked after certain
time spans.*

Thus both modeller and reality influence all characteristics of a
model. Both are 'on-going history-dependant processes'. Therefore
"modelling is an on-going history dependant process" too (Zeigler 1982).
This implies that one modelling process may pertain to more than one
model. Hence modelling deals not only with the definition of one such
4-tupel, but with DEFINITION AND MAINTENANCE of a SERIES OF such
4-TUPELS. Analogously to the software life_cycle such a series will be
called MODEL_LIFE_CYCLE in the following.
Therefore, while the nature of modelling support is given by the
model_life_cycle, it has yet to be decided upon the shape of the support
environment. For that reason let us consider the cause of a model_life_
cycle.
The model_life_cycle is· characterised by changes of the model; a
change of the model is caused by a change of the 'modeller's reality';
a change of the modeller's reality can be caused
(c1) either by a change w i t h i n   r e a l i t y
(c2) or by a change o f   r e a l i t y (a change of parts of reality,
including enlargement of reality)
(c3) or by a change o f the m o d e l l e r (change of the person)

(c4) or by a change w i t h i n the m o d e l l e r (eg. his attitude
     towards reality)
     or by a change w i t h i n the set of m o d e l l e rs (eg.
     change of one person of the set).

C1) usually describes 'numeric' changes. These are changes of
attributes of system elements. Respective support is inherent in
(almost) all recent modelling aids.

C2) describes changes of (factual) semantics and imposes the need
of a separate definition of model semantics. This need has been taken
into account in Zeigler's system entity structure (Zeigler(1982)). It
serves as a knowledge base for subsequent modelling tasks.

C3) and c4) express the distributed nature of modelling and the
resulting need of support for model communication (c3) and distributed
model composition(c4). If more than one person has access to a system
entity structure, it supports knowledge acquisition and maintenance in
a distributed way. However, support with respect to distributed model
composition is only rudimentary available (see ex20).

DISTRIBUTED modelling requires more than common access and
maintenance of a knowledge base. It is a consequence of and characterized by a set of modellers. Therefore - as long as support is based
on only one r-dual view or on only one form of description -
distributivity is achieved only for a homogeneous set of modellers.
Such modellers stick to the same form of description. Therefore they
have no problems of communication. With respect to support they can
be viewed as ONE modeller.

However, the set of modellers can and will be heterogeneous. The
consequences are two-fold. On the one hand, this influences the r-dual
partner: reality. Every component modeller has his 'personal reality'.
Whenever the intersection of any two personal realities is not empty,
any model which has been established distributively by modellers A
(with personal reality RA) and B (with personal reality RB) - this means
any model which is combined from a model established by A and a model
established by B - has to be noncontradictory with respect to the
intersection of the personal realities RA∩RB. The same requirement
pertains to 'adjacent' personal realities, where a model M is a union
of disjunctive partial models. Here suitable interfaces have to be
established.

On the other hand, heterogeneity of the set of modellers influences
all components of a model. This induces possible heterogeneity of all
components of the 4-tupel. Thus the shape of a modelling support
environment is determined by HETEROGENEOUS MODEL CHARACTERISTICS.
Therefore support is needed with respect to definition and maintenance
of models (considering change) and with respect to model composition
and validity (because of heterogeneous model components).

ex19: *For instance, let us view the component 'form of description'.
      From the viewpoint of reality, need of support for heterogeneous
      forms of description is illustrated by the numerous contributions
      on combined simulation or by the project of T.Kristiansen(1985)
      which is a pipeline of optimization and combined simulation.
      From the viewpoint of the modeller(s), problems arising from*

different world views tell their own tale.
ex20: *An example for a heterogeneous set of point of views is Zeigler's
example of cointossing (Zeigler(1979)).As a consequence the range
of views of the different models contain different variables.
The way they are related to each other is part of the system
entity structure. However, the responsibility for relating
them is allocated at the modeller. As a consequence, model
validity has to be checked by the modeller himself.*

3.1. Consequences of heterogeneous model components

We have seen in the previous chapter that the shape of a modelling
support environment is defined by the possibility of heterogeneous
components. Recalling that the form of description (abbreviated FOD
in the following) represents the pure conceptual knowledge which allows
a substantive reduction of the amount of work involved in modelling,
it is obvious, that with respect to the consequences of heterogeneity
(model composition and validation) the component FOD has a central role.

3.1.1. Heterogeneous form of descriptions

Heterogeneous forms of desctiption can be tackled in three ways:
Either by TRANSLATION: This means that a model defined in one FOD is
translated into another FOD. This procedure is problematic because of
the difficulty of finding general translating procedures which take
into account all default (intrinsic knowledge) of complex FODs
(compare compiler-compilers and translator-writing-systems).
Or by REDUNDANCY: This means that - given a model M1:=(R,P,F1,T) -
all possible Mi:=(R,P,Fi,T) for all FODs Fi are part of the model base.
The inpracticability of this way is obvious.
Or by RELAXATION with respect to FOD: The term relaxation comes from
combinatorial optimization and means that a given problem is replaced
            whose set of feasible solutions contains the set of all feasible
            solutions of the original problem. Therefore, relaxation of a
            model with respect to FOD means that in the relaxed model
            everything is ignored which is a consequence or a characteristic
            or an outcome of a special FOD. Thus any 'solution for a special
            FOD' is a model which is a subclass (specialization) of the
            (general) relaxed model. Here a 'solution' is a valid model.
            If the relaxation pertains to FOD only, than the relaxed model
            has to be valid too, but allows to apply more than one FOD.
            Expressed in other words, the same considerations which gave
            rise to separate semantics and numerics now give rise to
            separate (general) semantics and FOD-dependant semantics. As a
            consequence, a general basis for all possible FODs and
            procedures for validity check and for specialization with respect
            to FOD have to be sought. In fig.5,6 such a basis is proposed
            by applying a relational view to the general concept of a system.
Applying relaxation, every (factual) relationship is a specialization
of one type of basic relations and every (factual) aspect is a

Symbol	Meaning	Context
→⌈	" → is input of ⌈" "⌈ has input → "	systems theory
	"⌈ diminshes →" "→ is diminished by ⌈"	LINOPT
	"→ arrives at ⌈" "⌈ accepts →"	DES(transact.-or. view) (equipment-or. view) of arrival event
⌉→	"→ is output of ⌉" "⌉ has output → "	systems theory
	"⌉ enhances →" "→ is enhanced by ⌉"	LINOPT
	"→ leaves ⌉" "⌉ emits →"	DES(transact.-or. view) (equipment-or. view) of departure event
↑⌣	"↑ is control variable of ⊔"	systems theory
	not existent	LINOPT
	"in case of ↑ then ⊔"	MIP(mixed integer progr.)
	"if condition ↑ then ⊔"	DES
↑⌢	"↑ is control variable from ⊓"	systems theory
	not existent	LINOPT
	"in case of ⊓ is ↑"	MIP
	"if ⊓ has state ↑"	DES

fig.5: proposed basis for FODs and their meaning in some FODs.

specialization of one of the coupling operations. Note that more complex descriptions will need specializations of the proposed coupling operations (see ex21) and/or specializations of the basic elements (representing functions which are either not decomposable or used so much that composition is justified (see ex 22,ex23)). Note that for such elements translations or decompositions have to be available in the knowledge base in order to preserve the requirement of FOD-independancy and FOD-change.

ex21: a→ [*] ⟹ c=a*b <br> b→

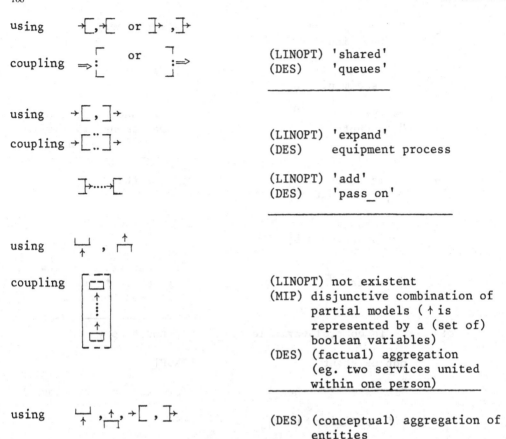

fig.6: coupling operations and their meaning in some forms of
description; (LINOPT) means linear optimization; (DES) means
discrete event simulation; (MIP) means mixed integer programming.
A detailed description of these coupling operations is given
in Maschtera/Schneider (1985a,1985b) for LINOPT and MIP, and in
Maschtera(1985,1985b) and Kohel/Maschtera (1985) for DES.

ex22: *Integral ∫, could be translated to ∑(eg. combined simulation
discrete simulation)*
ex23:*(DES) Basic types are interruptable processes with/without
resumption and a noninterruptable process.*

The advantages of relaxation are 1) that the basis contains only pure
conceptual knowledge; thus – given a mapping procedure (compare fig.1) –
also unsophisticated users can be supported; and 2) that the conceptual
knowledge is divided into two parts, the basis (which describes the
general semantics of the system) and the specializations (which
define certain FODs).

ex24: *For instance, specialization of a model with respect to
(LINOPT) needs the introduction of a component for LIMITATION
(MAXIMAL,MINIMAL,EXACTLY);   with respect to*

(DES) needs a time advance function (that is an aggregation of
*   time spans to a distribution).*
This comparison shows that 'everything which is a consequence' of
LIMITATION in LINOPT (eg. marginal costs of a resource; LIMITATION
defines the margin) will express itself in 'something which
pertains' to TIME advance in DES (eg. the DES-equivalent of
marginal costs are queueing strategies with dynamic priority;
compare the sheduling strategy "ageing" in operating systems.
(Peterson/Silberschatz (1983),p.109).)

3.1.2. Model composition and model (in)validation.

It has been derived
in chapters 2.2. and 2.4. that model composition is done by applying
coupling operations (*aggregation* procedures) to 'conceptually processed
basic factual units'(*specializations* of *general aggregative* units).
Furthermore it has been shown that a model – which has been composed in
this way – is a valid model in case 1) definition of factual units and
their mapping onto basic types of relations ('conceptual processing')
has been done correctly and 2) groups of elements – if existent – have
been formed according to the semantics of the universe. Thus coupling
can be done automatically.

If the responsibility for model validity is allocated solely at the
modellers, they have to know all the aspects and all the resulting
semantics of the universe, whenever they want to form a group of
elements, in order to uphold homogeneous group semantics. On the one
hand, this contradicts the requirements of distributive modelling. On
the other hand, the amount of conceptual knowledge needed for model
validation usually enables modellers to establish the model directly
(this is the 'modelling' arc $\Longrightarrow$ in fig.1).

Therefore support in model validation is necessary both for
distributed modelling and unsophisticated users. In accordance with
Quade (1980) ("...*models can, at best, be invalidated*") such a support
has the shape of invalidation aids. This means that semantic
inconsistency should be detected (→) by the user (→) in additionally
derived (factual) knowledge on the described problem domain.

Recall that models use conceptual knowledge in order to obtain a
minimal set of relations which have to be observed and input. Thus
'additional (factual) knowledge' means 'derived relations' and can be
obtained by applying conceptual knowledge (see ex6,8), which is inherent
in the coupling operations. Correctness of such derived relations has
to be checked by the user. (Therefore the derived relations have to
be expressed in user-adequate terms.)

3.1.2.1. Model invalidation, which is independant of a form of description

With respect to basic (FOD-independant) semantics model invalidation
aids can be subdivided into two groups:
a) inconsistency is detected because of violation of axiom '*system-*
input ≠ system-output'. Such inconsistencies can be the consequence
of inhomogeneous group semantics (see ex 25) or of insufficiently
discerned or incorrectly defined identifiers (see ex26).
b) inconsistency is detected because of violation of axiom '*system-input*

$\neq$ *system'* or *'system-output $\neq$ system'*. These two axioms express that
any relation has to contain two different components.
Such inconsistencies arise when identifiers are ambigously specified,
eg. when two different modellers use the same identifier for
different elements, or when identifiers pertain to different periods
(see ex 27).
Note that the axioms of both cases can be expressed by the requirement

$$R(x_1,x_2) \Rightarrow x_1 \neq x_2$$

where in case a) R denotes a derived relation and in case b) R denotes
a basic relation.

Note that such a derivation of semantic knowledge can be achieved
by using the semantic part of conceptually processed factual units and
the semantic part of coupling operations as production rules.

Furthermore note that model invalidation has the nature of
experimentation: firstly, model invalidation aids do not assure the
validity of the model. On the contrary, their statement is analogous to
statistical tests:*'there is no reason to suppose that the model is
invalid'* or *'the hypothesis of model validity cannot be rejected'*.
Secondly, model invalidation can be viewed as a semantic experiment.
This describes an experiment which is performed on semantic rules
instead of on a model (as it is the case in sampling experiments) or
on a real-life object.

3.1.2.2. Model invalidation, which is dependant on a form of description.
In the modelling methodology presented in this paper, every FOD is
viewed as a specialization of the general FOD of fig.5 and their coupling
operations are viewed as specializations of the general coupling
operations of fig.6. Therefore FOD-dependant semantics is inherent
in those specialized elements and coupling operations (see fig.7).
Thus the general procedure for model invalidation - described in the
previous chapter - need not be changed. However, additional axioms per
FOD can be defined. (see ex28).

ex25: *inhomogeneous group semantics (LINOPT)*
      store contains(IS_DIMINISHED_BY) bottles.
      full_bottles belong_to(ENHANCE) bottles.
      empty_bottles belong_to(ENHANCE) bottles.
      ==>
      derived relation: store contains(IS_DIMINISHED_BY) full_bottles?
      *   store contains(IS_DIMINISHED_BY) empty_bottles?*
      newly input basic relation:
      bottling_machine fills(DIMINISHES) bottles.
      ==>
      derived relation: bottling_machine fills(DIMINISHES) full_bottles?
      While the user will answer the first two 'questions' with YES,
      he will answer the last question with NO. This shows that the
      group bottles has inhomogeneous group semantics.
ex26: *loop (LINOPT)*
      a worker comes_to a teacher.
      a worker leaves the teacher.

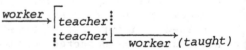

ex27: loop (LINOPT)
one worker teaches five workers (campare Dantzig(1966),p.66)

worker [5workers]

ex28:(DES) Queues with limited capacity belong to the special types of
DES-system-elements. Limitation of a queue is an axiom (this
means it is coupled with the existence of the queue and must not
be violated). Therefore DES-coupling operations have to comply
with queue limitations, which means they have to provide
alternatives when coupling would violate the axioms. If such
alternatives are missing, the user has to check whether defaults
can be applied or he has to define such alternatives. (compare
Maschtera(1985),Kohel/Maschtera(1985))

is specialized to $\dfrac{\text{numeral}}{}$

is specialized to $\dfrac{\text{numeral}}{}$

additional axiom: any derived relation may contain only one
component of type numeral.
(then a RATOM is built by coupling one basic
element and one specialized element, compare
Maschtera/Schneider(1985a))
additional axiom: a numeral can never be context of a derived
relation.
fig.7: specializations of basic elements for the special form
of description: linear optimization

3.1.2.3. Invalidation with respect to model connectivity. A valid model
is not only characterized by noncontradictory parts. Additionally, a
model has to contain all relevant aspects and only those aspects. In
order to check whether this requirement is violated, two structural
informations of a model can be used.

On the one hand, all basic and specialized descriptive elements
(eg. fig.5,fig.7) have to be connected to form one global system.
On the other hand, if different specializations of a system element
are combined within a model, an aspect has to be included, which
describes the transformation of the system element from one
specialization to another one. Such aspects can be defaults, but they have
to be checked by the user. (see ex16).

3.1.2.4. Model reformulation. In the previous chapters it has been
shown that models can be composed automatically. However, the resulting
model may not be tight with respect to the applied solution process.
In order to achieve or check tightness, reformulation procedures have
to be executed after model composition. They are based on structural
information which is inherent in a model and used by a certain algorithm.
Therefore the form of an expert system (containing answers/solutions
to concrete situations/problems) is adequate for that purpose.

3.2. Support for Model definition and maintenance

Support for model definition and maintenance can be planned similar to
software support systems (compare Hausen/Müllerburg(1982)). Besides
documenting and supporting any change of models by suitable interfaces
and file organisations, they should include a demon, who informs the
users when one of their models expires (because of the defined time span)
or whenever a change of data (range of view) or semantics (point of view)
occurs, which are shared between them and other users.

4. CONCLUSION

In this paper a methodology for constructing modelling support environments has been presented and demonstrated on examples from linear
optimization, mixed integer programming and discrete event simulation.
Application of the abstraction tools of conceptual modelling allows
decomposition and aggregation of factual and conceptual knowledge of
models. Thus factual and conceptual knowledge can be defined and stored
separately.
    Furthermore it has been shown that the conceptual knowledge of
models can be subdivided into one part which is independant of the
chosen target formulation and into one part which is dependant on the
chosen target formulation. Separate definition of these two parts
makes it possible to apply different target formulations to the basic
semantics of a system whereby only target formulation-dependant
information has to be added.
    With the help of such a support environment model composition is
done automatically. Model definition and model invalidation are carried
out by both users and the support environment, where conceptual
knowledge is provided by the support environment. Thus distributed
modelling with/without unsophisticated users becomes possible.

REFERENCES

Carnap R. (1960): *Meaning and Necessity*. University of Chicago Press
Dantzig G.B.(1966): *Lineare Programmierung und Erweiterungen*. Springer
    Verlag Berlin Heidelberg New York .
Frankowski E.N./Franta W.R.(1980): 'A Process Oriented Simulation Model
    Specification and Documentation Language', *Software P&E,10,721-742*
Greenberg H.J.(1981): 'Implementation Aspects of Model Management: A
    Focus on Computer-Assisted Analysis' in: *Computer-Assisted Analysis*
Hausen H.L./Müllerburg M. (1982): 'Software Engineering Environments:
    State of the Art, Problems and Perspectives', in: *IEEE*,p326-335
Kohel K./Maschtera U. (1985): 'Assoziation bei der Modellierung
    diskreter Simulationssysteme: ein Konzept und Überlegungen zu
    seiner Implementierung', in: *Simulationstechnik*, D.P.F.Möller (ed),
    Springer Verlag Berlin Heidelberg New York
kristiansen T.K. (1985): 'STATOIL Offsites Facilities Universal Simula-
    tor (SOFUS)', in:*11th IMACS World Congress on Sytem Simulation and*

Scientific Computation, Vichnevetsky R.,Wahlstrøm B., Henriksen R. (eds)

Maschtera U.(1984): 'Duality Concepts in Discrete Event Simulation!, in: *Applied Informatics*, Hamza M.H.(ed), Acta Press.

Maschtera U.(1985): 'Aggregation von Prozessen im Rahmen der konzeptionellen Modellierung diskreter Simulationssysteme',in: *Simulationstechnik*, D.P.F.Möller (ed), Springer Verlag Berlin Heidelberg New York.

Maschtera U.(1985b): 'MAGS - An Aggregation Tool for Discrete Event Simulation', Institutsbericht MUSIM85/1, J.K.University of Linz, Institut für Informatik.

Maschtera U./Schneider W. (1985a):'Structuring of Linear Optimization Models', in: *Modelling and Simulation Methodology in the Artificial Intelligence Era*, Elzas M.S, Ören T.I., Zeigler B.P. (eds), North Holland.

Maschtera U./Schneider W. (1985b):'A Relational View of a Linear Optimization Model and Its Consequences for the Modelling Process', in: *System Modelling and Optimization*, Prékopa A., Strazicky B., Szelezsán J.(ed), Budapest.

Minsky M. (1965): 'Models, Minds and Machines', in: *Proc. IFIP Conf.*, AFIPS Press, Montvale, New Jersey.

Peterson J./Silberschatz A. (1983): *Operating System Concepts*, Addison-Wesley Publishing Company.

Quade E.S.(1980): 'Pitfalls in Formulation and Modeling', in: *Pitfalls of Analysis*, Majone G., Quade E.S.(eds), John Wiley and Sons, New York.

Shannon R.E. (1975): *Systems Simulation*,Prentice-Hall, Inc.

Telichevesky R., Castilho J.M.V., Walter C.(1984): 'Transformation Systems: A Formalism for the Specification of Manufacturing Processes', in: *Modelling, Identification and Control*, Hamza M.H. (ed), Acta Press.

Wymore W. (1982): 'The Tricotyledon Theory of System Design' in: *Simulation and Model-Based Methodologies: An Integrative View*, Ören T.I., Zeigler B.P., Elzas M.S. (eds), Springer Verlag Berlin Heidelberg New York

Zeigler B.P. (1979): 'Structuring Principles for Multifaceted System Modelling', in:*Methodology in Systems Modelling and Simulation*, Zeigler B.P., Elzas M.S., Ören T.I., Klir G.J.(eds), North Holland

Zeigler B.P. (1982): 'Structures for Model-Based Simulation Systems', in: *Simulation and Model-Based Methodologies: An Integrative View*, Ören T.I., Zeigler B.P., Elzas M.S. (eds), Springer Verlag Berlin Heidelberg New York

HEURISTICS IN THE ABBOT-MONK PROBLEM

H.J. van den Herik, J.C. Stoop and P.R. Varkevisser
Delft University of Technology
Dept. of Mathematics and Informatics
Group 'Design of Knowledge-Based Systems'
Julianalaan 132 / 2628 BL DELFT
The Netherlands

ABSTRACT The future of expert systems lies in parallel processing. A combination of various AI techniques is considered for parallel knowledge-based systems. A careful examination of its organizational structure with respect to the relations between processes and data structures can result in a performance improvement. The appropriate tool for investigating parallel systems is simulation. In order to get some insight into the inter-dependency of the processes, a parallel computer simulator is constructed and tested.

The behaviour of the simulated parallel expert system HYDRA is studied with special attention to the Rule Agenda Manager (RAM). The relationship between the RAM and the simultaneously acting rule processors is reformulated in the Abbot-Monk problem. Adequate heuristics (when and to what extent should a process be curtailed or decomposed) are shown to influence the processing speed of a parallel real-time system.

1. INTRODUCTION

The use of knowledge-based systems (KBSs) is rapidly gaining acceptance in the world outside academic: they are now designed to be applicable in practice. Examples of fields for which KBSs are constructed are: production industries, service industries and even management (Steels, 1985). In the latter field, the treatment of the boundary conditions has been attempted only recently but looks promising. Service industries, in particular, employ KBSs to computerize their routine advice and to standardize their investments services, making for consistency. The best examples derive from the production industry, where KBSs are in use for tasks such as production planning, maintenance, process and quality control. In process control, especially with a man in the loop, KBSs act as intelligent advisers, controllers and analysers.

For instance, in a KB-controlled refinery, after the detection of a failure the KB system will attempt to minimize the failure's effect by

175

H. G. Sol et al. (eds.), Expert Systems and Artificial Intelligence in Decision Support Systems, 175–195.

looking for a bypass; in an emergency it must be capable of closing down the refinery. In the function of controller, the KBS replaces the supervisor of the conventional control system as a process supervisor. Process analysis is thought to be even more innovative: whereas ordinary control systems are not generally designed to react to anything not measurable, a KBS is expected to combine measurements and so to react to failures impending but not yet detected. Such rapid response could prevent major disasters. Still, the system is required not to take premature action which may result in grave damages.

Obviously, the more rules there are (and so the more knowledge) the stronger a competitor the knowledge-based supervisor will be to its real-life counterpart. Continuously adding knowledge finally leads to the problem of how to treat a very large number of rules adequately (Van den Herik, 1986). Regarding the abundance of information coming down in parallel to a human supervisor, a knowledge-based replacement can only be accepted if it satisfies the real-time contraints and acts in parallel. However, parallel computers and parallel programs dealing with knowledge are still in their infancy; therefore, many researchers resort to simulating a parallel computer for their parallel programs. The methodologies for designing the best, e.g., optimal in time, parallel algorithms are still in discussion. While looking for an optimal algorithm the investigation of the overheads caused by extra search, communication and synchronization must be combined with an analysis of the scheduling strategy (Marsland and Popowich, 1985).

In this contribution, efficient parallel computer programs are shown to be dependent on organizational structures as well as on heuristics guiding the order of the processes.

2. THE CONCEPT OF HYDRA

When building a parallel knowledge-based system the designer must be on the alert not to introduce a bottleneck in the form of a Master Control governing all (mutually parallel) inference engines. A centralized-control approach with such a Master Control is expected to be overloaded by the many tasks concerning jobs (selecting, assigning), control signals (receiving, sending), results (accepting, bookkeeping) and administration (updating, interrogating). Therefore, we have developed a decentralized approach to parallel KBSs (Groen et al., 1985).

The chief idea is to parallelize one inference engine into several administrative processes and a number of Rule Processors, performing only very specific tasks. In the expert system, termed HYDRA (HYpothesis Deduction through Rule Application), this idea is realized. Its fundamentals will be briefly discussed below; an extensive description can be found in Groen et al. (1985, 1986).

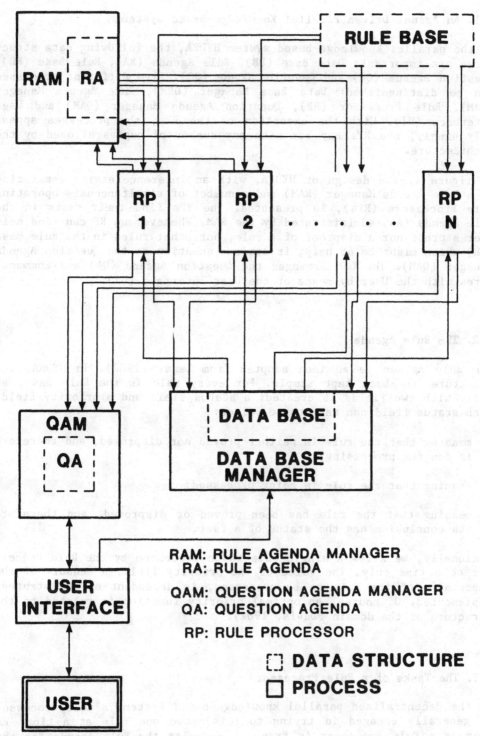

RAM: RULE AGENDA MANAGER
RA: RULE AGENDA

QAM: QUESTION AGENDA MANAGER
QA: QUESTION AGENDA

RP: RULE PROCESSOR

⬚ DATA STRUCTURE
☐ PROCESS

Figure 1: The Agenda-Driven Parallel Knowledge-Based System HYDRA.

2.1. An Agenda-Driven Parallel Knowledge-Based System

In the parallel knowledge-based system HYDRA, the following data structures are important: Data Base (DB), Rule Agenda (RA), Rule Base (RB),
Question Agenda (QA) and Question Queue (QQ). Five different processes
can be distinguished: Data Base Manager (DBM), Rule Agenda Manager
(RAM), Rule Processor (RP), Question Agenda Manager (QAM) and User
Interface (UI). With the exception of the RPs, the processes appear
only singly, the RPs may act with any number of copies allowed by the
architecture.

In figure 1, the design of HYDRA, with an inference engine consisting
of a Rule Agenda Manager (RAM) and a number of simultaneously operating
Rule Processors (RPs), is presented. The RPs find their tasks in the
Rule Agenda (RA) administrated by the RAM. Whenever an RP can find nei-
ther a proof nor a disproof of a rule, nor other rules in the Rule Base
(RB) which might be of help, it sends a question to the Question Agenda
Manager (QAM). The QAM arranges the Question Agenda (QA) and communi-
cates with the User by means of the User Interface (UI).

2.2. The Rule Agenda

The Rule Agenda is an idea adopted from Lenat (1982). In HYDRA, its
structure has been kept simple. For every rule in the Rule Base, an
entry with two fields is created: a status field and a priority field.
Each status field can take three values:

0   meaning that the rule is neither proved nor disproved, and therefore
    is due for processing;

1   meaning that the rule is being processed;

2   meaning that the rule has been proved or disproved, and therefore
    its conclusion has the status of a fact.

Rationally, we allow a single rule to be processed by one Rule Processor at a time only. The value of the priority field, a measure of the
importance of the rule to be processed, is dependent on the strategy
implemented. Of course, an optimal priority function is related to the
structure of the domain (Davis, 1982).

2.3. The Tasks of a Rule Processor

In the decentralized parallel knowledge-based system, a Rule Processor
is generally engaged in trying to (dis)prove one rule at a time. As
soon as a Rule Processor is free, it consults the Rule Agenda for the
next rule to be processed.

A Rule Processor performs its tasks in the following order.

1. <u>Take</u> a rule with the highest priority from the RA.

2. For all clauses <u>inspect</u> whether they are (dis)proved facts.

3. IF definite answer THEN <u>send</u> results to RAM and DBM
   [rule is proved or disproved], and terminate.

4. IF no definite answer THEN

   > <u>inspect</u> RB for further applicable rules;
   > <u>send</u> result to RAM

   [the rules selected will be included in the RA with their priority
   values updated], and terminate.

5. IF no further rules are applicable THEN <u>ask</u> the user via the QAM,
   and terminate.

Depending on the results of an RP's performance, one or more of the
following actions have to be executed:

- updating the Data Base;
- updating the Rule Agenda;
- updating the Question Agenda.

2.4. Relations between processes and data structures

In order to improve the performance of a parallel KBS or even to optimize it, a careful examination of the organizational structure with
respect to the relations between processes and data structures is required. For this purpose, it is important to know which processes operate on the distinct data structures. Which process is reading (R) or
writing (W) in a data structure and how is this action performed: by
direct access (D) or by sequentially following the complete data structure (S). In table 1 an overview is presented.

Some remarks on the accessibility are in order. As can been seen from
table 1, access to the RA is exclusive to the RAM and the set of RPs.
The RA is the most frequently used data structure, this is the more
clear when one takes into account that a set of RPs make use of the RA.
In all data structures, simultaneous reading is allowed, but in order
to keep the system consistent all reading while writing is excluded; as
a consequence simultaneous writing is not allowed either.

Only the RPs are reading in the DB; writing in the DB is the privilege
of the DBM, receiving its information from the RPs or the UI (see figure 1 and table 2). The RPs have concurrent access to the RB; no
writing is ever involved there.

data str. \ process	DB	RA	RB	QA	QQ
DBM	(W,D)				
RAM		(W,D)			
RP	(R,D)	(R,S)(W,D)	(R,S)		
QAM				(R,D)	(W,S)
UI				(W,D)	(R,S)

Table 1: How processes make use of the data structures in HYDRA.

Legend: (R,*) means reading   (*,D) means direct access to the
        (W,*) means writing   data structure
                                     (*,S) means sequentially follow-
                                           ing the data structure.

In table 2, the communication and the direction of the information flow
between the processes in HYDRA are outlined. Two types of communication
are distinguished: direct (X) and indirect (*). When the communication
is direct, the receiver will process the information as soon as possible; in case of indirect communication the receiver itself decides on
when to process the information delivered.

receiving process \ sending process	DBM	RAM	RPi	RPj	QAM	UI
DBM	▨		*	*		
RAM		▨	*	*		
RPi	X	X	▨	*	X	
RPj	X	X	*	▨	X	
QAM					▨	*
UI	X				*	▨

Table 2: The communication between processes in HYDRA.

Legend: X means direct communication   * means indirect communication

In table 2, it is made clear that HYDRA's decentralized-control approach leads to a structure of loosely coupled processes. Experiments have demonstrated that increasing the number of RPs raises the work load of the RAM (Groen et al. 1986). In a parallel environment, the RAM's access time to the RA is in competition with any RP's time. If every RP has to wait 100 msec due to the RAM's activity, the solution is postponed with 100 msec.

Before we can minimize the influence of the RAM's activity on the RPs' waiting times, a close investigation of the parallel processes and their critical actions, such as reading and writing, is required. To grasp the behaviour of the parallel expert system HYDRA on a simulated parallel computer we have generalized the mutual exclusion problem of the Dining Philosophers (Dijkstra, 1971).

3.   THE ABBOT-MONK PROBLEM

Anticipating the future importance of parallel knowledge-based systems, we shall examine some programming techniques and synchronization primitives which are crucial to their realization. A classic problem in concurrent programming is that of the Dining Philosophers. Though the problem was thought to be of greater entertainment value than practical value, it has shown significance as a vehicle for the comparison of synchronization primitives (Ben-Ari, 1982). We have reformulated the problem as the Abbot-Monk problem claiming that it is now a well-defined model representing the communication between the (loosely) coupled processes of the RAM and all RPs in HYDRA (cf. table 2).

3.1. Four Monks as an Example

The Abbot-Monk problem for four monks reads as follows. In a Himalaya monastry an abbot and four monks live together. Being dedicated worshippers they are happy to spend their time with transcendental meditation only, were it not occasionally necessary to eat. The abbot prefers to eat alone in the dining room. Monks may eat together provided that they fulfill the requirements of the dining room. In the dining room there is a round table; in the centre of the table is a bowl of rice which is inexhaustible. There are four numbered plates, each belonging to one of the four monks, and four chopsticks, one beside each plate. The abbot has his own set of plate and chopsticks (see figure 2). A monk or abbot wishing to eat enters the dining room, takes a seat, eats and then leaves the room. However, for eating rice the dining monk needs two chopsticks, which must to be adjacent to his own plate. In our experiments, the time that the monks and the abbot are allowed to spend in the dining room can be set by the user. A meal is defined as a certain quantity of rice to be eaten. To prevent a deadlock the maximum number of monks in the room simultaneously is set to three.

Figure 2: The Dining Room for One Abbot and Four Monks.

3.2. The Room-Door Concept

While many languages, such as Modula-2 and Concurrent Pascal, have formal primitives for solving the Abbot-Monk problem, they all lack a unified concept. We therefore introduce the concept of a Room (see figure 3). A critical action, such as eating, must be executed in a Room. In general, a Room has an arbitrary but stated number of Doors, the number of processes allowed to be in the Room simultaneously is fixed too. In the case of the Abbot-Monk problem, the processes are represented by the abbot or a monk. An abbot or monk attempting to enter by a Door he finds closed cannot enter the Room by that Door. When he finds a Door open, he may enter the Room only on the additional condition that his entering will not commit a breach of the Abbot-Monk problem rules. It can be thought rational to set the number of Doors to five (every person his own Door), but to set it to two is more appropriate (every class of actions its own Door).

When inside the Room any person is able to open and close any of its Doors. The privilege of closing Doors is also available to a person waiting before an open Door until the Room is empty; it is rational for the abbot to close the Room's other Doors collectively. In the implementation of this concept, extensive use is made of semaphores (Dijkstra, 1968).

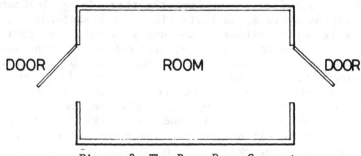

Figure 3: The Room-Door Concept.

An illustration of this concept Room is presented by showing how the abbot enters the dining room for his eating. In our solution the dining room has two Doors, one for the abbot's eating and one for the monks' eating.

```
WHILE the abbot still wants to eat DO WITH dining room
BEGIN

    Meditate;                                    (0)
    Close monks' Door;                           (1)
    Wait until empty;                            (2)
    Enter through abbot's Door;                  (3)
    Perform necessary eating actions;            (4)
    Open monks' Door;                            (5)
    Leave through abbot's Door                   (6)
END
```

We remark that the abbot never enters the dining room without attempting to eat. The abbot devotes himself to the mission in life, meditation (0). After (1) no monk is able to enter the dining room because monks are not allowed to open Doors from the outside. In our implementation, we have combined (2) and (3) into the procedure 'Enter when Room Empty', which guarantees the exclusive Room entrance for the abbot. The critical actions to be performed are represented in (4). The consequence of (5) is that all waiting monks are activated and will rush into the Room. The addition 'through Abbot's Door' in (6) is given for reason of symmetry; the abbot can leave the Room through any Door, because a closed Door may be opened from the inside.

4.   PARALLEL COMPUTER SIMULATION

On our way to achieve the aim of simulating the Abbot-Monk problem and HYDRA on a parallel computer, three different approaches have been investigated. All three have been implemented and examined on their merits. The first attempt, a concurrent process handler, was to simulate a parallel program by means of concurrent programming techniques (Ben-Ari, 1982).

Subsequently, to render it possible to record run and idle times, thus facilitating the understanding of the simulation, a time slicer was developed. This approach contained certain drawbacks, to be discussed below, resulting in the decision to construct a parallel computer simulator.

All three approaches rely on the same set of mechanisms for mutual exclusion and synchronization, the differences lie in the way of transferring to another process. The concepts on which the mechanisms are based are semaphores (Dijkstra, 1968), synchronizers (comparable with the Ada rendez-vous mechanism) and the Room-Door concept (discussed in 3.2.). In all approaches, the abbot and monk processes to be parallelized are put on a (circular) process list in order to provide the scheduler with easy access to the processes.

4.1. Concurrent Process Handler

Initially, in the simulation use was made of a Concurrent Process Hand-ler (CPH), determining the order in which the processes (abbot or one of the monks) should be processed. The scheduler of the CPH uses a random-number generator to choose which process is to be activated next. When a running process calls a procedure for performing some action critical for synchronization, this procedure in its turn will activate the scheduler and a transfer of control will take place. This being a random transfer, the same process, when not held up, might be re-activated. The method clearly is explicit and has the drawback of not being generally applicable.

Assume that the process list consists of n processes with n-1 processes loosely coupled and one process independent of the others. If the lat-ter is activated, it will never call a procedure for performing a cri-tical action or a synchronization. This implies that in such a situ-ation no transfer of control will take place, resulting in starvation. In the Abbot-Monk problem no independent process occurs, but in HYDRA the User Interface is more or less independent of the other processes; in order to prevent such a starvation we must introduce a dummy call in the independent processes with respect to the procedure which handles mutual exclusivity.

Disregarding this drawback, the main disadvantage of the CPH approach is the impossibility of estimating the impacts of parameters; in the Abbot-Monk problem there are the number of monks, the number of meals, the dining period, the abbot's strategy, etc.; in HYDRA, there are the number of RPs, the strategy in the RAM, the length of the QQ, etc. Such estimates presuppose exact measurings of the run and idle times of the parallel processes implying that a clock device is required. Since the Concurrent Process Handler provides no possibility for including a clock for such measuring, this approach was dropped.

4.2. Time Slicer

In order to estimate the parameters' impacts, a time slicer was built (Varkevisser, 1986), counting slices in multiples of n-hundreds of μs, n to be set by the user. It accumulates delays before individual ac-tions take place and it records them as idle times. Moreover, it fur-nishes estimates of the various processes' idle times. As already men-tioned the processes are placed in the process list and the scheduler inspects them in a round robin order imposed by the list. The scheduler is activated by a clock interrupt when a full slice has passed. The transfer of control is not due to an explicit procedure call as in the CPH, but by a clock interrupt, thus avoiding one of the CPH drawbacks; this transfer mechanism is therefore implicit. We shall elucidate this below.

In the examples, we assume the slices to be of the same size for every process; we have experimented with time-slice sizes which may vary with the nature of the processes, but this only complicates matters.
In all cases, the time slicer turned out to be accompanied by disadvantages, arising mainly from the fact that the results are dependent on the way in which the processes are ordered in the process list. We shall provide some simple instances to illustrate the problem of loosely coupled processes.

We assume the reader to be familiar with the semaphores as introduced by Dijkstra (1968). In our programs, the procedures 'wait' and 'send' are used as P- and V-operation, respectively. In a real parallel machine, two (loosely coupled) processes will be processed as shown in figure 4.

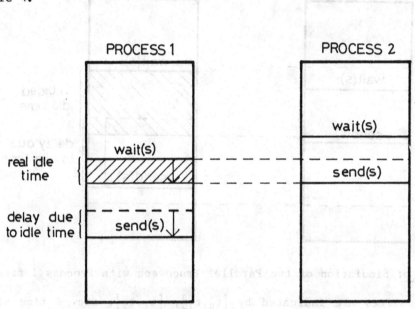

Figure 4: Two Real Parallel Processes

Looking at both processes in figure 4, we see that wait(s) is called first in process 2, allowing it to execute a critical action. At some time later, while process 2 is still occupied with its critical action, process 1 calls wait(s). Since the semaphore s is occupied, process 1 has to wait until s is set free. After process 2 has called send(s) the semaphore s admits process 1 to start its critical action. In figure 4, the real idle time constituting the part relevant to our discussion is indicated by a shaded area.

In a simulation environment with time slices, we would like to see that the amount of "real" idle time recorded is identical with the real idle time as presented in figure 4; or, if not identical, that the differences are at least acceptable, meaning that they can be accounted for.

However, experiments showed that the order of the processes in the
process list plays an exacting role. Different recorded idle times may
be arrived at, depending on the order in the list.

To state it more strongly, we cannot even predict whether the recorded
idle times will be smaller or larger than the real idle time, both may
occur with different ordering of the processes; it is even perceivable
that the recorded idle times interchange from one process to another,
as can be seen in the figures 5 and 6.

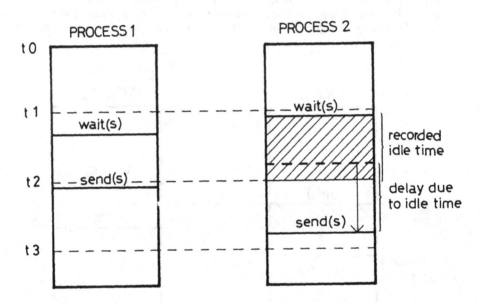

Figure 5: Simulation of two Parallel Processes with Process 1 first

The time slices are indicated by $[t_0,t_1]$, $[t_1,t_2]$, etc. A time slice
$[t_i,t_{i+1}]$ (i = 0,1,2,...) in figure 5 is first given to process
1 and then to process 2.   In the time slice $[t_1,t_2]$ process 1 calls
wait(s); semaphore s is not engaged and so process 1 starts its critical action. At the end of the time slice (at time t_2) when it is still
in its critical action, process 1 is interrupted. The scheduler offers
process 2 a time slice. In this time slice process 2 calls wait(s), but
the semaphore s is occupied, so process 2 cannot start its critical
action, implying that the rest of the time slice is recorded as idle
time (see the shaded area in figure 5).

In the next time slice $[t_2,t_3]$, process 1 resumes its critical action.
In our example, within this time slice process 1 calls send(s), it then
continues its normal actions until the end of the time slice. In its
turn, process 2 now finds the semaphore s free, and can perform a critical action.

We can see that the recorded idle time of figure 5 is clearly longer than the idle time in figure 4. But what is worse, in figure 4 the idle time is recorded for process 1, whereas in figure 5, the simulated case, the idle time is due to the waiting of process 2.

If process 1 in figure 5 would call send(s) a fraction before t_3 instead of just after t_2, the recorded idle time of process 2 would be the same. However, in case process 1 would call send(s) a fraction after t_3 the idle time of process 2 would be prolonged with a full time slice, making the simulation even worse. This implies that the simulation is also dependent of the time-slice size.

From figure 5 the conclusion may not be drawn that the recorded idle times will always be longer than the real idle time. In figure 6 we have depicted a simulation of the parallel processes of figure 4 again, but the order of processes are switched with respect to figure 5.

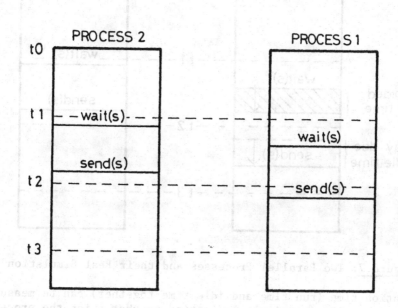

Figure 6: Simulation of two Parallel Processes with Process 2 first

Looking at figure 6, we see that the simulation shows no recorded idle time at all. In process 2 the wait(s) and send(s) are in the same time slice, implying that the critical action performed between wait(s) and send(s) has no influence on process 1's critical action to be performed.

Since the method of a time slicer turned out not to yield reliable results, a new method (see section 4.3) was introduced (Varkevisser, 1986).

4.3. Parallel Computer Simulator

To avoid the disadvantages of the time-slicer approach, another way of scheduling was developed in order to obtain more reliable estimates of the various processes' idle times. So far, no shortcomings have been discovered in this approach (Stoop and Varkevisser, 1985).

The approach, named the Parallel Computer Simulator (PCS), is based on the allocation of an own time space for every process. Since the PCS strategy results in a rather complex transfer of control, partly due to the presence of loosely coupled processes as well as independent processes, we shall elucidate its behaviour applied on the parallel processes given in figure 4.

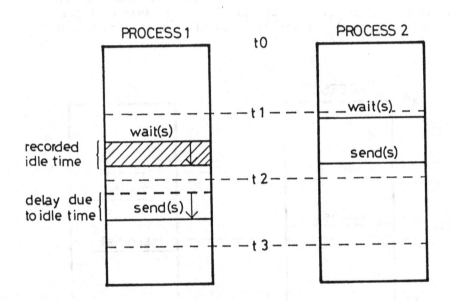

Figure 7: Two Parallel Processes and their Real Simulation

The execution time (run time and idle time together) can be measured in absolute time units (abstime), indicating to what point the process has advanced. The abstime of each process, accordingly called abstime 1, abstime 2, etc., is initialized at zero. The scheduler's general strategy is to select the first non-waiting process with the smallest abstime in the process list.

For our convenience we have placed some marks in the time space, e.g., $t_0 = 0$. Initially, abstime 1 and abstime 2 are both zero. The scheduler selects process 1 to be activated. The execution continues until wait(s) is called. The call wait(s) is a two-stage procedure. The first stage serves only to announce the "real" wait(s) execution. In the first stage of the wait(s) procedure the scheduler is activated. According to its general strategy, process 2, now with the smallest abstime,

is selected. Process 2 is executed until wait(s) is called, the first
stage of which activates the scheduler again. The scheduler sees that
abstime 2 is still smaller than abstime 1 and therefore (re-)activates
process 2. The second part of its wait(s) call is executed and process
2 can perform its critical actions until send(s) is called. The procedure send(s), also built up of two stages, activates the scheduler
before executing the "real" send(s) procedure. Since abstime 1 is
smaller than abstime 2 the scheduler activates process 1. Process 1
proceeds to execute the "real" wait(s) procedure (the second stage of
wait(s)) and finds the semaphore s occupied (in this instance, by process 2). Process 1 puts itself in a wait position and activates the
scheduler; meanwhile abstime 1 should increase as before (of course,
run time and idle time are registered separately). Since only process 2
is non-waiting it is activated. It executes the second stage of the
send(s) call (the "real" send(s) procedure) and sets the semaphore s
free. With the information available, it is easy to establish the abstime 1 and the idle time of process 1; thereafter the state of process
1 changes from waiting to non-waiting. The idle time of process 1 is
equal to the difference between abstime 1 and abstime 2; abstime 1
becomes abstime 2.

The rest of process 2 as shown in figure 7 is not (loosely) coupled
with process 1 and, therefore, treated as an independent process; process 2 may continue to its end, then the scheduler is activated. Since
process 1 is non-waiting and has evidently the smallest abstime, it is
activated and performs its delayed critical action. At the end of the
critical action it passes the two-stage send(s) procedure via the intermediate actions of the scheduler as described above and finishes all
its actions.

In figure 7, the shaded area indicating the idle time of process 1 is
identical in size to that of process 1 in figure 4. Furthermore, it is
situated at the same moment of time. The example presented gives insights in the way in which complex cases with n loosely coupled processes are treated by the PCS. Although no formal proof has been provided that the PCS always performs the simulation correctly, it seems
to us that the PCS appropriately records the run and idle times according to a parallel computer with n (loosely coupled) processes.

Finally, we would like to remind the reader of the potential presence
of independently acting processes. To deal with these processes we have
also adopted the techniques of implicit transfer of control by time
slicing in the scheduling mechanisms. Considering the scope of the
Abbot-Monk problem we will not discuss this matter here, but refer to
Varkevisser (1986).

5. KNOWLEDGE AND HEURISTICS IN SCHEDULING

The programming tools and techniques for dealing with parallel processes originated from solving the difficulties that were encountered when
programming operating systems. However, measuring the time used by the
processes of a parallel program differs from recording the time distribution of multitasking in operating systems, since in parallel programs
loosely coupled processes occur. When two loosely coupled processes are
mutually exclusive, as are the abbot and the monks, the order in which
they are processed may influence the total time needed for completion
of the tasks.
Using a time slicer in the simulation of a parallel computer, we have
seen in section 4.2. that the size of a time slice may influence the
performance. This implies that the scheduling mechanism might be optimized by exploiting heuristic knowledge about the domain in question.
Although an opportunistic designer, specialized in a particular domain,
could make much of such an optimization, it is not suited for an appropriate simulation of programs in parallel processing.

5.1. PCS's Performances

The PCS is a mechanism rendering it possible to record run and idle
times, exhibiting them and allowing careful examination of the results.
The performances of the simulation with the PCS have shown to be promising and we have also succeeded in realizing them with HYDRA. In September 1985, Stoop and Varkevisser (1985) converted HYDRA, written in
Modula-2, into the language C and made it run on a parallel machine
consisting of 2 to 15 MC68000 processors (De Bont, 1985). The results
on the parallel machine agreed with the simulation results when using
the PCS, be it that intricacies of the distinct managers still have to
be studied in order to get more insight into the inter-dependency of
the processes.

5.2. How to Optimize a Critical Action

Although the simulation with the PCS provides us with useful results,
the question of the program's optimality is still open. With the help
of the performances, the mutually exclusive actions of some processes
can be investigated in order to exploit the parallelism.

In the three examples below, it is assumed that the abbot and the four
monks have to eat 25 meals each. The following information about their
behaviour in the monastry is known.

For each monk : meditation takes 5 Asian hours;
                dinner takes 5 Asian hours.

For the abbot : meditation takes 0(zero) Asian hours;
                dinner takes 20 Asian hours.

An Asian hour is represented by the empty loop: FOR i = 1 TO 500 DO nothing. The configuration given above results in the figures presented in table 3; the monk's times are given as the average of the four monks' times.

	RUN TIME	IDLE TIME
Abbot	2980	2314
Monk	1960	4150

Table 3: Dinner with 25 abbot meals of 20 hours each.

The execution time of the whole process is the time of the longest process, being 1960 + 4150 = 6110. The times are measured in units of 100 µs, implying that the longest process takes somewhat more than 0.6 seconds.

In parallel processing, a critical action may constitute a bottleneck; in the Abbot-Monk problem, the eating procedure is a critical action. The output as given by the PCS indicates that the abbot finishes his 25 meals first; this is no surprise because the abbot is powerful. Furthermore, it implies that the abbot disturbs the monks in their eating. The conclusion is simple: the abbot is responsible for the longer processing time of the monks. This means that performance improvement is dependent on enhancements of the abbot's critical action.

Two suggestions for improvement can be thought of:
(i) curtailment of the abbot's critical action, if possible;
(ii) decomposition of the abbot's critical action, if possible and advantageous.

The idea of curtailment is to exclude anything not absolutely critical from the critical action. This can be performed only when a designer has reliable knowledge of the inter-dependency of the processes in the problem domain. If he is an expert in the domain, he may even attempt to exclude some actions on the base of heuristics. However, applying heuristics may jeopardize the advantage already gained by the use of knowledge; the whole system may even collapse when the inter-dependency is inappropriately affected.

We assume that the curtailment of the abbot's eating time results in the following partitioning of meditation and eating, whereas the times for the monks remain the same:

- meditation takes 6 Asian hours,
- dinner takes 14 Asian hours.

In table 4, the results are presented in the same manner as in table 3.

	RUN TIME	IDLE TIME
Abbot	2990	1670
Monk	1940	3400

Table 4: Dinner with 25 abbot meals of 14 hours each.

The execution time of the whole process amounts to 1940 + 3400 = 5340, which is less than 6110. The curtailment leads to a performance improvement of 780. In fact, this is an expected result.

The abbot's powerful behaviour can be assumed to reside in the indivisibility of his eating action, which takes 20 hours each meal (cf. table 3). A reasonable suggestion is to decompose the abbot's eating action into some smaller actions. The idea is that the waiting monks may eat somewhere in between the abbot's dinner periods. The abbot's waiting time may increase, but the hope is that the monks' waiting time decreases. The decomposition chosen for the abbot's actions reads as follows:

- meditation takes 0 Asian hours;
- dinner 1 takes 10 Asian hours;
- dinner 2 takes 10 Asian hours.

In table 5, the results are given.

	RUN TIME	IDLE TIME
Abbot	3314	3200
Monk	1980	3440

Table 5: Dinner with 25 abbot meals partitioned in 50 sessions of 10 hours each.

The execution time of the whole process amounts to 3314 + 3200 = 6514. Although we have succeeded in decreasing the time of an average monk process (1980 + 3440 = 5420), we are now faced with a increase of the total time claimed by the abbot. The result is even higher than without decomposition. Of course, the experiment can be repeated with another partitioning of the abbot's eating time, but it is clear that success also heavily depends on the structure of the inter-dependency. A tentative conclusion might be that decomposition is not of much help.

Regarding the Abbot-Monk problem with respect to HYDRA's RAM and Rule Processors, we may arrive at the idea that the RAM (or abbot) is not a

process like the other ones, but only an administrator. We assume that
the abbot first and foremost performs administrative tasks during which
he may also eat.
This changes the problem as follows: the four monks still have to eat
25 times, but the abbot's 'DO 25 TIMES' as indicated above (cf. the
algorithm in 3.2) will be 'WHILE a monk has not eaten his 25 meals DO'.

In table 6 the results are presented.

	RUN TIME	IDLE TIME
Abbot	4070	3250
Monk	1980	5300

Table 6: Dinner with the abbot as administrator, his critical action
         takes 20 hours.

The execution time of the whole process is 4070 + 3250 = 7320. It is
much higher then before, but we have to realize that the underlying
idea of the new model is in fact different from the previous one. We
apply subsequently the two suggestions, being curtailment and decomposition. In both cases, we have taken the partitionings as in the tables
4 and 5. The results of curtailment are given in table 7, while table 8
contains the results of decomposition.

	RUN TIME	IDLE TIME
Abbot	4000	2200
Monk	1990	4200

Table 7: Dinner with the abbot as administrator and curtailment ap-
         plied.

The execution time of the whole process amounts to 4000 + 2200 = 6200.

	RUN TIME	IDLE TIME
Abbot	2330	3230
Monk	1980	3582

Table 8: Dinner with the abbot as administrator and decomposition
         applied.

The execution time of the whole process amounts to 2330 + 3230 = 5560.

When the abbot acts as an administrator we see that both suggestions, the curtailment and the decomposition, reduce the execution time of the whole process. Applying heuristics in the curtailment and/or experimenting with other decompositions may result in further decrease of the execution time.

6.   CONCLUSIONS

In this article, we have established that simulation plays a prominent role when testing various AI techniques in parallel KBSs. As a result we mention that n simulated parallel processes may improve the processing speed, depending on the inter-dependency. The HYDRA concept for parallel machines therefore imposes high demands on the relations between the individual processes.

Moreover, the Abbot-Monk problem shows that the total execution time of a parallel process can be influenced by applying reliable knowledge and/or heuristic knowledge and by decomposing the process' critical action which forms a bottleneck. This leads to the following two conclusions. Firstly, an expert may invest a large amount of time in curtailment not using heuristics: all the actions he excludes from the critical actions assure a gain of time. Secondly, experiments with decomposition can result in enhancements of performances; the degree of improvement is dependent on the relation between the (loosely) coupled processes.

Finally, we may conclude that simulation of a parallel machine and a sequential machine using the Parallel Computer Simulator provides an excellent testing ground for models of which the structure is hard to characterize.

ACKNOWLEDGEMENTS

The authors wish to thank Ms. K.E. Börjars for the many valuable suggestions on the formulation of our results described in successive versions and for the scrutiny of the English text. They are grateful to A. Groen, A.G. Hofland, and Ir. E.J.H. Kerckhoffs for their co-operation in the HYDRA project.
Drs. E. van Utteren (Philips Laboratorium for Physics Research, Eindhoven) is acknowledged for giving permission to perform experiments on a parallel machine. Prof.dr. H.G. Sol's encouragements and advices are gladly recognized. We are grateful for the competent technical assistance of Ms. J.W. Pesch, who did all the typing; and for Mr. J. Schonewille's careful drawing of the figures.

REFERENCES

Ben-Ari, M. (1982). 'Principles of Concurrent Programming'. Prentice Hall International, Englewood Cliffs, New Jersey.

Bont, F. de (1985). 'Documentatie van het Multi-processor Systeem'. Intern Rapport, Natuurkundig Laboratorium Philips, Eindhoven.

Davis, R. (1982). 'Applications of Meta Level Knowledge to the Construction, Maintenance and Use of Large Knowledge Bases'. Knowledge-Based Systems in Artificial Intelligence (eds. R. Davis & D.B. Lenat), McGraw-Hill, New York.

Dijkstra, E.W. (1968). 'Co-operating Sequential Processes'. Programming Languages (ed. F. Genius), pp. 43-112, Academic Press, London, New York.

Dijkstra, E.W. (1971). 'Hierarchical Ordening of Sequential Processes'. Acta Informatica, Vol. 1, pp. 115-138.

Groen, A. & Herik, H.J. van den & Hofland, A.G. & Kasabov, N. & Kerckhoffs, E.J.H. & Stoop, J.C. (1985). 'Parallelizing Knowledge-Based Systems'. Expectations and Explorations (submitted for publication).

Groen, A. & Herik, H.J. van den & Hofland, A.G. & Kerckhoffs, E.J.H. & Stoop, J.C. & Varkevisser, P.R. (1986). 'The Integration of Simulation with Knowledge-Based Systems'. Proceedings of the Conference on Artificial Intelligence in Simulation (to appear).

Herik, H.J. van den (1986). 'Het Gebruik van Kennis in Expertsystemen'. Expert Systemen (eds. L. Steels and A. Nijholt), Academic Service, Den Haag.

Lenat, D.B. (1982). AM: 'An Artificial Intelligence Approach to Discovery in Mathematics as Heuristic Search'. Knowledge-Based Systems in Artificial Intelligence (eds. R. Davis & D.B. Lenat), McGraw-Hill, New York.

Marsland, T.A. & Popowich, F. (1985). 'Parallel Game-Tree Search'. Technical Report TR 85-1, 30 pp. Dept. of Computing Science, University of Alberta, Edmonton, Alberta, Canada.

Steels, L. (1985). 'Second Generation Expert Systems'. Future Generations Computer Systems, Vol. 1, No. 4, pp. 213-221.

Stoop, J.C. & Varkevisser, P.R. (1985). 'De implementatie van HYDRA op een parallelle computer'. Internal Report, TH Delft.

Varkevisser, P.R. (1986). 'Measurements of Idle Times of the Parallel Processes in HYDRA'. Internal Report, Delft University of Technology (in preparation).

MICROCOMPUTER BASED EXPERT SYSTEM SHELLS - THE SPREADSHEETS OF ARTIFICIAL INTELLIGENCE

Robert O'Keefe,Valerie Belton and Theresa Ball
Board of Studies in Management Science,
Rutherford College,
University of Kent at Canterbury,
Canterbury CT2 7NX, United Kingdom

ABSTRACT: Microcomputer based spreadsheets made simple financial modelling easy and cost-effective, opening the methods to those without previous experience in modelling or computing. Similarly, microcomputer based expert system shells promise those without an extensive background in Artificial Intelligence the opportunity to develop relatively simple, yet practical and useful, expert systems. The main types of shells are reviewed. In particular Micro-Expert, ES/P Advisor and Expert-Ease are discussed as examples of three distinct classes of shells, respectively using network based Bayesian inference, rule based logic, and deterministic decision trees as the basis for knowledge representation. An application in financial analysis is discussed. The weaknesses of the present range of microcomputer based shells is highlighted; it is concluded that flexibility, particularly access to a symbolic language, is an essential feature. Further, as spreadsheets have come to be used for a plethora of applications beyond those initially envisaged, declarative programming and knowledge based methods have applications beyond expert systems. As embodied in shells, they combine to provide a convenient structure for implementing many Decision Support Systems.

1. INTRODUCTION

1.1 Microcomputers and Spreadsheets

The arrival of the spreadsheet running on a desk top microcomputer can be viewed as a watershed for the Operational Research and decision support communities. It allowed simple numerical models to be built for direct use by clients with minimal investment in hardware and software; it allowed clients to build similar models for themselves.

H. G. Sol et al. (eds.), Expert Systems and Artificial Intelligence in Decision Support Systems, 197–211.
© *1987 by D. Reidel Publishing Company.*

Eight years after VISICALC, the first commercially available spreadsheet, was released in the U.S.A., Lotus 1-2-3 is easily the worldwide best seller among microcomputer packages. Many other types of microcomputer packages useful for decision support are widely available (examples include idea processors and project planning systems). However, the current vogue package is undoubtedly the expert system shell. In a recent paper (1) we listed 16 general purpose shells which ran on microcomputers. Most of these had been released since the start of 1984 - others have no doubt been released since the list was compiled.

This paper illustrates the present range of microcomputer based shells, and comments on their strengths and weaknesses from the context of OR and decision support.

1.2 Types of Expert Systems

Here we are solely concerned with consultative expert systems, where a user consults the system as an aid to a decision making task, not least because the present generation of shells is geared towards this. The early seminal expert systems, especially MYCIN and Prospector, were in this vein. However, other types of expert systems still very much at the research stage may ultimately also be of considerable importance to OR and decision support, particularly planning systems (2) and Intelligent Front Ends (3).

Further, here we are considering types of shells, rather than considering various knowledge representations, inference mechanisms, and methods of handling uncertainty. In our experience, separation of these matters is often difficult to achieve, and designers of shells have tended to stick to particular well tried or well documented combinations.

2. THREE TYPES OF SHELLS

2.1 An Example - Company Assessment

We have attempted to construct a system that supports a bank manager considering making a loan to a small company, some details of which are discussed elsewhere (1). It is based around the investigation of a number of key financial ratios, each of which can be calculated from submitted company accounts. Using knowledge represented as rule based logic, the system then assesses each ratio as favourable, unfavourable or satisfactory. Here we will consider the construction of a very simple expert system that combines the assessments of the five ratios for liability, assets, debtor/creditor, current and liquid. This would represent a financial assessment of a company based on information that is obtainable from the company's balance sheet alone.

2.2 Network Based Bayesian Inference

Currently, the most popular method employed in shells is network based Bayesian inference, as descended from Prospector (4). This is the basis of Micro-Expert, Savoir, Sage and Expert-Edge, amongst others. (For a detailed review of all the shells mentioned here, see the shell evaluation report produced at Loughborough University (5).) A system is perceived as a number of hypotheses or goals, dependant upon various assertions, which in turn may have dependants. Probabilities of the various assertions are propagated through the network using Bayesian techniques, where the effect of one assertion upon another is calculated using least sufficiency (LS) and least necessity (LN) weights (4). Encountering an assertion without a dependant results in the user being prompted to provide an assessment of its likelihood. For example, the user may be asked "How certain are you that the debtor/creditor ratio will increase ?", and the user must respond with a value in the range -5 to +5. Typically the inference mechanism will either backward chain from each goal in turn, or forward chain from the non-dependant assertions.

A Bayesian version of our example, coded in Micro-Expert, in shown in figure 1. It shows the top level goal for assessing the company financial position from the ratios, and the rules which combine assessments of the various ratios. (How these are gathered is not shown.)

GOAL   Balance_sheet_ratios 'Assessment of the balance sheet ratios'
            Bayesian Security ls 100 ln 0.01
                      Soundness ls 10 ln 0.1
            Prior 0.5

RULE   Security 'There is sufficient security for the loan'
            Bayesian Liability ls 100 ln 0.01
                      Solvency ls 100 ln 0.01
            Prior 0.5

RULE   Soundness 'The company is financially sound'
            Bayesian Asset ls 10 ln 1
                      Debtor_creditor ls 100 ln 0.01
            Prior 0.5

RULE   Solvency 'The company is sufficiently solvent'
            And Current Liquid

Figure 1 - a Bayesian version

Micro-Expert will backward chain from the Balance_sheet_ratios goal. Thus Security will be established as a sub-goal, and when a value for it has been obtained, Soundness will be likewise

established. Two details are worth noting. Firstly, the And in
Solvency provides the minimum of the Current and Liquid assessments.
Secondly, the LN value of 1 for the effect that Asset has on Soundness
means that a poor assessment of Asset does not decrease the liklihood
of Soundness. Both of these, and the other wieghtings, are a result of
viewing the company from the standpoint of lending. Other viewpoints,
for instance a company trying to assess the financial position of
another company they are considering trading with, would need
different weightings, and probably different knowledge.

The major problem with Bayesian inference is that it forces the
use of reasoning with probabilities, and both developers and users are
often not at ease with probabilities. Determination of the weights,
sensitivity analysis, and fine tuning of the system are all difficult
(6). Although most shells provide a number of functions whereby real
values can be reduced to probabilities (for instance, in Micro-Expert

```
RULE     Medium_to_long_term_debt 'Term of debt'
         Range Term 5 10
```

results in a proability of 1 for medium_to_long_term_debt if Term is
greater than 10, a probability of 0 if Term is less than 5, otherwise
its probability is calculated by linear interpolation) these are often
not powerful enough, and in any case, a situation may require direct
reasoning with these values.

2.3 Rule Based Logic

Using rule based logic, knowledge is represented as a number of
rules of the form

```
if { c1;c2.....cj}
then action
```

where the various conditions c1...cj are combined using logical
operators. This is the representation imposed by Prolog and shells
constructed in Prolog such as ES/P Advisor and Xi. Typically an
inference mechanism backward chains from a goal by looking for the
actions that will prove or disprove the goal, establishing the
necessary conditions as sub-goals, or forward chains from a number of
conditions thus inferring actions. If a situation can not be
established from the knowledge base, the user may be prompted to
provide relevant information.

The top level part of the example as coded in ES/P Advisor
in shown in figure 2. In ES/P, top level rules are composed of a
condition contained within braces, followed by text (ie. the action
taken if the condition is proved true is to display the text) and/or a
Prolog clause that should be established. These are attempted top
down. Hence here, if the assessment can not be established to be
favourable or unfavourable, it is assumed to be satisfactory. Both

favourable_bs_ratios and unfavourable_bs_ratios are boolean
parameters, with rules that establish their values. In this instance,
these rules represent the situations under which an extreme
classification can be made.

Unlike most Bayesian inference shells, rule based logic allows
for reasoning with absolute values. If the final estimate required can
be reduced from a continuous scale to a discrete scale, such reasoning
is probably more appropriate than Bayesian inference. However, when
capturing the logical conditions which lead to classification, it is
quite easy to miss a rule. The completeness of the knowledge can not
be easily validated. For instance, the above includes four rules for
the final classification, two for each extreme. Other experts may
suggest more rules.

section financial_assessment: 'Assessment of balance sheet ratios'.

{favourable_bs_ratios}
'The balance sheet ratios indicate a favourable position', quit.

{unfavourable_bs_ratios}
'The balance sheet ratios indicate an unfavourable position', quit.

'The balance sheet ratios indicate a satisfactory position'.

favourable_bs_ratios: 'Favourable balance sheet ratios'
    fact
    rules
    true if liability_ratio_favourable and drcr_ratio_favourable
        and current_ratio_favourable and liquid_ratio_favourable,
    true if liability_ratio_favourable and asset_ratio_favourable
        and current_ratio_favourable and liquid_ratio_favourable
        and drcr_ratio_satisfactory,
    false.

unfavourable_bs_ratios: 'Unfavourable balance sheet ratios'
    fact
    rules
    true if liability_ratio_unfavourable or liquid_ratio_unfavourable
        or (drcr_ratio_unfavourable and current_ratio_unfavourable),
    true if (drcr_ratio_unfavourable or current_ratio_unfavourable) and
        (not liability_ratio_favourable or not liquid_ratio_favourable),
    false.

Figure 2 - a rule based logic version

Where detailed uncertain reasoning is required, explicit
uncertainty must be employed. This can be added to rule based logic by
associating certainty factors with the various actions. Descended from

MYCIN (7), this is available in a number of shells including INSIGHT 2 and M.l. Alternatively, the logic can be extended to include aspects of one or more fuzzy logics (8), but as yet the only shell that provides comprehensive facilities for fuzzy sets with appropriate operators is REVEAL.

2.4 Deterministic Decision Trees and Induction

Shells based upon deterministic decision trees are conceptually simpler than most others. Knowledge is represented as a tree, where the leaves are conclusions or pieces of advice. The inference mechanism starts from the root, taking branches (perhaps deciding upon which branch after prompting the user for some information) until a leaf is encountered.

What makes deterministic decision trees of interest here is that an algorithm called ID3 (9) is available to induce the tree from a set of examples. With the Expert-Ease shell, a system is built by providing examples and subsequent induction, not by directly specifying the tree.

Using Expert-Ease, examples are presented in a table as shown in figure 3. The resultant decision tree appears in figure 4. In part this is incorrect, simply because only 11 examples have been presented to the induction algorithm. A valid tree is only guaranteed if all possible combinations are presented - in this instance numbering 243. Thus the ID3 algorithm is only viable where certain crucial combinations can be identified and/or the number of attributes and their possible values is small. However, the induction here has captured the importance of the liability ratio, and as with the previous hand coded rule based logic has indicated that the position of the company is unfavourable if the liability ratio is unfavourable, regardless of the other factors.

A futher limitation of ID3 is that it can not handle contradictions. Hence the choice of attributes from which the tree is induced is crucial. However, advances are being made which overcome a number of these problems (10), and research into machine learning will result in other techniques and tools that aid the construction of a knowledge base.

Apart from some simple fault finding problems, the deterministic decision tree would appear to be inapplicable. Extending it by uncertainty results in the decision tree employed in decision analysis (11), well known within OR (12), and implemented in packages such as ARBORIST.

2.5 Some Weaknesses

In general, there are a number of weaknesses common to the majority of shells available on microcomputers. Firstly, they do not represent the state of the art in expert systems - increasingly used knowledge representations such as frames (13), and extended methods of reasoning such as causal reasoning (for an example of this, see Roach et al (14)), are not available. The developer requiring these must directly employ Prolog or Lisp, or obtain one of the increasing number of environments that run on dedicated Lisp machines, such as LOOPS, ART or KEE. (These are expensive, not the least because of the need to purchase the Lisp machine.) However, it is likely that the next generation of microcomputer shells will include some of these features.

Secondly, facilities for communication with other software is rarely provided for. Expert-Edge can read DIF files generated by spreadsheets, but too many shells are self contained.

liability	asset	dr-cr	current	liquid	class
fav	fav	fav	fav	fav	fav
un	fav	fav	fav	fav	un
fav	un	fav	fav	fav	fav
fav	fav	un	fav	fav	sat
fav	fav	fav	un	fav	sat
fav	fav	fav	fav	un	un
sat	fav	fav	fav	fav	sat
fav	sat	fav	fav	fav	fav
fav	fav	sat	fav	fav	fav
fav	fav	fav	sat	fav	sat
fav	fav	fav	fav	sat	sat

Figure 3 - example table for induction
(fav=favourable, sat=satisfactory, un=unfavourable)

```
liability:
        fav : liquid
            fav : current
                fav : dr-cr
                    fav : fav
                        un : sat
                        sat : fav
                    un : sat
                    sat : sat
                un : un
                sat : sat
            un : un
            sat : sat
```

Figure 4 - resultant decision tree

Access to other software is possible if program code can be embedded or linked into the knowledge representation lanaguge (KRL). This is also necessary for extending the system beyond the restrictions of the KRL. Many shells, including Micro-Expert, provide hooks for inserts written in FORTRAN or Pascal. We have generally found this inadequate. ES/P Advisor allows Prolog to be embedded in the KRL, and this provides considerable flexibility. In using ES/P, we are increasingly writing comparatively more Prolog and less KRL with each project. Our experience suggests that the best shells are those that are based on an appropriate symbolic language, and allow direct access to that language.

2.6 The Use of Shells

Despite the specific and general criticisms above, simple but useful expert systems can be constructed. Some diagnostic type systems can be produced using network based Bayesian inference; rule based logic can adequately handle knowledge that is well defined, for instance, machine operating procedures. However, the developer quickly meets the need to integrate the expert system with other software, organise data by traditional means (ie. in files and arrays), and use techniques that are not available. For the OR scientist, this often means the ability to be able to implement OR techniques. This is possible only if the shell allows access to a language.

It should be remembered that use of a shell is only part of the process of building an expert system. Knowledge aquisition is still a black art. Yet it is the elicitation of knowledge that is the prime problem in many expert system projects, not the choice and use of software tool (15).

3. DECISION SUPPORT

3.1 A Basis for Decision Support

Many systems now being built with shells, including the example above, are not expert systems in the sense that they satisfactorily perform some routine task that normally requires the judgement of an expert. They are systems that aid users in one or more decision making tasks - in short, they are Decision Support Systems.

Shells provide a number of features useful for developing microcomputer based DSS. Firstly, where a shell uses a KRL, it is declarative ie. the relationship between the various objects does not have to be specified explicitly (although in most cases some rules have to be inserted so as to maintain some procedural requirements, for instance, dynamically alter the order in which questions are asked so they appear sensible to the user). In comparison with using a traditional procedural language (and most financial planning and DSS generator languages are procedural, let alone the popular high-level languages such as FORTRAN) declarative programming results in code that is highly readable, and thus easy to maintain and extend.

An obvious extension of this is that knowledge can be coded declaratively as if it were data. Relationships between data objects can be succinctly and simply expressed. DSS's that explicitly employ knowledge can be built.

Finally, many shells provide a good interactive interface. Thus, in comparison with using a traditional high-level language with a run time system, when using a shell a reasonable and robust user interface is obtained "for free".

3.2 Sketching an Example - Production Planning

To show how a DSS might be developed using a shell based upon a symbolic language, we will sketch out an example in production planning using the ES/P shell and Prolog. (We will not dwell on the details of the Prolog code, since explanation would take more space than available here. Interested readers should consult Clocksin and Mellish (16).).

Suppose a DSS that advises on production in a job-shop, whilst also keeping track of inventory, is to be developed, and we wish the DSS to suggest candidates for production if the users first choice can not be produced. Prolog can be used to construct a data base of the inventory thus

```
store(partA,3).
store(partB,4).
store(partC,0).
```

where each clause shows how much of a particular part is in store.(A separate Prolog program can perhaps update what's in store following the arrival of inventory.) Further clauses can be used to specify the parts needed to make any product thus

```
needed(body,[partA,1,partB,2]).
needed(chassis,[partB,1,partC,1]).
needed(nothing,[]).
```

The first clause shows that to produce a body 1 of partA and 2 of partB are needed. The third clause is useful for housekeeping, simply showing that it takes no parts to produce nothing.

Given the above, futher useful clauses can be programmed. To find out if a particular product can be made, the following

```
make_one([X,W|Y]) :-
        store(X,Z),
        Z>=W,
        make_one(Y).
make_one([]).

make_product(Product) :-
        needed(Product,Parts),
        make_one(Parts).
```

can be employed, where, for instance, make_product(body) would succeed
if enough of the needed parts are in store. Further, make_product(X)
would instantiate X to a product that could be made. (In Prolog,
variables begin with an upper-case letter.) Note that this would
always succeed, as it is always possible to make nothing. Another
version of the clause could be

```
make_product(Product,Yes) :-
        needed(Product,Parts),
        make_one(Parts),
        Yes=true .
```

where make_product(body,X) would instantiate X to true if it is
possible to make body. For updating inventory, the following could be
used

```
update([X,W|Y]) :-
        retract(store(X,Number)),
        New is Number-W,
        assertz(store(X,New)),
        update(Y).
update([]).

update_product(Product) :-
        needed(Product,Parts),
        update(Parts).
```

where update_product(body) will update the store clauses for the parts
needed to make body. This is done by retracting the appropriate clause
in update, and making a new assertion. (Prolog afficiaondos note - the
newly established clauses would have to be explicitly saved in most
Prolog systems.)

Such Prolog development gives a data base for inventory,
knowledge about what parts are needed to make products, and working
clauses that can be used from within ES/P. Figure 5 shows ES/P code
for part of the DSS. Its action is to

(1) ask the user to choose a product to be produced,
(2) if it can be produced, update the inventory,
(3) if it can not, suggest an alternative, which the user can
    accept or override.

The first action taken when figure 5 is executed is to try to establish confirm. The action text for the rule contains the value of choice, so this must be established first. This can be done by asking the user to supply the value. If choice can be produced, the user is informed, the inventory updated, and this section quitted. Otherwise the inference mechanism will try to establish the next condition, which here involves establishing possible.   (For further details of the KRL see the ES/P manual (17). An example consultation is shown in figure 6.)

```
choice: 'choose a product for production'
  category
  options body - 'main body',
          chassis - 'associated chassis',
          nothing - 'nothing'
  askable 'What is your first preference for production ?'.

confirm: 'try and make first preference'
  fact
  rule use make_product(choice,confirm),
      false.

{confirm}
@choice .. ' is to be made', do update_product(choice), quit.

{not confirm}
'It is not possible to make ' .. @choice.

possible: ' possibility for production'
  category
  options body,chassis,nothing
  rule use make_product(possible).

{possible<>nothing}
'However, it is possible to make ' .. @possible.

{want_to} do update_product(possible).

want_to: 'is this desired'
  fact
  askable 'Do you want to do this ?'.
```

Figure 5 - KRL code for the production planning example DSS

What is your first preference for production ?

    (1) - main body
    (2) - associated chassis
    (3) - nothing

Enter the number of the relevant entry : 2

It is not possible to make chassis

However, it is possible to make body

Do you want to do this ? y

Figure 6 - an example consultation with the "system" of figure 5

3.3 Discussion

The example shows how declarative programming with a symbolic language can ease the development of a DSS, and the advantage of using knowledge alongside data.

The above combination of Prolog and ES/P is comparatively readable, and fairly compact. Consider the numbers of lines of FORTRAN necessary to do an equivalent task. Extension of it is easy - more parts can be added by including another store clause; more products by another needed clause, and altering the various options in the KRL. For a job-shop with 200 products and 2000 parts, the basic structure would be the same. Knowledge, in this case concerning the parts necessary to make a product, is represented by a number of Prolog clauses. It is not hidden in a data structure, or distributed around a data base.

The decision support task here was very simple. However, this is where OR can contribute. Various algorithms could be included in the DSS. Despite Prolog having a depth-first search mechanism, it is quite straightforward to implement the breadth-first branch and bound search that so many scheduling algorithms are based upon. (An example can be found in Clocksin and Mellish (16).) Clauses can be set up to implement an inventory control policy.

There are a number of problems in using shells as decision support tools, beyond the criticism of shells as tools for producing expert systems presented earlier. The previously mentioned good user interface does not extend to graphic capabilities. The range of arithmetical and mathematical functions available in most spreadsheets and many languages is missing. However, such facilities are likely to be included as shells are increasingly seen as general purpose software tools, and not just expert sytem generators.

4. CONCLUSIONS

Are microcomputer based expert system shells the spreadsheets of Artificial Intelligence ? The answer is a qualified no. They employ a few tried and tested techniques, and are some way behind the state-of-the-art as available on dedicated Lisp machines. They are pitched at a level of complexity that makes them easy-to-use tools for those with modelling experience, such as OR workers; it is unlikely that they will be directly used by managers.

They do provide an opportunity to develop simple but useful expert systems, but not to the extent that the developers of many such shells claim. However, they are useful tools for developing microcomputer DSS, especially if they can be used in combination with a symbolic languge such as Prolog or Lisp.

Acknowledgements

This work was supported by grants from the United Kingdom Science and Enginneering Research Council, the University of Kent at Canterbury, and Ernst and Whinney (Chartered Accountants).

The various packages mentioned in this paper are marketed by the following companies. Some are trademarks.

VISICALC:	VisiCorp
Lotus 1-2-3:	Lotus Development Corporation
Micro-Expert,	
Savoir:	ISI Ltd.
Sage:	SPL International Ltd.
Expert-Edge:	Helix Expert Systems Ltd.
ES/P Advisor:	Expert Systems International Ltd.
Xi:	ExperTech Ltd.
M.1:	Teknowledge
REVEAL:	Tymshare
ARBORIST:	Texas Instruments
LOOPS:	Xerox Corporation
KEE:	IntelliCorp
ART:	Inference

References

1. R.M. O'KEEFE, V.BELTON and T.BALL (1985) 'Getting into expert systems'. Paper presented at the 27th Annual Conference of the O.R. Society, Durham, September 1985.

2. A. TATE (1985) 'A review of knowledge-based planning techniques'. The Knowledge Engineering Review 1, number 2, 1-17.

3. A. BUNDY (1984) 'Intelligent Front Ends'. In Research and Developments in Expert Systems (M. Bramer, ed.), Cambridge University Press, 117-126.

4. R.O. DUDA, P.E. HART, P.BARRETT, J.GASCHNIG, K. KONOLIGE, R. REBOH and J. SLOCUM (1978) 'Development of the Prospector system for mineral exploration'. SRI International, Menlo Park.

5. R.J. ALLWOOD, D.J. STEWART, C.HINDE and B. NEGUS (1985) Report on expert system shells evaluation for construction industry applications. Department of Civil Engineering, Loughborough University of Technology.

6. J. GADSDEN (1984) 'An expert system for evaluating electronic warfare tasking plans for the Royal Navy'. In IEEE Proceedings of the First Conference on Artificial Intelligence Applications, IEEE, Silver Spring, Maine.

7. E.H. SHORTLIFFE (1976) Computer-Based Medical Consultants: MYCIN. Elsevier, New York.

8. T. WHALEN and B. SCHOTT (1985) 'Alternative logics for approximate reasoning in expert systems: a comparative study'. Int. J. Man-Mach. Stud. 22, 327-346.

9. J.R. QUINLAN (1979) 'Discovering Rules by Induction from Large Collections of Samples'. In Expert Systems in the Microelectronic Age (Michie, Ed.). Edinburgh University Press, 168-201.

10. A.E. HART (1984) 'Experience in the use of an inductive system in Knowledge Engineering'. In Research and Developments in Expert Systems (M. Bramer, ed.), Cambridge University Press, 117-126.

11. P.G. MOORE, H. THOMAS, D.W. BUNN and J.M. HAMPTON (1976) Case Studies in Decision Analysis. Penguin, London.

12. L. PHILLIPS (1982) 'Requisite decision modelling: a case study'. J. Opl. Res. Soc. 33, 303-312.

13. M. MINSKY (1977) Frame-system theory. In Thinking (P.N. Johnston-Laird and P.C. Wason, Eds.), Cambridge University Press.

14. J.W. ROACH, R.S. VIRKAR, M.J.WEAVER and C.R. DRAKE (1985)
    'POMME: a computer-based consultation system for apple orchard
    management using Prolog'. Expert Systems **2**, 56-69.

15. M. WELBANK (1983) A Review of Knowledge Aquisition Techniques
    for Expert Systems. British Telecom Research Laboratories,
    Ipswich, U.K.

16. W.F. CLOCKSIN and C.S. MELLISH (1984) Programming in Prolog
    (Second Edition). Sringer, Berlin.

17. EXPERT SYSTEMS INTERNATIONAL (1985) ES/P Advisor manual.
    Expert Systems International, Oxford, U.K.

EXTENSIONS TO THE EXPERT SYSTEM SHELL DELFI-2

P.J.F. Lucas
Centre for Mathematics and Computer Science
P.O. Box 4079
1009 AB AMSTERDAM

H. de Swaan Arons
Department of Mathematics and Informatics
Delft University of Technology
P.O. Box 5
2600 AA DELFT

ABSTRACT. DELFI-2 is an empty expert system shell designed and developed at Delft University of Technology [1,2]. It has been and still is being used in both industry and institutes for building expert systems and for research on knowledge-based systems. Not unexpectedly, however, one of the intermediate conclusions of research and practical experience with the system has been that it proved to be inadequate, in some circumstances, to apply just one of the available knowledge representation formalisms when building an expert system.

In this paper some extensions to the DELFI-2 system are presented, which will be carried out in collaboration between Delft University of Technology and the Centre for Mathematics and Computer Science.

1. INTRODUCTION

The representation of human knowledge in computers is a key issue in expert systems research, because earlier systems that included only general purpose problem solving knowledge have demonstrated to be insufficient in dealing with complex real-life problems. Therefore, the subject of knowledge representation is emphasized in this paper. There are several knowledge representation schemes. To represent heuristic knowledge, for instance, production rules are widely used. Further, object-attribute-value triplets can be taken to represent facts. There are also other, more sophisticated schemes such as semantic nets and frame representations.

Until now, knowledge representation in DELFI-2 has been restricted to object-attribute-value triplets and production rules. Rule-based expert systems are the most successful systems to date, with a variety of applications in several technical (e.g. maintenance, trouble-

213

H. G. Sol et al. (eds.), Expert Systems and Artificial Intelligence in Decision Support Systems, 213–225.

shooting) and non-technical (e.g. medical, managerial) domains of expertise.

Not unexpectedly, however, one of the intermediate conclusions of research and practical experience with the system has been that it proved to be inadequate, in some circumstances, to apply only these two available knowledge representation formalisms.

The knowledge encoded in the knowledge base is applied by a tool for automatic reasoning, called the inference engine of DELFI-2. Knowledge representation and inference methods are strongly related, thus it is not surprising that the algorithms encoded in the inference engine also require further investigation. DELFI-2 uses a backward chaining inference algorithm, one of the few possible algorithms. However, it would make the system more widely applicable if it incorporated other inference algorithms as well.

The DELFI-2 system is a university product and has been constructed to investigate the fundamentals of knowledge-based systems such as knowledge representation, inference techniques, knowledge engineering and user interface design. At present, research is being focused on developing methods to integrate various knowledge representation schemes in DELFI-2 such as production rules, semantic networks and frames. A major part of research will be directed to interfaces between these representation schemes. The modular set-up of the system facilitates the extensions necessary to investigate the above-mentioned research topics. The paper discusses how these features will be included in DELFI-2.

In the next section an overview of the system DELFI-2 is presented. In section 3 extensions to the inference engine are discussed and in section 4 knowledge representation is discussed. In both sections, applicability in the DELFI-2 system is the central issue. The resulting system will be called DELFI-3.

2. THE DELFI-2 SYSTEM

In many aspects DELFI-2 is similar to the well-known EMYCIN [3,4,5] system and the architecture of DELFI-2 is based on this system.

Unlike this famous system that was developed at Stanford University, the DELFI-2 system has not been written in the programming language LISP, but in Pascal. LISP certainly has obvious advantages due to its symbol manipulation capability, but on the other hand languages such as Pascal allow for a more straightforward application of techniques from software engineering and other well-established fields of computer science (such as the study of algorithms and data structures, program verification, time and space complexity analysis etc.).

An overview will now be given of the architecture of the DELFI-2 system. Also some aspects of knowledge organization will be discussed. The DELFI-2 program needs a knowledge base to function as an expert system. Therefore, in an expert system developed with DELFI-2 two separate components can be distinguished. The first part being the DELFI-2 consultation program, which consists of a set of modules,

manipulating the second part, the knowledge base. The knowledge base
is kept in a file system separately from DELFI-2 and can be constructed
using an ordinary editor or a specially designed editor, called a
knowledge base editor. The structure of these files are more or less a
mapping of the internal data structures of DELFI-2. The file
organization itself is determined by the procedures reading in the
data. The knowledge base consists of two separate parts:

- a set of production rules, called the rule base

- a so-called object tree or schema, which is used to supply
  declarative information during a consultation

In the DELFI-2 system the production rules are basically used to encode
the heuristic expert knowledge.
Principally, the inference engine, which is one of the components of
DELFI-2, uses backward chaining as its control strategy. This is one
of the possible implementations of the more general form of inference,
called top-down inference. In top-down inference, information is
gathered starting with one or more goals and working back to the
necessary data. A well-known alternative to top-down inference is
bottom-up inference, which essentially starts with the data the system
already has, and generates information with this data. This process is
most often implemented as forward chaining in rule-based expert
systems. In the DELFI-2 system only backward chaining is available.
There are two kinds of user of an expert system shell: on the one hand
the expert or a knowledge engineer, whose task it is to fill the
knowledge base with domain-specific knowledge, and on the other hand
the client, whose prime interest in the system is its possibility to
supply advice. Important additional facilities of the consultation
program are the explanation and the trace facilities.
Highly crucial to the proper application of expert systems is an
explanation capability. Without such a facility, it is impossible to
monitor the way the knowledge base is used. Basically two types of
questions can be asked by the user, i.e. it is possible to determine
WHY a question has been asked and to verify HOW a certain fact has been
established.
The trace facilities are mainly useful in the design stage of a
knowledge base. It is very hard to develop an expert system without
having such facilities available. The trace facility supplied with the
DELFI-2 system reports on searched data and on selected and applied
production rules. Information is generated on request and with as much
detail as desirable.
In order to reach conclusions the expert system needs input data, which
could be derived from the following four potential sources:

- a general data base (for example an Hospital Information System)

- the knowledge base

- external subroutines, linked to the system

- the user, asking for advice

It is feasible to restrict an application to only a few of these.
The knowledge base contains general information on the domain of
expertise and all the other sources supply the system with more
specific data.
During a consultation of an expert system, so-called facts are derived
from one of these four sources. Facts are created (instantiated)
dynamically, using static object information as a kind of template.

3. EXTENSIONS TO THE INFERENCE ENGINE

The expert system shell DELFI-2 has been found to be quite appropriate
for various applications. However, the DELFI-project is directed to
developing software tools that have a general applicability to building
and consulting expert systems. Some applications have been established
in which DELFI-2 did not appear to have this characteristic. This
observation has challenged the designers of the DELFI-2 system to adopt
another course.
Many modifications are possible, but essential extensions to the DELFI-
2 system must be related to the core of the system: the knowledge
representation techniques and the inference algorithms. The latter
will now be considered in more detail first.
The inference engine can be modified in several ways. For instance, by
implementing better search methods or more appropriate conflict
resolution techniques. However, there is a pragmatic reason for not
giving much attention to this kind of improvements. As long as DELFI-
2's performance does not suffer from simpler and less efficient
techniques, these search methods will have lower priorities in the
project.

3.1. Forward chaining

DELFI-2 is very appropriate for solving classification problems.
Examples of this class of problems are technical and medical diagnosis.
The most important characteristic of this kind of problem is that the
expert is able to precisely indicate the set of possible solutions from
which the actual solution must be selected. For instance, in the
expert system B747/ATA-21 that helps to detect disorders in the
airconditioning system of Boeing 747 airplanes, what could be wrong in
a malfunctioning system, is very well known . For example, when
applying for a subsidy the set of possible outcomes is also known
beforehand: granted or denied.
For these applications backward chaining has appeared to work
reasonably well. However, not all applications show these
characteristics. A good example is the design process that is
characterised by seeking for a more or less unknown solution i.e. the
design of an object [6]. The inference engine must support this task:
reasoning from data to goals. This reasoning process is known as
forward reasoning. It uses a fixed set of data together with the rules
present in the knowledge base to produce new facts.

From an informatics point of view backward reasoning is preferred to forward reasoning. However, as explained above, in various applications it is not possible to determine a set of a priori solutions or recommendations, which is required from backward chaining. Therefore, the implementation of forward reasoning in DELFI-2 is of utmost practical importance.

There are also other reasons why forward chaining can be considered a necessary component of the inference engine. It could be an advantage to use production rules that do not actually contribute to the inference process itself, but that cause execution of one or more externally defined procedures, when some conditions are satisfied. For example, in the following rule:

```
IF
   Same object identity sphere ;
THEN
   Execute object I(mass,radius) ;
FI
```

the moment of inertia I(mass,radius) will be computed if it is known that the object of interest is a sphere. If this is the user's only purpose, then there is no need via backward chaining to trace other parameters than those necessary to determine I(mass,radius). In this case forward chaining must be preferred.

Experience with the development of the B747/ATA-21 expert system made clear that forward chaining is also suited to easily switching from one object to another. During the consultation of hierarchical expert systems, it is often wanted to descend to one or more sub-objects without bothering the user with a lot of questions not directly concerning the corresponding transition. In this case backward chaining can be used, but it makes the consultation less transparent. Forward chaining facilitates this procedure by placing the corresponding objects in the IF-part and THEN-part respectively of a forward chaining rule.

There are applications for which a combination of both inference techniques is most appropriate. The rule base can then be seen as a combination of two separate rule bases: one containing the production rules that are subject to forward chaining (so-called F-rules), and one with only backward chaining rules (B-rules). The results produced by either rule base are communicated to the other via the collection of facts. How to use rule base components is determined by the characteristics of the application. Definitions, transitions between objects and the execution of tasks based on certain conditions can be embodied in the forward chaining rules. The analytical aspects of the application and the actual heuristic reasoning can be modelled by backward chaining rules.

Of course, there is the choice when to activate which rule base. For various reasons it is considered better to take backward reasoning as the prime reasoning process. Each time it produces new data the system swaps to the forward reasoning process. The forward reasoning process cyclicly uses its rules until it is no longer able to infer new data based on those already available in the system's data base. In that case the system returns to the backward chaining process. Naturally, there are some technical complications, but these are beyond the scope of this paper. In figure 1 an outline is given of an expert system using both forward and backward reasoning.

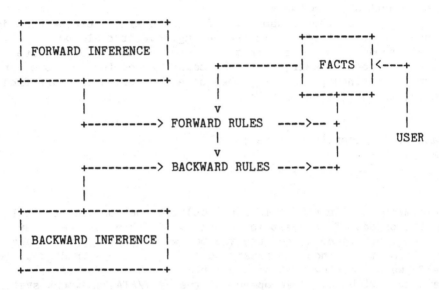

Figure 1. An expert system using both forward and backward reasoning

3.2. Meta-rules

Expert system shells will never be able to completely fullfill the designer's wishes with respect to building expert systems. One of the reasons for this is the inference engine. Despite its complexity, it can only contain the general control strategies. However, in many applications these are far from sufficient. In such a case it would be very desirable if the control strategy could be more directed towards the specific application's characteristics.

Meta-knowledge offers such a possibity. It is an advanced and more flexible way to control the set of production rules. This kind of knowledge can be formulated in meta-rules containing inferential information. As a consequence, inferential algorithms are partly moved to the rule base, so that the rules can be used on a more domain-dependent manner. For instance, in a meta-rule it can be dynamically decided, based on available facts, to have a parameter to be traced.

For instance, suppose an expert must establish either A or B to reach a conclusion C, and suppose he knows that it could be done faster by starting with A. This approach cannot be modelled in the present DELFI-2 system. However, in the new expert system shell DELFI-3, meta-rules will be able to cope with this problem. A meta-rule could state, for instance, that if there are rules concluding A and there are rules concluding B, then start with the rules concluding A.

As a consequence of the foregoing, the rule base will contain three different types of rule: forward chaining rules, backward chaining rules and meta-rules. There are much more types of rule possible, but we do not discuss these here.

4. EXTENSIONS TO THE KNOWLEDGE REPRESENTATION SCHEMES

Knowledge representation has always been one of the key issues in Artificial Intelligence. This is not surprising, of course, since a good description of the domain knowledge is a necessary condition for an efficient AI-system, and thus also for expert systems.
DELFI-2 combines two well-known representation techniques. On the one hand it uses a set of production rules. These are primarily meant to contain the heuristic knowledge. On the other hand facts are described by the so-called object-attribute-value triplets.
In AI literature there are also other, more powerful techniques available that can play an important role: semantic nets and frames. We will devote a brief discussion to both.

4.1. Semantic nets

A semantic net describes a collection of objects and how they are related [7,8]. These relations have a semantic nature, that is, the relation has some defined meaning. An object can be a physical entity, but also a concept. Further, it is possible that it is not the object itself that is concerned but only its description. The objects and the descriptions are the nodes in the net. In many cases the net is graphically represented, with arcs indicating the relations.
Many relations can exist between the objects. Simple types are the Is-A relation ("Rameau Is-A composer", or "composer Is-A person"), and the Has-A relation ("person Has-A name", or "magazine Has-A subscriber"). Some of these relations actually express a definition, others could contain heuristic knowledge.
In a semantic net various types of meaning could be distinguished. First, the semantic net is meant to describe an application domain. The information present in the semantic net only specifies certain relations between the objects. Another type of semantics is of great importance to expert system research: procedural semantics. The meaning of the semantic net is derived from the operators operating on it. Important concepts in this context are generalisation and specialisation.
In generalisation the Is-A relation plays an important role. Via an Is-A arc an object or concept in the net can be reached that is more general than the one that was under consideration. For instance, in figure 2 the object "Rameau" is less general than another object in the net: "composer". This is called generalisation. Going the other way around then we deal with specialisation. By introducing in a semantic net the principle of generalisation, it is possible to place certain concepts second to more general concepts.

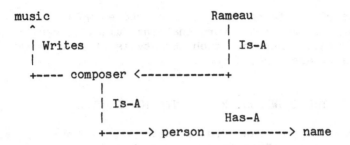

Figure 2. A simple semantic net

Apart from the meaning of a semantic net, there is the problem of how
to represent the semantic net in some specification language. This is
accomplished quite often in symbolic logic, since this offers methods
and inference techniques utilising the information stored in the
semantic net. The example in figure 2 can be converted into symbolic
logic as follows [9]:

F1   Is-A(Rameau,composer).
F2   Is-A(composer,person).
F3   Has-A(person,name).

The fact that Rameau is a name can be deduced by the following
inference rules:

R1 Is-A(x,y) if Is-A(x,z) and Is-A(z,y).
R2 Is-A(x,y) if Is-A(x,z) and Has-A(z,y).

In these two rules x, y and z are variables. The deduction is as
follows:

  1. Apply R2 to F2 and F3. This leads to x=composer, y=name and
     z=person, so to the intermediate conclusion Is-A(composer,name)

  2. Then R1 is applied to F1 and the intermediate conclusion. If the
     possibility x=Rameau, y=name and z=composer is chosen, then
     application of rule R1 leads to Is-A(Rameau,name).

Semantic nets have some disadvantages. In this context, the most
important one is that they do not allow non-elementary descriptions of
the objects that are contained in the net. Since frame structures do
offer such facilities, we are more interested in integrating semantic
nets and frame structures. Therefore, in the next section we first pay
some more attention to the characteristics of frame.

4.2. Frames

Much research in knowledge representation focuses on imbedding knowledge in frames [2]. A frame associates an object with a collection of features (also called attributes) e.g., facts, rules, defaults, and active values. Each feature is stored in a slot. The frame structure resembles the record data type that is used in programming languages such as Pascal.

Frames can be compared with the objects in DELFI-2's object tree, but they offer much more descriptive power. This also allows to describe semantic relations between the various objects.

We can distinguish two types of frame: static frames and dynamic copies of the static frames. These copies are called instantiations, since in most cases only a part of the information available in the general frame is copied. The remaining information will be adjusted to the individual case.

A new frame will be created (instantiated) when it is first needed during the consultation process. It will have a structure similar to its model frame present in the static knowledge base. Consequently, a frame-based expert system has a dynamical nature: during the consultation new frames are instantiated and related to frames that already exist.

A frame is defined by its name and by one or more slots each having a number of facets. Most often used facets are those for values, defaults and tasks, but there are many more. In AI literature tasks are known as demons. For DELFI-3 the following frame structure describes a physical object.

```
FRAME : physical object

    SLOT : identity
      FACETS :
        VALUE : unknown
        DEFAULT VALUE : sphere
        LEGALVALUES : CYLINDER, SPHERE
        TRANSLATION : unknown
        DEFAULT TRANSLATION : the sphere
        PROMPT : What is the identity of the object?
        TYPE : singlevalued
      END FACETS
    END SLOT
    SLOT : weight
      FACETS :
        VALUE : unknown
        DEFAULT VALUE : 10
        LEGALVALUES : real in [1,100]
        TRANSLATION : the weight
        PROMPT : What is the weight of the object?
        TYPE : singlevalued
      END FACETS
    END SLOT
    .
    .
```

{other slots}
       .
       .
    SLOT : Moment_of_Inertia_I
      FACETS :
        VALUE : if_needed execute function
                    I(weight,radius)
        DEFAULT VALUE : 100
        LEGALVALUES : real in [1,1000]
        TRANSLATION : the moment of inertia
        PROMPT : unknown
        TYPE : singlevalued
      END FACETS
    END SLOT
       .
       .
    SLOT : ISA   unknown

    END FRAME

This static frame is used for instantiation purposes. When
instantiated, a number of fields will consequently be changed, which is
in particular true for the facets which have "unknown" as a value.
Suppose that a particular object is a sphere. The corresponding
instantiation is depicted next. Just as in DELFI-2, it is the aim of
the system to establish values needed to accomplish a given problem.
The instantiated frame is considered at a given moment during the
consultation process.

    FRAME : physical object #1

      SLOT : identity
        FACETS :
          VALUE : sphere1
          DEFAULT VALUE : sphere
          LEGALVALUES : CYLINDER, SPHERE
          TRANSLATION : the sphere number one
          DEFAULT TRANSLATION : the sphere
          PROMPT : What is the identity of the object?
          TYPE : singlevalued
        END FACETS
      SLOT : weight
        FACETS :
          VALUE : 20
          DEFAULT VALUE : 10
          LEGALVALUES : real in [1,100]
          TRANSLATION : the weight
          PROMPT : unknown
          TYPE : singlevalued

```
        END FACETS
      END SLOT
      •
      •
{other slots}
      •
      •
    SLOT : Moment of Inertia I
      FACETS :
        VALUE : if_needed execute function
                I(weight,radius)
        DEFAULT VALUE : 100
        LEGALVALUES : real in [1,1000]
        TRANSLATION : the moment of inertia
        PROMPT : unknown
        TYPE : singlevalued
      END FACETS
    END SLOT
      •
    SLOT : ISA  unknown

  END FRAME
```

The Is-A slot refers to the static frame physical object with general
properties. The foregoing relation can be depicted as follows:

```
            physical object #1 (sphere1)
                        |
                        | ISA
                        |
                        v
                physical object
```

With the Is-A relation it is made possible to get information from
frames that are not available in the frame itself. This way of
information acquisition is called "inheritance of properties". For
instance, in the frame pysical object #1 it could first be attempted to
establish a certain value by consulting the rule base. If this is not
successful, then a routine (a task) could be executed. If no such task
is defined, then the default facet could be used. If no default value
is present, then, via the Is-A relation to the tenant frame the value
could be found. At last, the user can be requested to provide the
necessary information. The information that is inherited could be
applied in the production rules. For example, in the rule

```
IF
   LessThan physicalobject weight 2 ;
   Between physicalobject radius 0.05 1.0 ;
```

```
   Between physicalobject I(weight,radius) 0.03 3 ;
THEN
   Conclude physicalobject applicable yes ;
   CF = 0.9
FI
```

only general frames, slots and values are mentioned.
During the consultation of the knowledge base, the identifier
"physicalobject" is replaced by the identity of "physicalobject1", i.e.
"sphere1". The value of the weight of this object is inherited from
"physicalobject" if the inference engine was unable to derive a more
specific value for it. This value is used in the specified production
rules.
It is mentioned before that DELFI-2 already has a similar structure.
The object tree very much resembles the frame structures. Of course,
there are a few important differences. First, frames have a better
organised structure. Second, DELFI-2 could execute tasks, but in a
less general way. Third, the principle of inheritance is not known in
the DELFI-2 system.

5. CONCLUSIONS

The modifications described above leading to the DELFI-3 system, can be
characterised as real improvements. It will make the expert system
shell wider applicable. The modular set-up of the DELFI-2 system allows
a rather quick redesign. Completion within a few months can be
expected.

6. LITERATURE

1. de Swaan Arons H, Lucas PJF. 'Expert Systems in an application-
   oriented environment'. Informatie, 1984; 8: 631-637. (In Dutch).

2. Lucas, PJF, Stienen H, de Swaan Arons H. 'Knowledge manipulation in
   a rule-based expert system'. NGI-symposium. Utrecht, 1985.

3. van Melle W. 'A domain-independent system that aids in constructing
   knowledge-based consultation programs'. Stanford, California:
   Stanford University, 1980.

4. Buchanan BG, Shortliffe EH. 'Rule-based expert systems: the MYCIN
   experiments of the Stanford Heuristic Programming Project'.
   Addison-Wesley, Reading Massachusetts, 1984.

5. van Melle W, Scott AC, Bennet JS, Peairs M. 'The EMYCIN manual'.
   Report no. HPP-81-16. Stanford, Carlifornia: Stanford University,
   1981.

6. Final Report of the Project Groep CAD and AI: 'Expert systems in engineering practice'. CIAD, Zoetermeer, 1985.

7. Winston PH. 'Artificial Intelligence'. 2nd edition. Addison-Wesley, Reading, Massachusetts, 1984

8. Knowledge representation. Computer, vol. 16, 10, 1983.

9. Kowalski R. 'Logic for problem solving'. North-Holland, New-York, 1979.

ASPES: A SKELETAL PASCAL EXPERT SYSTEM

Georgios I. Doukidis and Ray J. Paul
Statistical and Mathematical Sciences Department
London School of Economics and Political Science,
Houghton Street, Aldwych, London WC2A 2AE, England.

ABSTRACT. There are several knowledge engineering techniques in use for building expert systems. One approach is to write the system from scratch in a high level programming language which is generally available, such as Pascal, LISP etc. Another approach is use a specially constructed domain independent system or skeletal system made up of a domain independent inference engine and a domain specific knowledge base. Such a system requires the user to formulate his model using input data rather than adding code. ASPES is a skeletal system written in Pascal which is a mixture of the above two approaches. It is an expert system building tool to which the user adds pascal code for the particular application. The virtue of this approach is that the modelling process is entirely under the control of the user in that Pascal can be written transparently and is well supported.

ASPES consists of a general purpose inference engine to which the user adds his domain specific knowledge base. The knowledge base is held in an external text file in the form of IF-THEN rules and is created with ease using a text editor. ASPES converts the knowledge base text file into linked lists of records when the system is used. ASPES is a product of research into the formulation phase of simulation modelling. References to this work and the general applicability of ASPES to Operational Research problems will be given.

1. INTRODUCTION

Although expert systems are much talked about, they have not yet proved as effective as might have been expected. One of the main reasons for this is that expertise in the construction of such systems lies in the hands of a few people. One approach adopted has been to write the system from scratch in a well supported generally available high level programming language such as Pascal, LISP, PROLOG etc. This is a very expensive method of approach. Little literature exists of such developments. This is presumably because where successful, the authors have appreciated the more general applicability of the system and have developed an expert system skeletal system from it. Unsuccessful applications in any field rarely get reported.

The second method of approach has been to take one of the many available skeletal expert systems or expert system shells and hope the problem to be tackled can be handled by the system. O'Keefe et al [1985a] report on many such systems with comments on their applicabilty.

H. G. Sol et al. (eds.), Expert Systems and Artificial Intelligence in Decision Support Systems, 227–246.

Such systems are domain independent and typically comprise a domain independent inference engine and a domain specific knowledge base. The user formulates his model via input data rather than by adding code. As with any software package, the applicability of any skeletal expert system is restricted to the class of problem envisaged by the system designer. Obviously improvements in new systems are rapid since the subject is so new, but the structures are very restrictive.

This paper describes the development of ASPES, a skeletal expert system. ASPES came into being because the authors, Doukidis and Paul [1985] and Paul and Doukidis [1985] constructed an expert system to solve a problem they had - in this case formulating discrete event simulation problems. ASPES is a research tool, both for developing and experimenting with expert systems. It is also used as a teaching aid at the School to explain by example what expert systems are. It is a mixture of the two approaches described above, writing the whole system from scratch and using an expert system shell. The user adds code to a suite of Pascal routines to construct the particular inference engine or algorithmic approach designed for his application, and assembles a knowledge base.

A brief description of what an expert system is, and how an expert system application might be tackled is given in the second section. ASPES is described in section three. Experiences of using ASPES, development and future work are described in section four. The fifth and final section discusses the place of ASPES in Operational Research.

2. EXPERT SYSTEMS

2.1. Definition and history

Artificial Intelligence (A.I) is that part of computer science concerned with designing intelligent computer systems, that is, systems that exhibit the characteristics we associate with intelligence in human behaviour -understanding language, learning, reasoning, solving problems and so on. An important development, arising largely from A.I research is the idea of an expert system.

Some define expert systems by placing the emphasis firmly on methodology and some on performance. For example, in the first case Basden [1983] states that:

> "they are loosely assumed to be computer systems that can hold human-like knowledge of (in theory) any kind and can process knowledge in a more human-like fashion than do conventional computer systems".

In the second case Bramer [1982] defines it

> "... as a computing system which embodies organized knowledge concerning some specific area of human expertise, sufficient to perform as a skillful and cost-effective consultant. Thus it is a high-performance special-purpose system which is designed to capture the skill of an expert consultant such as a doctor of medicine a chemist or a mechanical engineer".

Stefic et al [1982] give a more complete definition by presenting the relationship between expert systems and AI research. They say that

"Expert systems are problem-solving programs that solve
substantial problems generally conceded as being difficult and
requiring expertise. They are called knowledge based because
their performance depends critically on the use of facts and
heuristics used by experts. Expert systems have been used as a
vehicle for AI research under the rationale that they provide
a forcing function for research in problem solving and
reality".

The one thing upon which most writers agree is that expert systems
are designed to perform as a consultant to problems that are difficult
and require human expertise for their solution. Example of expert
systems are scattered in various journals, books, conference proceedings
and technical reports. It is very obvious, based on these examples,
that systems with seemingly similar tasks sometimes have radically
different organizations, and seemingly similar tasks are sometimes
performed with only minor variations. The variations reflect the
immaturity of the field, in which most of the systems are experimental.
Expert systems can vary considerably from one another in terms of system
design and capabilities -not least because the term 'expert system' is
not yet precisely defined. Bramer [1982] states that:

"it could be argued that virtually any A.I system written in
Lisp, for example, was an expert system if its performance
was sufficiently good".

In general, an expert system consists of a knowledge base and a
control structure. The knowledge base contains the knowledge of an
expert(s) in an organised way. A control structure is a program which
tries to solve a problem based on the knowledge base, the user's
responses and the status of the conversation.

Many of the early systems are considered as domain-dependent,
systems developed for a specific application area. But as the demand
for expert system personel (in research laboratories) exceeded the
supply, and as the discovery that knowledge for different domains could
be expressed in a similar fashion, it followed that systems were
designed with more than one application area in mind. Hence from the
mid 1970s new kinds of systems started to be developed which can be
considered as domain-independent expert systems building tools. The
most well known are: AGE [Nii & Aiello 1979], which provides guidance on
building expert systems and a set of tools for doing so; EMYCIN [Van
Melle 1979], a domain-independent version of MYCIN, used for developing
rule-based consultation programs for many fields; EXPERT [Weiss &
Kulikowski 1979], a system for designing and building models for
consultation. Other domain independent expert systems which run on
microcomputers include XI [Expertech 1985] and ES/P Advisor [Expert
Systems International 1985].

All these systems are called "expert systems shells". In general,
they provide facilities to develop the knowledge base interactively
(hence they automate the knowledge acquisition process) and then they
drive the compiled knowledge base by using a specific control mechanism.
Hence their task is quite similar to that of program generators.
Details of many of the domain-dependent and domain-independent systems
are given in Hayes-Roth[1981], Bramer [1982] and Feigenbaum [1979].

2.2. Characteristics of expert systems

Although expert systems can vary considerably from one another in terms of system design and capabilities, many of them have some common characteristics at various levels. These are used, usually, to define if a program is an expert system or not. This sub-section covers the classification of expert systems in terms of their common characteristics and features.

2.2.1. Knowledge. In expert systems, a representation of knowledge is a combination of data structures and interpretive procedures that, if used in the right way in a program, will lead to "knowledgeable" behaviour. Work on knowledge representation has involved the design of several classes of data structures for storing information in computer programs, as well as the development of procedures that allow "intelligent" manipulation of these data structures to make inferences. The type of knowledge which can be represented by the system and the ease with which that knowledge can be represented can be experimented with. This aspect takes account of the fact that knowledge is not a concrete entity, it is not easily described and is not tangible. In fact, some writers believe (see for example [Leith 1983]) that the subject is so intangible that most expert system researchers have avoided providing a definition of the knowledge that their particular system handles.

Of the many ways in which knowledge has been represented in expert systems, four in particular have achieved widespread acceptance (for a critical review see Barr and Feigenbaum [1981]) :

- Production rules
- Semantic nets
- Frame systems
- Procedural representation

When using production rules, the basic idea is very simple; we have a database and a collection of production rules each of the form [situation ---÷ action]. The situation part of each rule expresses some condition about the state of the data base, and at any point is either satisfied or not. The action part of each rule specifies changes to be made to the database every time the rule is used ('fired'). The system conceptually goes through an evolutionary process. At each cycle, one rule whose situation is satisfied is selected and fired, changing the data base and so affecting the rules that could possibly be fired on the next cycle.

The basic unit of a semantic network is a structure consisting of two points, or "nodes", linked by an "arc". Each node represents some concept and the arc represents a relation between pairs of concepts. Such pairs of related concepts may be thought of as representing a simple fact. Nodes are labelled with the name of the relevant relation. Figure 1, for example, represents the fact that:
"Smith works in the production department"

```
                  works-in
      Smith  ----------------->  production-department
```

FIGURE 1   A UNIT OF A SEMANTIC NETWORK

Note that the arc is directed, thus preserving the "subject/object" relation between the concepts within the fact. Moreover, any node may be linked to any number of other nodes, so giving rise to the formation of a network of facts.

In frame systems the kernel of the idea is the representation of things and events by a collection of frames. Each frame corresponds to one entity and contains a number of labelled slots for things pertinent to that entity. Slots in turn may be blank, or be specified by terminals referring to other frames, so the collection of frames is linked together into a network. An interesting, much discussed feature of frame-based processing is the ability of a frame to determine whether it is applicable in a given situation. The idea is that a likely frame is selected to aid in the process of understanding the current situation (dialogue, science, problem) and this frame in turn tries to match itself to the data it discovers. If it finds that it is not applicable, it could transfer to a more appropriate frame.

In a procedural representation, knowledge about the world is contained in procedures -small programs that know how to do specific things, how to proceed in well-specified situations. For instance, in a parser for a natural language understanding system, the knowledge that a noun phrase may contain articles, adjectives, and nouns is represented in the program by calls (within the noun phrase procedure) to routines that know how to process articles, nouns and adjectives.

Although there is a serious concern about the validity of the various representation schemes, it is not yet possible to prove that one scheme captures some aspect of human memory better than another. As Barr and Feigenbaum [1981] said

> "There is no theory of knowledge representation and we do not yet know why some schemes are good for certain tasks and others not".

2.2.2. Explanation facility. In the early days it was thought that computer based consultation would be confined to the conventional performance goal of earlier computing technologies, namely to deliver good answers to the client's input question. This turned out to be wrong in expert systems. As Michie [1980] says "the user demands explanation as well as answers". The ability to explain the line of reasoning in a language convenient to the user is necessary for application and for system development (e.g for debugging and for extending the knowledge base). Thus most expert systems make available an explanation facility for the user, be it an end-user or a system developer.

What constitutes 'an explanation' is not a simple concept, and considerable thought needs to be given, in each case, to the structure of the explanations. It seems that the best explanation facility is given by systems which present the knowledge as production rules. For example, using MYCIN at any stage of the consultation, the user can ask WHY (to query the significance of a request by MYCIN for information) or HOW (to ask how deductions so far considered as established by MYCIN were arrived at).

2.2.3. Automatically acquiring or refining knowledge. To emulate human thinking a machine intelligence must be flexible and expandable. These

are two hallmarks of expert systems. They can be expanded by the
addition of new knowledge, and corrections to the knowledge base can be
made and immediately assimilated. In this way an expert system
continues to build up its knowledge base by adding new information
incrementally. Thus the expert system is not static; it can be said to
"learn".

The critical factor affecting the speed at which the new technology
can take off is the degree to which expert systems can be made capable
of adding to, or refining their knowledge (or part of it) in the light
of observations either presented by the user or sampled directly. Most
expert systems have such facilities in one degree or another; various
"learning" systems are listed in Michie [1980].

2.2.4. Manipulating partial descriptions. One interesting set of
problems that occurs in expert systems involves finding ways of
effectively manipulating incomplete descriptions in the data base, when
it is incrementally constructed. Expert systems are consultantative
interactive systems where the user is bound to make mistakes, especially
when the interaction is done through a natural language. Thus
deductions may be made which are consistent with the available
information but may, in fact, turn out to be incorrect in the light of
information subsequently obtained.

Although this problem has not been taken into account in many
expert systems developments (see for example Bramer [1982]), we can
describe a set of facilities for dealing with partial descriptions found
in those few systems that have taken it into account. These facilities
make deductions using incomplete data (i.e make whatever deductions are
possible, given the data that is available in a description), recognize
and combine multiple descriptions of the same situation, and sort and
merge collections of partial descriptions.

2.3. PRODUCTION SYSTEMS

A production system is the most popular type of expert system
because it is easy to develope, it originates from MYCIN (the most well
known expert system) and it is the type of expert system adopted by the
British Computer Society. It consists of four main elements: the
knowledge base which has the form of production rules; the inference
engine which drives the execution; the working memory (or database)
which keeps track of the status of the problem; and an explanatory
interface which explains the line of reasoning. The architecture of a
production system is shown in Figure 2.

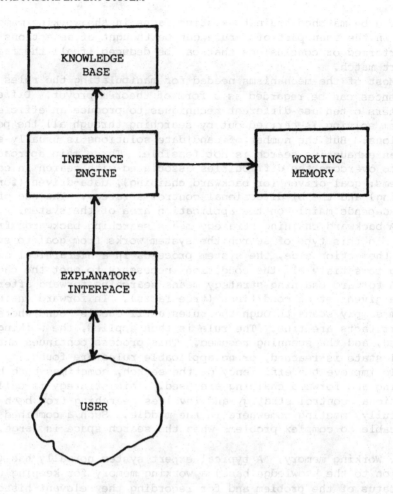

FIGURE 2.   THE STRUCTURE OF A PRODUCTION SYSTEM

2.3.1. Inference engine. In addition to the knowledge base containing
rules, a mechanism is needed for manipulating the rules to form
inferences, to make diagnoses and so forth. In order for a system to
reason, it must be able to infer new facts from what it has been told
already. The rules have the following general form:

    IF   trigger fact 1 is true
            trigger fact 2 is true
                            .
                            .

    THEN   conclusion fact 1 is true
            conclusion fact 2 is true
                            .
                            .

The facts in the if-part of a rule can be thought of as patterns that can be matched against existing facts in the working memory. The facts in the then-part of a rule can be thought of as actions that can be performed or conclusions that can be deduced if all the facts in the if-part match.

Most of the mechanisms needed for manipulating the rules to form inferences can be regarded as a form of theorem prover. Different designers often use different techniques to produce an efficient system. Problem solving is carried out by searching through all the possible solutions. But the number of candidate solutions is usually so great that an exhaustive search is not feasible. Three main approaches are used to overcome the difficulties associated with search in complex problems: goal-driven (or backward chaining), data-driven (forward chaining) and the bi-directional control strategy. The use of one of these depends mainly on the application area of the system.

A backward chaining strategy means searching backwards from the goal. In this type of search the system works from goal to sub-goal. Using the action side, the system proceeds in a hierarhical search trying to satisfy all the conditions necessary to meet the chosen goal.

A forward chaining strategy means searching forward after starting from a given set of conditions (true facts). In forward chaining the system simply scans through the rules until one is found where all the if-part facts are true. The rule is then applied, the working memory updated, and the scanning resumed. This process continues until either a goal state is reached, or no applicable rules are found.

To improve the efficiency of the search, sometimes both backward chaining and forward chaining are used. This strategy is called the bi-directional control strategy and involves searching from both ends and (hopefully) meeting somewhere in the middle. Such a combined search is applicable to complex problems when the search space is large.

2.3.2. Working memory. A typical expert system normally has (in addition to the knowledge base) a working memory for keeping track of the status of the problem and for recording the relevant history of what has been done so far. For example: the facts that are true (given at the beginning of the conversation or proved during the conversation), the facts that proved to be false, the rules that we try to prove etc.

2.4. How to build expert systems

Bonnet [1985] proposes that "constructing an expert system is an informal activity, more of an art than an exact science." The first requirement is that the problem to be solved should suit an expert systems approach. Typical applications to date have tackled interpretation and/or understanding of a complex mass of data, classification, diagnosis (medical and equipment faults), fault finding in equipment design, evaluation of situations and crisis management.

The second requirement is access to an expert or experts. Expertise readily acccessible in books, whilst essential, should not be sufficient otherwise the need for an expert system does not exist. Hence the 'hunches' or 'best-guesses' of experts are required to be encapsulated in some fashion in the system. Since expert opinion is usually given in special or unusual cases (otherwise the opinion would be well known and hence not 'expert'), it is necessary to develope the system in collaboration with the expert in order to encapsulate the knowledge and heuristics used.

Further requirements for building an expert system are to determine the level of information to be incorporated in the system i.e. to include only that expertise that has a sufficiently sound technical basis. This is obviously a matter of judgement. Given the state of the art, building a system in stages or prototyping makes sound practical sense. Staged development of the system avoids dramatic errors in design, and enables the expert to be involved in the improvement stages rather than waiting some time for the 'completed' version.

The final requirement for building an expert system is to evaluate it. This is impossible to achieve in a validation sense, since experts disagree and for a complex problem area, the number of possible combinations of outcomes is too large to test. Testing of known outcomes is obviously essential, but at the end of the day, user acceptance will be based on confidence which is developed over time as the system is successfully used. Hayes-Roth et al [1983] provide an excellent guide to building expert systems.

3. ASPES

3.1. The need for ASPES

As will be further explained in section 5 below, ASPES was developed from a particular expert system application. Many other skeletal expert systems have similiar origins. The disadvantages in general of using skeletal expert systems for an application are manyfold. The old framework may be inappropriate to the new task. The control structure embodied in the inference engine may not sufficiently match the new expert's ways of solving problems. The old rule language may be inappropriate to the new task. Task-specific knowledge may be hidden in the old system in unrecognised ways.

However in spite of these problems, the advantages of a skeletal expert system that overcomes these difficulties are obvious. The development of a new application will be relatively quick. For teaching and research purposes, such a system is potentially invaluable. ASPES has been developed at the LSE with this purpose in mind. However, the expectation is that ASPES will not only be used for teaching and research, but that it will be modified and expanded with its use in research. In order to make this task easier, ASPES is written in Pascal.

The advantages of Pascal as a high level programming language for OR modelling has been discussed by O'Keefe [1984] among others. However, it is not the most obvious choice for A.I. work. Various high level languages have been used to build expert systems (e.g FORTAN, BASIC and Pascal), but most expert systems currently employ PROLOG [Pereira et al 1978] or LISP [McCarthy et al 1962] or some language based on either of them.

Since its invention in 1958 by John McCarthy and others, LISP has been the primary A.I programming language, used by the vast majority of A.I researchers in all subfields. The reasons for this is in part historical: Lisp was established early, several large systems have been

developed to support programming in the language, and all the students
in A.I laboratories (mainly in the U.S.A) learn Lisp, so that it has
become a shared language. The language also continues to be the natural
vehicle for expert system research because there are features of Lisp
that are critically important in expert system programming. For
example: it is a symbol manipulation language; the representation of the
programs themselves are in the same data structure as all the other data
(list structure); it is a recursive language (any program can be defined
in terms of itself); and there are good editing and debugging tools.

The most prominent feature of Lisp is the "property list" which has
proved valuable for constructing specialised forms of knowledge
representation. Simply stated, each "atom" may have "properties"
associated with it. These may be defined by the programmer and provide
a convenient method of representing associations between objects. A
"property" is defined as a "property/value" pair which is linked to an
"atom". Semantic networks and frames are easily implemented in Lisp
using property list structures. The main disadvantage of Lisp is that
the programs are not portable; there are many Lisp versions (with basic
differences between them) and it seems that each computer runs only a
specific version. For a critical review of Lisp see Barr and Feigenbaum
[1982]. Winston and Horn [1981] gives a good introduction to the theory
and the practice of Lisp programming.

In spite of the high usage of Prolog and Lisp, they have
disadvantages for teaching and research purposes. They are not as well
supported as the more commonly used high level programming languages,
they are expensive to purchase if the intended application is a large
and complex task, and new researchers often need to learn the new
language. ASPES attempts to overcome these problems by incorporating
the spirit of Lisp, it's atoms and property lists, in Pascal routines
forming a library or skeletal expert system.

3.2. Using ASPES

Basically, the system consists of 3 components - a database, knowledge
base, and inference engine.

(i) The knowledge base contains knowledge about a particular type
of problem domain expressed in production rules.

(ii) The inference engine (interpreter) controls the system's
activities, deciding which production rule to fire next.

(iii) The database contains information about the specific problem
at hand as well as information created by activation of the production
rules.

Separation of the knowledge base and the inference machine ensures
"portability". Here "portable" is taken to mean that the program is
capable of dealing with many types of problem domains. Many expert
systems available in the market today are designed to deal with only a
specific area of expertise. It is, therefore, important to design a
system that can be easily adapted by others to deal with their
individual problems, thus providing the user with greater flexibility.

Production rules in the knowledge base have the general format of:

      IF   antecedents
      THEN   consequences

The antecedents are strings of characters which can be matched against

the entries in the database. The consequences are conclusions that can
be deduced. Knowledge is stored in a text file written by the user. A
very simple and popular example of such a file is given in Appendix 1.

The file begins with a list of hypotheses to be proved by the
system. Next comes the production rules. Each rule consists of 2
parts,the "identify rule" number and the "production rule", e.g.

        IDENTIFY5
        IF
        ANIMAL EATS MEAT
        THEN
        ANIMAL IS CARNIVORE

The use of text files allows the user to inspect the knowledge base. It
also makes adding, deleting and modification of rules easier.

The interpreter has two functions: it finds the rules which are
enabled and it decides which rule to apply. The control strategy is
goal-driven. The process of proof is backward chaining. A set of
hypothesis is read first, then one by one the inference machine will try
to prove their truth. The system first decides which rules can
establish the goal statement. The antecedents of these rules would
require other rules to be applied. This continues recursively until
there are no more rules. The system then asks the user for the required
information to be entered into the database.

For example (with reference to Appendix 1), in order to prove that
ANIMAL IS ZEBRA, the program has to prove that ANIMAL is UNGULATE and
ANIMAL HAS BLACK STRIPES. ANIMAL IS UNGULATE becomes a new hypothesis
to be proved. To prove that ANIMAL IS UNGULATE, the program has to
prove that ANIMAL IS MAMMAL and ANIMAL HAS HOOFS. ANIMAL IS MAMMAL
becomes a new hypothesis to prove. To prove that ANIMAL IS MAMMAL, it
has to prove that ANIMAL HAS HAIR.   At this point, the program will not
be able to find any other identify rule that has ANIMAL HAS HAIR as the
consequence. When this happens, the system will ask the user the
question whether ANIMAL HAS HAIR is true or not. If the user answers
YES, then the consequence ANIMAL IS MAMMAL becomes true. However, this
does not mean that ANIMAL IS UNGULATE is true. In order to prove this,
the system has to prove that ANIMAL HAS HOOFS. A similar procedure will
be carried out to prove that ANIMAL HAS HOOFS is true and until it is
done, ANIMAL IS UNGULATE is an unknown fact.

The search through the goal tree is thoroughly explored in turn and
the search is exhaustive because all applicable rules are invoked. The
program adopts an "evidence collecting strategy". This means that it
will consider all possibilities every time by collecting all evidence,
both favourable and unfavourable, about a subgoal from the activation of
every applicable rule.

The program has a dictionary which is built during the operation of
the system. It contains all the facts that have been asked and proven.
Therefore the user will not be asked the same question again when the
program tries to prove the next hypothesis.

3.3. Architecture of an ASPES Expert System Program

The ASPES program is composed of 3 parts: initialisation, file reading
and diagnosis. Initialisation involves setting all the necessary Pascal
linked lists to nil. They are HYPOTHESES, RULES, FACTS and ASKED.

(i)   HYPOTHESES is the list used to store the list of hypotheses
to be proved. With reference to Appendix 1, the list HYPOTHESES
consists of :
              ANIMAL IS ALBATROS
              ANIMAL IS PENGUIN
              ANIMAL IS OSTRICH
              ANIMAL IS ZEBRA
              ANIMAL IS GIRAFFE
              ANIMAL IS TIGER
              ANIMAL IS CHEETAH
The system will go from one hypothesis to the next, until one
hypothesis can be proved or when it has exhausted the list.
     (ii)   RULES is the list that contains all the identify rules. The
system will go through the list searching for those that it requires to
prove a hypothesis or subgoal.
     (iii)   FACTS is the list that contains those identify rules already
proven to be true.
     (iv)   ASKED is the list that contains those identify rules already
proven to be untrue.
     After initialisation, the system will read the knowledge base (text
file) requested by the user as his or her particular problem domain.
The system will go through the file, first reading in all the hypotheses
and storing them in individual records of the list HYPOTHESES. After
hypotheses, it will start reading in all the identify rules. The
IF_PART of the record of list RULES contains the antecedents whereas the
THEN-PART of the record contains the consequences.
     After setting up the appropriate knowledge base, the system will
move into DIAGNOSE. This is a procedure that performs the inference
part of the system. The most important component of DIAGNOSE is VERIFY.
     VERIFY is a recursive function that attempts to prove the truth of
a statement until either it succeeds or fails. If the statement is
proved true, VERIFY returns a true value, otherwise it returns a false
value. When VERIFY returns a true value, the system will inform the
user that a particular hypothesis has been proven to be true. If it
returns a false value, the system will switch to the next hypothesis in
the list HYPOTHESES.

4.   EXPERIENCES WITH ASPES

4.1 Teaching

ASPES has been tested on M.Sc. Operational Research and B.Sc. Computing
students with encouraging results. The students are given a dictionary
of the system's routines, a knowledge base, and a basic program
structure. The M.Sc. O.R. student has to write the DIAGNOSE procedure
so that it goes through the list of hypotheses until one has been proved
true or all have been found false. Hence this procedure requires the
repetitive use of the Boolean function VERIFY until it returns the value
true or until all possible hypotheses have been tested. The B.Sc.
Computing specialist student has to write both the DIAGNOSE and VERIFY
routines. The expectation is that the students will produce a program
that operates in a similar fashion to one that is demonstrated during

the preceding lecture. The ability to use ASPES for different purposes for different student specialisms is due to its flexible design.

The knowledge based used by the students represents knowledge about the particular domain of classifying a human being as a male or female child or adult. For obvious reasons this knowledge base is somewhat simple and rather incomplete. The students are invited to extend the knowledge base by modifying existing rules or adding new ones. Since the subject matter allows personal humour to be publicly displayed, the chosen knowledge base has the desirable outcome of arousing keen student interest and participation°

4.2 Experimental Developments

ASPES is simple enough to easily demonstrate how an expert system is built, and how its inference power operates. However, it only performs the basic function of verification and only when it fails will the program inform the user accordingly. In this sense, the program is not at all user friendly. The user will have no idea what path the system has gone through, or how it can or cannot successfully carry out a particular mission. A good expert system should have the ability to explain to the user the process it has gone through when requested.

With this in mind, a number of improvements to ASPES have been attempted. The experimental expert system developed by Ip (1985), a postgraduate student at the LSE, shows that a more user friendly and efficient system than the original program could be developed. The experimental system is called ARTINTS by its author.

ARTINTS was designed as an interactive system that provides a "general" purpose inference machine to deal with a wide variety of problem domains. It includes two programs: ARTINTS ADVISER and ARTINTS TUTOR. It is "general" in the sense that it is written to cope with all types of problem domain provided that the knowledge base is represented in the required format.

4.2.1 The Adviser. ARTINTS ADVISER is used to advise a user on the specific problem domain. The users are assumed to have minimum knowledge of the problem domain and also are not interested in knowing the process of deduction. All they are concerned with is the result. Under these circumstances, it is more important to reduce the time that users have to spend with the system. There are a number of ways of achieving this.

(i) The user could be asked to volunteer some information to the system to enhance the power of deduction by moving the system in the right direction.

(ii) The system could possess the power of automatic logical deduction.

The adoption of goal driven backward chaining has limited ASPES'S ability to allow the users to interrupt and guide the line of reasoning by volunteering information. Therefore the second approach was adopted. A list of opposite facts were built into the knowledge base file.

Whenever a fact is established, its opposite statement will automatically be added into an ASKED list (facts that have been asked and proven not true) at the same time the true fact is added into a FACTS list (facts that have been asked and proven true). For example, if it is proven that HUMAN IS MALE is true, then its explicit opposite HUMAN IS FEMALE will be logically deduced to be untrue. This reduces the amount of time that the expert systems takes to prove that HUMAN IS FEMALE is untrue. The power of logical deduction depends on the amount and accuracy of opposite statements incorporated into the knowledge base.

The storing of the untrue statement in the ASKED list will eliminate the system's need to ask the user any questions leading to the proof that HUMAN IS FEMALE is untrue. When the opposite statement cannot be found from the knowledge base, this facility becomes redundant.

In order to achieve the above, a few modifications to ASPES were necessary. Apart from adding into the knowledge base the required list of opposites, a new Pascal record type called OPPOSITES is used to hold all available opposite facts. During the initialisation stage, it is set to nil. The list of opposite statements is read and added into the list OPPOSITES after the list HYPOTHESES is constructed during the process of file reading.

A lot of care has to be put into the designing of the list of opposite statements. Ambiguity and inaccurate statements can not only confuse the system but may cause a total breakdown of the system itself. The ease of drawing up such a list depends very much on the availability of explicit opposite statements. It also depends on the type of problem domain one is facing. In some complex problem domains, explicit opposites cannot be easily found and therefore the use of ARTINTS ADVISERS as a facility to reduce time is limited.

In general, the number of questions asked can be greatly reduced by using ARTINTS ADVISER. The advantage of ARTINTS ADVISER is that not only is it time saving, but it also reduces the boredom that could occur should every single rule need testing by questions and answers.

4.2.2 The Tutor. ARTINTS TUTOR is a tutoring device. The assumption underlying the tutor is that the user knows something about the problem domain but is unable to make deductions from it. It is assumed that the user wants to know and understand the train of thought adopted by the system. Time in this case is not a crucial factor. The user will not complain if many questions are asked as long as it helps the understanding of the problem at hand.

ARTINTS TUTOR, modified from the ASPES expert system program, has the ability to explain to the user why it is doing what it is doing. When the user is asked to answer a question with "YES" or "NO", the user can, instead of doing either, ask the expert system "WHY" (by inputting "?"). That is, why has it asked that question. The system then displays a series of messages giving the reasons why a particular question was asked. This is achieved by stepping forward through the chain of rules to be verified.

The use of backward chaining has facilitated the adoption of this explanation ability. A hypothesis is first set up to be the goal and all rule identifiers that can be used to prove its truth directly are collected and linked. Then the IF_PART of this list of rules becomes the sub-goal to be proven. This goes on until no more rules can be found, i.e. the sub-goal to be proven is the basic prime statement. Then the user is asked to state "YES" or "NO" to a question. At this

point, the user is allowed to ask the system "WHY". Should this happen,
the system simply displays the records of rules identified on the
current linked list of rules. These show that the reason that the
particular question is asked is because certain intermediate conclusions
have to be proven.

The other facility of ARTINTS TUTOR is the question "HOW". When a
particular statement, be it the sub-goal or the final hypothesis, is
deduced and the user informed, the user is given the opportunity to
either accept the deduced result or ask the sytem "HOW" it has arrived
at the conclusion. When "HOW" is asked, the system will step backward
through the chain of reasoning that led up to this intermediate or final
conclusion showing which rules were used. The system looks up the
current rule list and identifies those rules that have the deduced fact
similar to the THEN_PART. This should be the reason why the system
arrived at the particular conclusion. The user will also be reminded of
the facts he has provided with a positive answer (YES) and those that he
has provided with a negative answer (NO).

The global list that is used throughout the program is WHYS. Since
ARTINTS uses backward chaining, WHYS contains the list of records
visited during the process of backward tracking.

There are many advantages and limitations of the explanation
facility:

(i) Users, particularly those who don't know much about computers,
are impressed with a system that acts in such a human fashion that it
can explain itself when asked to. This can be dangerous as Weizenbaum
(1984) eloquently explains.

(ii) During the process of knowledge acquisition, it is useful to
allow the user (or expert) to query why an apparently stupid question is
asked so that he can get some idea of what has gone wrong (with a view
to putting it right by adding another rule or modifying some old rules).

(iii) During program development and at the point when the
system has made a mistake - by asking an inappropriate question - the
knowledge engineer may wish to know how it managed to get where it is
now.

(iv) It encourages a higher degree of interaction than would be
possible if the user just sat there staring at the screen all the time.

Unfortunately, the explanation power is limited by the fact that
explanation consists of simply showing all the relevant rule
identifiers. It would be more useful to the user if the explanation
could be derived from first principles. For example, why is it that a
human who wears a shirt is a male? (Although the identify rule has
already been explicitly stated that if HUMAN WEARS SHIRTS, HUMAN IS
MALE.) A facility like this would definitely enhance the power of being
a tutor.

4.3 Future Developments.

The work of Ip (1985) described above will be incorporated into ASPES
with a view to maintaining system flexibility for future developments.
The next planned development is to incorporate forward chaining as well
as backward chaining, firstly as an alternative, and then later in
combination under inference control.

5. EXPERT SYSTEMS AND OPERATIONAL RESEARCH

5.1. Computer aided simulation modelling

ASPES was developed as part of the research being undertaken by the
Computer Aided Simulation Modelling (CASM) project at the LSE. The
general aims of CASM are described by Balmer and Paul [1985]. Part of
the research has entailed an examination of the problem formulation
stage of a simulation project. In attempting to provide a computer
based aid to problem formulation, an expert system approach was
initially adopted. A description of the system produced is given by
Doukidis and Paul [1985], along with reasons for its failure. Later
work moved the research into the area of Natural Language Understanding
Systems, which is described by Paul and Doukidis [1985].

Apart from the proposed extensions to ASPES outlined in section 4.3
above, it is expected that other aspects of simulation modelling as a
solution method will lend themselves to an expert systems approach. For
example, the analysis of simulation output and the determination of an
experimental design might be semi or fully automated with an expert
system. In this event, ASPES will provide a useful vehicle for such
research.

5.2. Operational Research

The rapidly growing interest and publicity in expert systems at the
beginning of the 1980s made various professions, with aims similar to
those of expert systems workers, start to investigate them and play an
active role in their development. A leading example is the O.R.
community which has often played a major role in all the phases of
designing a software system - from the feasibility study of introducing
such a system to its implementation.

It can be said that the relationship between expert systems and
O.R. started in the mid 1970s. The two papers published by Tate [1977]
and Goldestein & Roberts [1977] were the first examples of systems which
combined expert systems methods within O.R techniques. Tate's system is
a critical path analysis program and Goldstein's system is a scheduling
program. Although both systems employ mainly A.I. methods (rather than
expert systems methods), they marked the start of a new era. The
beginning of the 1980s, with the growing interest in the U.K on expert
systems resulting from the Alvey Report, raised a couple of important
issues for the O.R. community:
- do major applications for expert systems exist which guarantee
  the validity and durability of the concept?
- is there a role for the O.R. professional in the design and/or
  implementation of expert systems?

This interest brought some active research in the subject with some
theoretical and practical results. In the first category lies the work
by Thorton [1983] and O'Keefe [1985b]. Thorton identifies a natural
role for O.R. in the feasibility study, requirements and design phases
of an expert system project. O'Keefe argues that the liasion of expert
systems and O.R. will produce mutual benefits.

In the second category lies the work by Doukidis and Paul [1985],

Hollocks [1984], Ip [1985], and O'Keefe [1985c]. Hollocks demonstrated
a commercialy available expert system - produced by the O.R department
of British Steel - for use in the diagnosis of a plant's fault(s).
Doukidis and Paul [1985] describe an unsuccesful attempt at using an
experimental expert system to aid simulation model formulation. Ip
reports on a prototype expert system that has been developed to aid in
the process of debugging simulation programs. O'Keefe describes an
expert system (which has been developed by using the ES/P Advisor shell)
for giving advice on experimentation with transaction flow models.

Based on discussions with the participants in the one-day event on
'Expert Systems in Practice' organised by the O.R Society in April 1985,
and on reading the above papers, it can be seen that at present there
are two parallel approaches to expert systems in the O.R. community.
One approach is to buy off-the-self expert systems so that a knowledge
base can be built in. The other approach is an actual attempt to
develop expert systems suitable for O.R purposes.

The first approach is taken due to either a shortage of time or of
the technical know-how to develop a system for the particular purpose.
The focus is on the acquisition and presentation of the knowledge for a
specific application. This approach will obviously provide a quick
solution. However, bearing in mind that the resulting knowledge base
will always be very much constrained by the way the shell is designed,
the solution may only be short term. Furthermore, this approach has the
disadvantage of pretty low portability. The expert system adopted by
the company may not be compatible with the existing hardware used. One
also has to be aware of the fact that the solution in the end may not
even be a good one due to the generality of the inference engine.

The second approach is more difficult but looks more promising.
The process of designing an expert system should be a reiterative
process. That is, once the system and the knowledge base are designed,
they should run together. Feedback from the test runs should be used
for restructuring both the system and the knowledge base. This process
should continue until the system and the knowledge base are refined to a
satisfactory level. The reiterative process would help the O.R. analyst
grasp the concept of the expert system and, through the knowledge
acqusition process, a better understanding of the problem in hand. This
approach will provide a good theoretical and practical background for
O.R's future role in the development of expert systems.

It is this latter approach that ASPES is designed to fulfill for
O.R. researchers at the LSE. The flexible and open design of ASPES,
plus the transparency of the Pascal code it is written in, enables a
quick and iterative development of an expert system. This approach has
proved correct for teaching purposes, where students can quickly see
what is going on and can construct simple expert system models. The
research examples of expert systems applications in simulation described
above are the start of an increasing experimentation with expert systems
in O.R. at the LSE. ASPES and later developments will be one of the
major supports for this work.

APPENDIX 1

```
ANIMAL IS ALBATROS              IDENTIFY7
ANIMAL IS PENGUIN               IF
ANIMAL IS OSTRICH               ANIMAL IS MAMMAL
ANIMAL IS ZEBRA                 ANIMAL HAS HOOFS
ANIMAL IS GIRAFFE               THEN
ANIMAL IS TIGER                 ANIMAL IS UNGULATE
ANIMAL IS CHEETAH
                                IDENTIFY8
IDENTIFY1                       IF
IF                              ANIMAL IS MAMMAL
ANIMAL HAS HAIR                 ANIMAL CHEWS CUD
THEN                            THEN
ANIMAL IS MAMMAL                ANIMAL IS UNGULATE

IDENTIFY2                       IDENTIFY9
IF                              IF
ANIMAL GIVES MILK               ANIMAL IS MAMMAL
THEN                            ANIMAL IS CARNIVORE
ANIMAL IS MAMMAL                ANIMAL HAS TAWNY COLOUR
                                ANIMAL HAS DARK SPOTS
IDENTIFY3                       THEN
IF                              ANIMAL IS CHEETAH
ANIMAL HAS FEATHERS
THEN                            IDENTIFY10
ANIMAL IS BIRD                  IF
                                ANIMAL IS MAMMAL
IDENTIFY4                       ANIMAL IS CARNIVORE
IF                              ANIMAL HAS TAWNY COLOUR
ANIMAL FLIES                    ANIMAL HAS BLACK STRIPES
ANIMAL LAYS EGGS                THEN
THEN                            ANIMAL IS TIGER
ANIMAL IS BIRD
                                IDENTIFY11
IDENTIFY5                       IF
IF                              ANIMAL IS UNGULATE
ANIMAL EATS MEAT                ANIMAL HAS LONG NECK
THEN                            ANIMAL HAS LONG LEGS
ANIMAL IS CARNIVORE             ANIMAL HAS DARK SPOTS
                                THEN
IDENTIFY6                       ANIMAL IS GIRAFFE
IF
ANIMAL HAS POINTED TEETH        IDENTIFY12
ANIMAL HAS CLAWS                IF
ANIMAL HAS FORWARD EYES         ANIMAL IS UNGULATE
THEN                            ANIMAL HAS BLACK STRIPES
ANIMAL IS CARNIVORE             THEN
                                ANIMAL IS ZEBRA
```

```
IDENTIFY13                      IDENTIFY15
IF                              IF
ANIMAL IS BIRD                  ANIMAL IS BIRD
ANIMAL DOES NOT FLY             ANIMAL FLYS WELL
ANIMAL HAS LONG NECK            THEN
ANIMAL HAS LONG LEGS            ANIMAL IS ALBATROS
ANIMAL IS BLACK AND WHITE
THEN
ANIMAL IS OSTRICH

IDENTIFY14
IF
ANIMAL IS BIRD
ANIMAL DOES NOT FLY
ANIMAL SWIMS
ANIMAL IS BLACK AND WHITE
THEN
ANIMAL IS PENGUIN
```

REFERENCES

D. W. BALMER and R. J. PAUL (1985), 'CASM - The Right Environment for
    Simulation', paper given at the O. R. Society Annual Conference,
    Durham, England, 10-13 September
A. BARR and E. A. FEIGENBAUM (1981), The Handbook of Artificial
    Intelligence, Volume 1, Pitman.
A. BARR and E. A. FEIGENBAUM (1982), The Handbook of Artificial
    Intelligence, Volume 2, Pitman.
A. BASDEN (1983), 'On the application of expert systems', International
    Journal Man-Machine Studies, 19, 461-477.
A. BONNET (1985), Artificial Intelligence : Promise and Performance,
    Prentice-Hall International
M. A. BRAMER (1982), 'A survey and critical review of expert systems
    research', in Introductory Readings in Expert Systems (D. Michie
    Ed), pp 3-29, Gordon and Breach Science Publishers.
G. I. DOUKIDIS and R. J. PAUL (1985), 'Research into expert systems to
    aid simulation model formulation', J. Opl. Res. Soc, 36, 319-325.
EXPERTECH (1985), Xi User Manual, Expertech, Slough,
    England.
EXPERT SYSTEMS INTERNATIONAL (1985), ES/P Advisor Manual, Expert Systems
    International, Oxford, England.
E. I. FEIGENBAUM (1979), 'Themes and case studies in Knowledge
    Engineering', in Expert Systems in the Micro-Electronic Age (D.
    Michie Ed), pp 3-25, Edinburgh University Press, Edinburgh,
    Scotland.
I. P. GOLDESTEIN and R. B. ROBERTS (1977), 'Generating Project Networks'
    in the Proceedings of the Fifth International Joint Conference on
    Artificial Intelligence, M.I.T, 888-893.
F. HAYES-ROTH (1981), 'AI the new wave. A technical tutorial for R & D
    Management', in Proceedings AIAA Annual Meeting.

F. HAYES-ROTH, D. A. WATERMAN and D. B. LENAT (Eds.) (1983), Building
    Expert Systems, Addison-Wesley

B. HOLLOCKS (1984), 'Expert Systems on Micros', paper presented at the
    O.R. Microcomputing Study Group meeting, The London School of
    Economics, London, February 1984.

B. W. F. IP (1985), Expert Systems and Operational Research: ARTINTS,
    M.Sc O.R project, The London School of Economics, London.

P. LEITH (1983), 'Hierarhically Structured Production Rules', Computer
    Journal, 26, No 1, 1-5.

J. McCARTHY, P. W. ABRAHAMS, D. J. EDWARDS, T. P. HART and M. I. LEVIN
    (1962), LISP 1.5 programmer's manual, MIT Press, Cambridge, Mass.

D. MICHIE (1980), 'Expert Systems', The Computer Journal, 23, No 4,
    369-376.

H. P. NII and N. AIELLO (1979), 'AGE (Attempt to Generalize): A
    knowledge-based program for building knowledge-based programs',
    in the Proceedings of the International Joint Conference on
    Artificial Intelligence, pp 645-655.

R. M. O'KEEFE (1984), 'Programming Languages, Microcomputers and O.R.',
    J. Opl. Res. Soc., 35, 617-627.

R. M. O'KEEFE, V. BELTON and T. BALL (1985a), 'Getting Into Expert
    Systems', paper presented at the O. R. Society Annual Conference,
    Durham, England, 10-13 September

R. M. O'KEEFE (1985b), 'Expert Systems and Operational Research- Mutual
    Benefits', J. Opl. Res. Soc., 36, 125-130.

R.M. O'KEEFE (1985c), 'Simulation and Expert Systems - A taxonomy and
    some examples'; paper presented at the O. R. Society Annual
    Conference, Durham, England, 10-13 September

R. J. PAUL and G. I. DOUKIDIS (1985), 'Further Developments in the use
    of Artificial Intelligence Techniques which Formulate Simulation
    Problems', paper presented at the O. R. Society Annual Conference,
    Durham, England, 10-13 September

L. M. PEREIRA, F. PEREIRA and D. H. D. WARREN (1978), User's Guide to
    DEC system - 10 Prolog, Dept of Artificial Intelligence, University
    of Edinburgh.

M. STEFIC, J. AIKINS, R. BALZER, J. BENOIT, L. BIRNBAUM, F. HAYES-ROTH
    and E. SACEROTI (1982), 'The organization of Expert Systems: A
    Tutorial', Artificial Intelligence 18, 135-173.

A. TATE (1977), 'Generating Project Networks', in Proceedings of the
    Fifth International Joint Conference on Artificial Intelligence,
    MIT, 257-263.

P. THORTON (1983), 'Expert systems and O.R meeting the challenge', paper
    given at the O.R Society meeting on Expert Systems, London Tara
    Hotel, London, June 1983.

W. VAN-MELLE (1979), 'A domain-independent production rule system for
    consultation programs', in the Proceedings of the Joint
    International Conference on Artificial Intelligence, 923-925

S. WEISS and C. KULIKOWSKI (1979), 'EXPERT: a system for developing
    consultation program', in the Proceedings of the Joint
    International Conference on Artificial Intelligence, 942-947.

J. WEIZENBAUM (1984), Computer Power and Human Reason : from Judgement
    to Calculation, Penguin

P. H. WINSTON and B. K. P. HORN (1981), LISP, Addison-Wesley.

DECIDEX, A MULTI-EXPERT SYSTEM FOR STRATEGIC DECISIONS

P. Lévine	J.Ch. Maillard	J.Ch. Pomerol
Dept. Informatique	Université de	Université
E.N.A.	Picardie	P. et M. Curie
13, rue de l'Université	48, rue Raspail	4, Place Jussieu
75007 PARIS	02100 SAINT-QUENTIN	75005 PARIS
FRANCE	FRANCE	FRANCE

ABSTRACT. DECIDEX is an intelligent decision support system, which is intended to help the decision maker in strategic planning and strategic decision making. The main feature of this system is a scenario developer which is connected to various expert systems.

1. STRATEGIC PLANNING AND STRATEGIC DECISIONS

1.1. Main Features

In this paper, we are mainly concerned with the problem of managerial decisions. At every level in the management of the firm or more generally, in the management of any complex task, the decision makers (D.M.) are obliged to choose between many possible actions, according to the state of the environment.

Decision making generally begins with an analysing and planning phase. During this analysing process it often appears that the decision is actually divided in many subdecisions which will take place at various dates according to many possible schedules. For each of these subdecisions the D.M. gathers facts and estimations so that he is confronted to numerous data, mainly expectations, it is the first aspect of strategic planning. These data are characterized by their uncertainty and incompleteness.

Uncertainty refers to probabilistic events which may occur with a known probability. It also refers to non-probabilistic situations, for instance the possible occurrence of a political revolution in a given country. Generally the decision makers or experts have some a priori ideas (not probabilities) about these possible outcomes. So we must cope with qualitative information about the future events.

The uncertainty also comes from the reactions of the other actors. For example, in business management the results of your own actions heavily depend on the responses of your competitors, customers and workers. Every possible reaction of the other actors must

247

H. G. Sol et al. (eds.), Expert Systems and Artificial Intelligence in Decision Support Systems, 247–255.

be evaluated, so that you are obliged to develop several different scenarios or decision trees (see e.g. [1] and [3]). Moreover the decision maker is absolutely unable to give realistic probabilities to most of the events that occurs in his decision tree. So we are confronted to qualitative judgments or evaluations. In order to be acceptable by the user, a practical system must capture these qualitative information. (see e.g. [2] and [4]).

The second characteristic of strategic planning is complexity.

Every important step in the decision process requests a very large amount of information in various fields.

The D.M. needs technical, organizational, psychological, sociological and political informations. The first component of this complexity is therefore that the relevant information is scattered in various data bases or librairies. The second is the hugeness of the data bases which are relevant for the analysis of the situation. For example, there exist many historical data about some events or decisions which occured and were in some sense close to your present problem. The question is to know either where these informations are available or who is able to manage them.

The third point is a consequence of the two previous ones. Complex, uncertain and incomplete environments require appropriate expertises. So high level planning is a domain where the knowledge of several experts is necessary in order to obtain pertinent expertises in each of the concerned fields.

Expert knowledge outside of the firm is useful but also the knowledge of the different actors within the firm who are concerned with the project. Thus strategic planning has to be regarded as a multi-expert cooperative and interactive process (see [6]).

As an example of a complex task as described above, we will consider the case of the entrepreneurial decision of the introduction on a market of a new product or service.

1.2. The functions of a realistic system

To manage the multiple occurences of the various subdecisions, we can agree that the basis of the system is the scenario (or a decision tree) developer

The first purpose of this scenario developer is to allow the easy preparation and retrieval of the files. Then the scenario developer permits an interactive building of the decision tree. It means that the D.M. can easily explore different paths, he also can easily enter his qualitative informations about the different nodes of the tree. The D.M. can, at every step, modify the tree. According to his qualitative and intuitive informations the D.M. estimates the plausibility of the different paths in the tree. The more plausible ones are firstly developed, but all the plausible paths are stored and should be developed if the current path appears to be unusable. Some evaluations of the D.M. should need an expert advice, so the expert modules may be called at every decisive step.

The reader is refered to [5] for further developments on effective interactive decision support systems.

When the decision is made, the scenario tree as it results from the first phase is still useful to control the realization of the project, to react quickly to any change in the state of the world, to eventually replan some subprocesses.

So at the end of this process it is useful to keep a trace of the planning assumptions and of the expertises confronted with the effective results. When the consequences of the decision are completely known, it is the moment to make an "a posteriori" analysis and to improve the system, to understand the mistakes (if any) and make profitable the firm and manager experiences for future decisions.

2. THE ARCHITECTURE OF THE SYSTEM

The organization of the system is displayed on the figure 1.

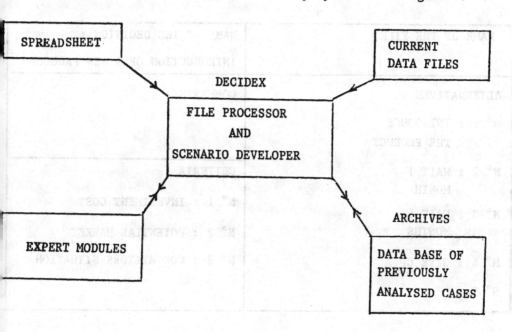

FIGURE 1. DECIDEX ARCHITECTURE

The heart of the system is the file processor and scenario generator named DECIDEX. This module gathers the data from different files about decisions and events. It progressively and interactively aids the D.M. to build scenarios. Moreover it organizes the expert module consultation.

The ARCHIVES data base contain the experience that has been accumulated from the previously completed cases.

A spreadsheet is connected to DECIDEX in order to make easier the intermediate calculations of the user, for instance the calculation of a ratio which has not been already calculated.

Let us describe more accurately the different modules.

3. DECIDEX

The first step consists of identifying the decisions and the events which are relevant for achieving your task.

A decision is a choice of the decision maker at a certain step of the process. You have to choose between certain known alternatives. This choice is made according to some criteria. So, a decision record appears on the screen as shown on figure 2.

NAME OF THE FILE	NAME OF THE DECISION :
	INTRODUCTION OF A NEW PRODUCT

ALTERNATIVES :
 	
 N° 1 : INTRODUCE
       THE PRODUCT
 	
 N° 2 : WAIT 1
       MONTH
 	
 N° 3 : WAIT 6
       MONTHS
 	
 N° 4 : GIVE UP
 	
 N° 5 :
	COMMENTS :

	CRITERIA N° 1 : INVESTMENT COST N° 2 : POTENTIAL MARKET N° 3 : COMPETITORS SITUATION

FIGURE 2. THE DECISION "INTRODUCTION OF A NEW PRODUCT"

An event is a situation which results of the surrounding world such as a reaction of a competitor, a sale or a demand state (growing decreasing, high, low), a political change and so on.

The screen for an event record is displayed figure 3

NAME OF THE FILE	NAME OF THE EVENT : DEMAND GROWTH
POSSIBLE VALUES : N° 1 : HIGH N° 2 : MODERATE N° 3 : LOW N° 4 : UNCERTAIN N° 5 :	COMMENTS :

FIGURE 3. THE SCREEN FOR THE EVENT "DEMAND GROWTH"

Each event takes different values according to the state of the world and to the possible responses of the other actors. For example, the demand growth may be "low" "moderate", "high" or "uncertain".

All the usual facilities of word processors are provided by DECIDEX for modifying, updating, deleting the decision and event records. These records are connected to a data base named "ARCHIVES" in which is stored the whole story about the decisions or events ; it contains the numerous and detailed information and comments that are only displayed on request. This data base permits an interactive developing by several users, in different divisions of the firm, who share the same files, but follow the fixed syntax of the base and refer to the same comments.

The second task of DECIDEX is to provide an aid for generating scenarios. Each scenario is a sequence of decisions and events.

The scenario begins with the first decision one wants to test, then it continues with events (such that the reactions of competitors, customers) and afterward, with other decisions and events. For instance the D.M. study the introduction of a new product. For this introductory decision he has four alternatives to consider : introduce the product, wait one month, wait 6 months, do not introduce the product (fig. 2). The D.M. chooses the alternative that he prefers, for example "introduce the product". Then the system asks him an evaluation of the alternatives according to the scale. (+,0,-). The value + means that the decision maker feels that it is a good decision, - a bad ones, and 0 that it is an uncertain decision. Afterward the event to consider is for example "demand growth" (fig. 3). The decision maker gives to this event its more probable value. Assume that it is "demand growth" = "high". Then once more the D.M. has to say by +, -, or 0 if he feels that it is a good, bad or uncertain situation.

What are the important features of this scenario developer ? The first point is that DECIDEX keeps the values of every decisions and events and it is able, when the current path arrives to a bad situation (which means only with - values), to propose alternative paths with

pending values + or O. From the root of the scenario tree to the
current node DECIDEX has is memory all the partial promising paths and
of course the already fully developed scenarios.

As a consequence, it allows the development of scenarios by the
same person at various dates or by different people.

The second point is not forgetting any decision or event. It is
done by means of rules. In your experience of D.M. you have already
noticed that some decisions or the consequences of some events have
to be chained following a given sequence. DECIDEX allows you to keep
this experience by encoding it in a rule. Let us give such a rule :

Rule N° 3
If demand growth is on the current path, and demand growth is
different from high, and long term marketing plan has not been yet
considered.
Then consider long term marketing plan.

Before developing a new node on the path the system tests
whether any rule applies and, if any, displays the conclusions. So
the D.M. experience is saved and the possibility of forgetting a
decision or an event is avoided. The path N° 7 is shown on figure 4
with the conclusion of the rule N° 3.

THE RULE N° 3 PROPOSE	PATH N° 7
EVENT : LONG TERM MARKETING PLAN	BEGINNING CHOICE : INTRODUCE THE NEW PRODUCT + COMPETITION : UNCERTAIN O DEMAND GROWTH : LOW O

FIGURE 4. APPLYING THE RULE N° 3

Thus the whole story of your project with the chosen decisions,
the neglected scenarios which at every moment, before the decision,
may be pursued, is recorded. When the decision is made and the task
is completed, it is possible to analyse why the decision was or was
not successful and to increase if necessary the number of the rules
and, by the way, the skill of the expert modules.

4.   EXPERT MODULES

At every important point, mainly for the critical events the D.M. can make a misevaluation. For instance, the D.M. may think that demand growth will be high. A mistake on this particular point may have catastrophic consequences. In the introduction of new products some other capital points are, for instance, competition, venture management, contractor behavior and distribution.

In order to examine these important points, DECIDEX is connected with expert systems. The task of each of these expert modules is to contradict the D.M.'s valuation. They are goal-directed, which means that starting from the negation of the decision maker's point of view and applying their rules, they try to prove that this negation is true contradicting the D.M.'s assertion. Besides the rules the information of the expert system comes from the scenario or is improved by the D.M.'s answers via a dialogue interface. When the expert system does not succeed in contradicting the D.M., it does not prove that he is right, it only proves that his valuation does not contradict the experience of the expert. On the other hand, when the expert system successfully contradicts the D.M., it is a strong signal which should incite him to a further reflexion. Perhaps the D.M. has some information which was not considered by the rules. Is this information reliable ? Perhaps some rules are wrong, but more often the reason of the disagreement lies in the D.M.'s willfulness to arrive at some desirable issue.

It must be stressed that the "computer advice" which is neutral, is frequently more easily accepted, than a contradictory advice of a collaborator. Moreover the expert system has the power to show its entire reasonning chain, thus it is easy to find the exact point, or assumption, where the user does not agree with the system. When the disagreement point is identified, the user is able to forward some further examination and to reduce, if possible, the uncertainty.

5.   THE DATA BASE "ARCHIVES"

The last but not least module is the "ARCHIVES" data base. It is a relational data base which records the story of the previous experiences of the firm in the field. As these stories are structured by DECIDEX, it allows an easy retrieval of the actors, decisions and events. So this data base can answer the following queries :
- In which project the firm X intervenes as a contractor ?
- List the successfully completed projects. Give the followed strategy.
- What decisions were taken after this event ?
- Why does this decision was chosen ?

It is a worthwhile task to conceive an "a posteriori analysis program" in order to analyse the past decisions and their results according to the events that really occurred. This program is able to compare your decision tree, the valuations you have given when studying the problem, and the results as they appear at the end of the realization of the project. At each divergent point, you can enter your comments and your a posteriori explanations.

This "a posteriori program", interactively help you to answer the questions such as :
- Why this project does not succeed ?
- Where are the wrong values which explain the failure of this scenario ?

The responses to the above question are recorded in the "ARCHIVES" data base. Then when we develop a scenario having some analogies with an already stored story, it is easy to refer to the past scenario tree and to keep in mind the success or failure that happened.

We do insist on the fact that "ARCHIVES" is not intended to induce the D.M. to adopt some standard strategy, but at the opposite, "ARCHIVES" keeps in its memory the whole D.M.'s experience and tends to make him remember the complexity of the possible situations and the variety of the practicable responses.

6. CONCLUSION

We have already tested the main features of this system, i.e. DECIDEX and the expert modules derived from the expert system developer ARGUMENT, in the field of the introduction of new services or products.

The four following expert modules are completed :
- Demand forecast
- Contractors behavior
- Competition analysis
- Distribution

This system, which is designed to be used by high level managers and planners, as well as by people whose job is to prepare decisions, has already given some fruitful results, and has proven some of the qualities that were expected.

The interactivity is provided by the interfaces at different levels :

a) The file processor of DECIDEX gives a framework which allows that several divisions or persons may contribute to project planning.

b) Various people may suggest some scenarios thanks to the developer. However the rules make them respect the coherence of the project.

c) The interactivity with the manager is provided by the dialogue with the expert modules.

The uncertain, incomplete and qualitative informations are managed by the expert systems. Moreover the qualitative valuation method adopted by DECIDEX for the scenario evaluation fits with the intuition and the partial information of the manager.

The multi-expert architecture of the system captures the complexity and the multidisciplinarity of any decision process. It also allows to progressively increase the system knowledge and it ensures its modularity.

Thus we think that this decision support system is realistic and reliable. Moreover, its learning components should increase the manager experience and the firm competitiveness by avoiding hazardous unfounded strategies.

7. REFERENCES

[1] A. LEAL and J. PEARL, 'An interactive program for conversational elicitation of decision structures' I.E.E.E. Trans. Systems Man and Cybernetics 5, 1977, p. 368-376.

[2] J. PEARL, A. LEAL and J. SALEH, 'GODDESS : a goal-directed decision structuring system' I.E.E.E. Trans. Pattern Analysis and Machine Intelligence 3, 1982, p. 250-262.

[3] J. RAVIN and M. SCHATZOFF, 'An interactive graphics system for analysis and business decisions', I.B.M. Systems Journal 3, 1973 p. 238-256.

[4] R. SELTEN, 'The scenario bundle method' Research Conference on strategic decision analysis focusing on the Persian Gulf, 1977.

[5] R.H. SPRAGUE Jr and E.D. CARLSON, Building effective decision support systems, Prentice-Hall, Englewood Cliffs, 1982.

[6] N.S. SRIDHARAN and J.L. BRESINA, 'Knowledge structures for planning in realistic domains', Computer and Mathematics with applications 11, 1985, p. 457-480.

A KNOWLEDGE BASED APPROACH TO BUSINESS PLANNING

Paolo Gallo and Rosa Massa-Rolandino
Artificial Intelligence Laboratory, CSI-Piemonte
C.so Unione Sovietica, 216 - 10134 TORINO (ITALY)

Franco Canepa
Aeritalia-SAIPA G.V.C. (Combat Aircraft Group)
C.so Marche, 41 - 10148 TORINO (ITALY)

Francesco Borazzo
Istituto di Matematica Finanziaria, Università di Torino
Via Assarotti, 3 - 10122 TORINO (ITALY)

ABSTRACT. Business planning and evaluation is one of the management
activities in which man is flooded by data and information.
Computers can help to handle them, and crucial is the role of knowledge
to manage the whole decision process that allows an efficient decision
making based on searching for effective "real time" solutions.
A knowledge based system, integrated with data bases, tools and models to
solve specific structured subtasks can raise the level of management
activities. Some critical conditions for the correct and effective design
and development of expert systems are highlighted.
In this paper, an updated summary of our experience about knowledge
acquisition is presented, involving three main phases, problem
identification, conceptualization and structurization.
A short example shows the interweaving between the model performances and
the knowledge manipulating it.

1. BUSINESS PLANNING AND EVALUATION

Business planning is here intended as the continuous activity aimed at
keeping the Company alive and growing, changing its product/market mix
through the environment evolution.

Possible examples of these activities are monitoring of the existing
portfolio and selecting new business, both based on the evaluation of
possible future situations for the company.

257

H. G. Sol et al. (eds.), Expert Systems and Artificial Intelligence in Decision Support Systems, 257–270.
© 1987 by D. Reidel Publishing Company.

The class of problems evoked are respectively the control towards strategic objectives and the choice among alternative actions.

Business planning and evaluation is a task performed within the company by human experts of planning, budgeting and financial analysis areas, working in the midst between the assistance and the participation within the decision-making process. The task of these experts is fed by data and information coming from the whole management environment, both internal and external, and feeds the management itself with data, information, forecasts, evaluations and reports that strongly affect the final decision.

The analysis of ill-structured problems involves the whole set of variables related to the company's behaviour and it requires handling and reasoning using huge and highly differenciated amounts of data and information.

The temporal correlation between (and inside) different sets of planned events may become a critical item.

The most extended way of communication is usually the accounting formalism, the only one that is familiar to the management, regardless of nationality or type of business, which allows a critical comparison among different roles and functions.

We can assume that the above mentioned process is supported by some sort of simulation model of the company's behavior.

In the current practice, the most diffused approach is developed through a specific sequence of logical steps. The first phase includes:

1) collection of data and information

2) their critical evaluation

3) inferring missing information

4) the final evaluation of the full set of data and information (in terms of coherence, relationships etc.)

The purpose of this phase is to make available a "current model data base" about the current problem, keeping in mind that it is the minimum reasonable amount and quality of information that runs "some sort of model" mentioned before.

The second phase deals with the processing of data and information handled by simulation models. During this process a large amount of reasoning is spent on intermediated results; they help the expert to be conscious about final results. Strictly interwoven with this step is the last reasoning phase, dealing with the analysis and the interpretation of the final results in order to prepare meaningful reports on relevant facts and variables to be submitted to the management.

2. THE CRUCIAL ROLE OF KNOWLEDGE

It looks as though that available tools and techniques are becoming
increasingly less suitable in order to face more and more complex and
risky decisions, characterized by uncertainty and need for effective
"real time" solutions.
While the knowledge used to solve structured problems can be embedded in
deterministic models and computationally processed, a totally different
matter is posed by the knowledge that is employed to solve unstructured
problems.

As complex unstructured problem solving highly depends on human
uncoded knowledge, it seems logic to pick up the part of this knowledge
dealing with the resolution of less structured aspects of the main
problem, and treat it separately. There are different kinds of knowledge
involved:

1) knowledge to collect data and information (what, where from, at
   what level of detail) testing their coherence and evaluating
   their reliability
2) knowledge dealing with the correct and effective use of
   calculation models which can be evoked to solve some special
   problems arising
3) knowledge to interpret results, to reason about them, to guide
   the "back-tracking" towards relevant causes focusing the
   management attention

and, in terms of personal strategy and expertise:

4) an overall "strategic" knowledge to guide management activities
   through the phases of intelligence, design and choice
5) a specific "tactical" knowledge to face and manage every single
   subproblem

An expert system embodying and managing these kinds of knowledge could
strongly help the manager through the whole decision-making process,
leaving him time for more creative activities of reasoning and permitting
the management to work at a higher level.

3. HOW CAN AN EXPERT SYSTEM MANAGE PROBLEM

The main goal of an Expert Sustem is to achieve, in dealing with
unstructured problems, the same performance levels exploited by human
experts.

However, computers will never be final decision-makers, but they
will be able to play the role of intelligent and expert advisors, capable
of increasing and improving, quantitatively and qualitatively, the
effectiveness of management activities.

Expert systems perform reasoning to solve problems by generating candidate resolutions and evaluating them /5/6/. One of the most interesting features of an expert system is the possibility of providing the user with a complete explanation of these candidate solutions, not only in the form of a "trace" of logical steps, but also in terms of general representations of the specific decision-making process in which the user can recognize his own behaviour /7/.

3.1. Interfacing the Expert System with Data Bases, Tools and Models

The integration of an Expert System with data bases, tools and models, grants the power and the effectiveness of the expert system to increase considerably.

3.1.1. <u>Data bases</u>. The availability of large data bases, inside and outside the company, using data base management systems (DBMS), has a great importance because it provides the expert system direct access to the information associated to its current knowledge level, leaving man free from "data flooding".

Data and information are usually collected and organized within a company according to a hierarchical structure having at the bottom the large amount of data generated by the detailed company transactions and at the top the small set of data contained into the financial statements, and often further concentrated into relevant data only (fig. 1).

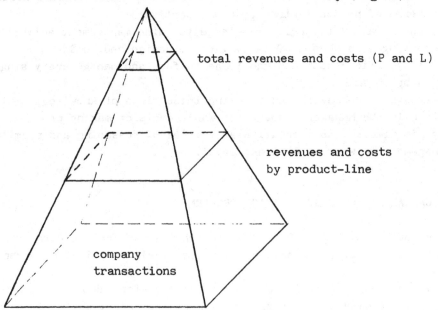

Figure 1. Possible data aggregation levels

Nobody can handle the huge amount of detailed information: for everybody it is relatively easy to generate aggregated data sets simply by following common schemata, for example the chart of accounts or the hierarchical line from the single product, through the product line, up to the business unit.

The same capabilities can be given to an expert system, which is able to handle information much more quickly and efficiently than a human being.

A set of rules can drive the system through the data structure so that the level of the data set used to solve a specific subproblem, can be tailored to the current case, as well as human experts commonly do.

3.1.2. <u>Tools and Models</u>. In our approach, tools and models are whatever is able to process and solve structured subproblems, such as for example accounting models, tools and models employing O.R. techniques, tools for time series forecasting, simulation models etc.

These tools and models can have different characteristics and tasks, and act at different conceptual levels.

The topic that joins them is that of its capability of behaving as a "specialist" in the solution of a specific structured subtask.

The expert system activates each one of these "specialists" whenever the solution of a related subproblem is requested, therefore involving data, information and models which that particular analysis requests.

It is obvious that just as humans access to, and interact with these "specialists", a knowledge-based system needs to speak to each of the "specialists" in there own appropriate language /5/, that is to say that knowledge includes the capability of correct interfacing, effective using and interacting with each one of them.

3.2. Critical conditions

Two key conditions for the acceptability and the effective use of the expert system within the company organization are the following:
1) The end user must rely on the capabilities offered by the expert system
2) The expert system must have the ability to interweave and integrate itself in the specific company organization.
Concerning the first point, it is highly desirable that the human experts fully rely on the expert system, being sure that the latter follows the same reasoning flow they are familiar with. So, while logical and conceptual moments of reasoning should be the same for both of them, the structural and running modularity becomes a critical factor to perform this task.

The use of formalisms by which the company economics are usually represented is a consistent aid to face the problem.

Software interfacing the user with the Expert System plays an important role provided it is able to show the parallelism between the two reasoning flows.

A great help in this direction is given by powerful explanation and justification qualities confered to the Expert System.

Seeing that the system is based on knowledge, the involvement of domain experts from the very beginning is a crucial condition for the correct design.

The second point is strictly connected with the capabilities of the expert systems to collect and aggregate data from large data bases and traditional existing packages, and to use them with enough interdisciplinary knowledge to be accepted by the company functions which are involved.

4. KNOWLEDGE ACQUISITION: OUR EXPERIENCE

One of the major problems in designing and developing an expert system is the method through which knowledge from experts can be acquired.

Our approach consisted in organizing the knowledge according to the use that the expert makes of it in his reasoning, keeping the phase of acquisition separated from that of the system's implementation.

The task for knowledge engineers is to bridge the gap between verbal data from experts and the actual implementation of a system /11/.

The methodology used for knowledge acquisition involves three main phases: problem identification, conceptualization and structurization.

4.1. Problem Identification

The first phase includes the selection and acquisition of an expert, as well as knowledge sources and resources, and a clear definition of the problem.

This was performed by a series of interviews and discussions with domain experts.

In order to capture knowledge about the reasoning steps, relations and strategies, a set of criteria for the qualitative evaluation of new business has been assembled, investigated and tested.

The comprehension of high level relations among the different topics involved in the qualitative evaluation of a new opportunity gave us the possibility to observe more carefully those data which were directly or indirectly involved in the analysis. The use of thinking and reasoning about data in knowledge acquisition is crucial, as they provide the most informative window to expertise in action.

It has been proved by psychology of problem solving that the analysis of thinking about data is feasible when an initial model of the task is used as an interpretative framework /12/ taking in consideration what has previously been said, to knowledge engineers.

4.2. Conceptualization

The second task is articulated in the following points:

1) an analysis of the static domain knowledge starting with the collection of a lexicon ending with concepts structured in hierarchies
2) analysis of functions, environment and potential users of the expertise to obtain a definition of the operational characteristics of the prospective system. The functional analysis defines the procedures by which the expertise can be applied
3) analysis of expertise in action and the way problems are solved. This initial model gets refined and modified into a detailed structure of knowledge objects, knowledge sources and strategies. The final conceptual structure of expert reasoning represents the basic behaviour of the prospective system.
    In the conceptual structure the descriptive knowledge and the actions performed become integrated.
    These tasks have been performed by spotting the logical moments of the most common experts approach, reasoning and work, from the first product/market scanning to the company's new configuration, through the first screening as a differential analysis, the selection of alternatives and the overall analysis, including the matching with quality and quantity of available or required resources.
    Clarification of terms used in a technical way and description of any additional organizational mechanism constitutes the structural expertise about the domain.
    A lot of this expertise lies in the basic strategies and justifications the expert adduces while performing the task.

4.3. Structurization

There is a parallel between the behaviour of an Expert System and that of a human expert, in terms of justifications and evaluations.
This can be made explicit using the following approaches during the phase of knowledge structurization:

1) top-down refinement

   2) least-commitment principle
   3) strategies concerning knowledge control and use.

4.3.1. <u>Top-down refinement</u>. The approach named top-down refinement
configures an abstract representation to fit each instantation of the
problem class /13/.
   The most important aspects should reasonably be:
   1) abstractions for each problem are composed by terms to fit the
      knowledge structure with the problem structure
   2) during the problem-solving process these concepts represent
      partial solution that are combined, evaluated and reshaped
   3) the concepts are defined at predetermined abstraction levels
   4) the problem solution proceeds top-down looking in breadth before
      and leaving the reasoning to be driven by evidence
   5) the problem's solution is completed at one level before moving
      down to the next more specific level
   6) within each level, subproblems are solved in a problem -
      independent order.
      (this creates a partial ordering on the intermediate abstract
      states).

4.3.3. <u>Least-commitment principle</u>. As one of the major difficulties with
top-down refinement is the lack of feedback from the problem solving
process, it becomes important to integrate the treatment of abstraction
deepening levels with a mechanism for guiding the reasoning process
through one of the least-commitment principle.
   Its basic idea is that decisions must not be arbitrarily or
prematurely taken.
   This makes it necessary for the system as well as the human expert
to have:
      - the ability to know when there is enough information to make a
        decision about the problem that is currently being exploited
      - the ability to suspend problem-solving activity on a subproblem
        when the information is not available
      - the ability to move among subproblems, restoring work as
        information becomes available
      - the ability to combine information from different subproblems.
The least-commitment principle coordinates decision making with the
reliability of information and moves the focus of problem-solving
activity among the permitted subgoals.

4.3.3. <u>Strategies concerning knowledge control and use</u>. The ability to
orient the reasoning flows consists in making the different reasoning
models, inherent to knowledge, explicit.

A goal defines a strategy agenda which is considered correct only at a certain moment of the reasoning chain: when the strategy accomplishement gives rise to facts which deny its validity (from that moment onwards), this causes the strategy to be rejected and replaced by one considered better for that case.

4.4. An example

We now see an example (figg. 2,3,4) useful to highlight the generality of the approach for the need to move through different knowledge levels.

Let's suppose that at a certain point of the expert system work, an analysis of the sales report is required. The modeling scheme used is the same regardless it is a budget/actual report (control mode) or a "run to run" comparison (simulation mode). Even though the modeling scheme is the same, the deduction mode can be very different, because results and the whole situation are interpreted accordingly to the two different standpoints.

The typical (restricted) content of a sales report is shown in table 1.

TABLE 1

Five years plan and Sales Report at Top level.

TOTAL SALES	SITUATION 1		SITUATION 2		TOTAL VARIANCE	
YEARS	Sales	MKT-Share	Sales	MKT-Share	Sales	MKT-Share
ALL	2000	=	1800	=	200	=
1	300	5.0	300	4.0	=	1.0
2	350	5.0	300	3.8	50	1.2
3	400	5.5	350	3.0	50	2.5
4	450	6.0	400	3.0	50	2.0
5	500	6.0	450	4.0	50	2.0

Comparing two situations that may be interpreted as a budget vs/ actual report for the same accounting period or as two different runs of a simulation for a policy choice, the Expert System can easily infer that sales are decreasing and that the company is loosing market share (confirmation stage). This inference can be used as a "trigger" to motivate and evaluate the reasons at a more detailed level, accordinghly to the least-commitment principle:

how is the market going?
what product is responsible?
why?
where?

A chain of processes will be evoked to pinpoint and focus the critical and relevant moments of the described situation.

```
 TOP LEVEL SALES
┌─────────────────────────────────────────────────────────────┐
│  CONFIRMATION                                                 │
│  ┌────────────────────────────────────────────────────────┐  │
│  │  CONTROL STRATEGIES                                     │  │
│  │  ┌──────────────────────────────────────────────────┐  │  │
│  │  │  Trigger one of the following sequence of rules  │  │  │
│  │  │                                                  │  │  │
│  │  │  1. if total sales variance is negative and > x% │  │  │
│  │  │     then deduce that:                            │  │  │
│  │  │          total sales are decreasing              │  │  │
│  │  │          market share is also decreasing         │  │  │
│  │  │                                                  │  │  │
│  │  │     SUBGOALS:                                    │  │  │
│  │  │       ┌─────────────────────────────────────┐    │  │  │
│  │  │       │  - which product is responsible:    │    │  │  │
│  │  │       │      sales analysis (by product)    │    │  │  │
│  │  │       │  - where major decrease is focused: │    │  │  │
│  │  │       │      sales analysis (by product/zona)│   │  │  │
│  │  │       │  - how is the market going          │    │  │  │
│  │  │       └─────────────────────────────────────┘    │  │  │
│  │  │                                                  │  │  │
│  │  │  2. if total sales variance is positive and > x% │  │  │
│  │  │     then deduce that:                            │  │  │
│  │  │          .....................                   │  │  │
│  │  │          ....................                    │  │  │
│  │  └──────────────────────────────────────────────────┘  │  │
│  └────────────────────────────────────────────────────────┘  │
│                                                              │
│  DISCONFIRMATION                                             │
└─────────────────────────────────────────────────────────────┘
```

Figure 2. Illustration of knowledge strategy and concepts organization in the structurization phase.

SALES ANALYSIS (BY PRODUCT)

CONFIRMATION

CONTROL STRATEGIES

Move down into the hierarchical data level:
remaining into the current context
execute the following nested actions

CONTEXT: PRODUCT

1. select family product accounting for 80% of the
   total variance

2. within them select individual products accounting
   for 90% of the family variance

3. evalutate their variance (volume & price)

SUBGOALS:

... why: variance analysis
....
....

Figure 3. Description of more detailed sales knowledge level.

VARIANCE ANALYSIS

CONFIRMATION

CONTROL STRATEGIES

Trigger one of the following sequence of rules

1. if volume variance is < 0 and
       price variance is > 0
   then deduce that:
       a price increase policy
       may be the reason of
       volume drop

   SUBGOALS:

   ....
   ....

2. if volume variance is > 0 and
       price variance is < 0
   then deduce that:
       the price decrease policy may be the
       reason of a loss not balanced by major
       revenues due to the volume increase
       gained on the market

   SUBGOALS:

   .. look at the product price/performance
   ....
   ....

3. ...

Figure 4. Illustration of hypothesize and test mechanism for
evaluation of policies.

CONCLUSIONS. Business planning and evaluation is a fruitful field (even
though it is not exactly easy) for expert system applications, in which
there is room for knowledge representation both for structured problems
(modeling) and for the more challenging areas of less structured ones.
The task of our group is based on the feeling that Computer Science is
fast moving from data processing to knowledge processing, and for this
reason we are more interested in its second aspect (i.e. less structured
problems) regarding the first point (modeling) as a tool which knowledge
actually uses in every day company operations.

REFERENCES

1. H. Simon, The New Science of Management Decision, Harper (NY 1960)
2. R. H. Sprague and E. D. Carlson, Building Effective Decision Support
   Systems, Prentice-Hall (1982)
3. P. Kenn and M. S. Scott-Morton, Decision Support Systems: An
   Organizational Perspective, Addison Wesley (1978)
4. F. Canepa, "Modelli di gestione aziendale e strumento di R. O. in
   expert systems: ipotesi di lavoro sulla loro interazione", Ricerca
   Operativa 35 (1985)
5. F. Hayes-Roth, "The Knowledge-Based Expert System: A Tutorial", IEEE
   Computer (September 1984)
6. F. Hayes-Roth, "Knowledge Based Expert Systems", IEEE Computer
   (October 1984)
7. F. Hayes-Roth et al., Building Expert Systems, Addison Wesley (1983)
8. J. S. Aikins "Prototypical Knowledge for Expert Systems", Artificial
   Intelligence 20, pp. 163-210, North-Holland (1983)
9. R. Davis, "Meta-Rules: Reasoning About Control", MIT - AI Laboratory:
   AI Memo NO 576 (March 1980)
10. M. Milanese "EDSS: Expert Systems for Decision Support", invited
    paper at the Seminar "New Information Technologies for Productions",
    Sperry International Management Science, Saint Paul de Vence (1985)
11. P. de Greef and J. Brenker, "A Case Study in Structured Knowledge
    Acquisition", Proc. of the 9th IJCAI, 1, pp. 390-392, (LA 1985)
12. K. A. Ericcson and H. A. Simon, A Protocol Analysis: Verbal Reports
    as Data, the MIT Press, Cambridge Mass (1984)
13. M. Stefic et al., "The Organization of Expert Systems, A Tutorial",
    Artificial Intelligence 18, pp. 135-173, North Holland (1982)
14. W. J. Clancey, "The Epistenology of A Rule-Based Expert System, A
    Framework for Explanation", Artificial Intelligence 20, pp. 215-251,
    North Holland (1983)

KNOWLEDGE ACQUISITION FROM USER PROGRAMS BY COMPUTER WITH OWN KNOWLEDGE-BASED SYSTEM

Jan Kazimierczak
Institute of Engineering Cybernetics
Technical University of Wroclaw
Wyb. Wyspianskiego 27
50-370 Wroclaw, Poland

ABSTRACT. This paper deals with the problem of knowledge acquisition from user programs for the knowledge base of the computer. Various forms of knowledge included in user programs are considered. First, knowledge expressed in the form of rules included in a user program is discussed. It is shown that this knowledge, extracted from the user program, can be transformed into a symbolic expression. This symbolic expression is compared with the symbolic expression that represents the knowledge contained in a knowledge base. Such elements are then extracted from the symbolic expression which, as acquired knowledge, should be added to the knowledge base. Moreover, knowledge expressed as an algorithm for the solution of problems is considered. It is shown that such knowledge is contained both in the structure and in the sequence of operations of user programs. These parts of user prgrams are transformed into symbolic expressions. On the basis of these expressions the knowledge acquisition process is realized. The method of knowledge acquisition, presented in this paper, can be used in decision support systems.

1. INTRODUCTION

A knowledge-based system is a computer system that stores knowledge in some problem domain and applies such knowledge to usefully assist the user of the system. Expert Systems form a class of knowledge-based systems (KBS). This class has archieved the most significant results so far, with some major cost benefits. Knowledge-based systems are particularly useful in decision support systems. A major problem in the development of a knowledge-based system (e.g. an expert system) is the acquisition of knowledge from information included in the user programs run by the computer.

This paper discusses a method of acquisition of knowledge from user programs and a way of storing it in computer memory. This is an offspin of the research that is done on programs using machine intelligence, in other words it is a problem of artificial intelligence. The current type of computer has no ability in the domain of machine intelligence because it does not remember knowledge included in user programs. It is clear however that each user program contains some

. G. Sol et al. (eds.), Expert Systems and Artificial Intelligence in Decision Support Systems, 271–292.
1987 by D. Reidel Publishing Company.

problems to be solved by the computer. When the running of a given
user program is completed, it is erased and the computer will not
remember what scientific problem was solved. Since the computer has not
stored the knowledge included in the completed user program, it does
not possess an own intelligence. Such behaviour of the computer,
controlled by it OS-nucleus, is contrary to the behaviour of Man, who
studies scientific problems, remembers them and, on the basis of the
acquired knowledge, is able to form his own scientific opinion.

For this reason, human knowledge included in a user program
should not be erased from the memory after running, but should be
stored in the knowledge base (KB) of the computer. The knowledge,
extracted from different user prgrams, should be integrated in the KB
in such a way that similar elements of knowledge appearing in other
programs would be stored as one element only.

For an explanation of the above we assume that user programs
are written in some higher-level language, e.g. in Pascal. Moreover, we
assume that knowledge included in a given program is concealed in the
structure of such a program as well as in the sequence of operations
appearing inside such a structure. We note that a given structural
component of the user program, and a given operation included in the
program, can appear in several user programs, For suitable organization
of the computer's knowledge base, the same structural component appearing
in different user programs should be stored in one and the same memory
location. The same applies to similar operations contained in different
user programs. This means that knowledge acquired from user programs
should be added to knowledge which is already included in the knowledge
base. This integration of knowledge must be executed in such a way
that the information included in the KB can be easily found and easily
modified. A solution for such problems is introduced in this paper.

Firstly, so that the problem can be more easily understood,
we assume that in the user programs there are decision rules stored in
the knowledge base. These rules, written in ordinary language, are
transformed by the computer into symbolic expressions. The first rule
transformed into a symbolic expression is treated, by the computer, as
an initial knowledge base. The second rule is treated as new knowledge
and is also transformed into a symbolic expression. Then, the symbolic
expression of the newly acquired rule is compared in the computer memory
with the symbolic expression representing the initial knowledge base. If
a part of the symbolic expression of the newly acquired rule is already
included in the symbolic expression representing the initial KB, then
such a part is omitted in the knowledge acquisition process. However,
if the part of the symbolic expression is not included in the symbolic
expression representing the KB, this part must be stored in the computer
memory. In this way, the symbolic expression representing the KB is
complemented by the part of the symbolic expression of the newly
acquired rule.

This means of acquiring knowledge, expressed in the form of
decision rules, can be applied to all elements of knowledge included in
the given user program. In the fourth and fifth sections of this paper
are, as an example, two very simple user programs considered. These
programs, written in Pascal, do not contain rules but algorithms for
the solution of problems.

After completion, the user program is first split by the computer into a structural part and an operating part. The structural part is split into structural components expressed in the form of clauses. Each structural component is transformed into the form of a rule. This rule assigns to the given structural component a symbol denoting it. Then, the rule representing a given structural component is transformed into a symbolic expression. This symbolic expression is stored in the KB, in the part entitled "The set of structural components". The same structural components are represented in such a set only by one symbolic expression in which a symbol denoting the given type of the structural component is contained.

Next the sequence of the symbolic names of the structural components, belonging to the first program, is determined. This sequence is itself transformed into a symbolic expression, thus representing the structural part of the first program. This symbolic expression will be stored in the KB, in the set of program structures.

The operating part of the first user program is derived in a similar manner. This part of the user program is also transformed into symbolic expressions. The relationship between the structural part and the operating part of the program is contained in the symbolic expressions describing such parts.

Next the second user program is considered. It is the knowledge acquiring program. This program is also divided into structural and operating parts. However, the computer does not know whether the structural components of this program are already included in the KB. Therefore, each structural components is searched for in the KB, in the set of structural components. If the given structural component is already included in the set, the symbol denoting such a component from this set will be overlooked. However, if the given structural component is not included in the set of structural components, such structural component will be denoted by a symbol and will be inserted, as acquired knowledge, in the set of structural components. After for all structural components of the second program symbols have been determined, the symbolic expression representing the structural part is built out of these symbols. This symbolic expression, treated as acquired knowledge, is added to the knowledge held in the set of program structures. Similar operations are performed on the operating part of the second program. As a result the KB is extended.

The problems and operations mentioned above will be considered in more detail in the following sections of this paper.

2. NOTATION OF KNOWLEDGE AS A SYMBOLIC EXPRESSION

Suppose that an initial knowledge base contains the following rule:

RULE 1

IF: THE RUNNING PROCESS IS BLOCKED
          AND THE READY LIST OF PROCESSES IS NONEMPTY

THEN: MOVE THE RUNNING PROCESS TO THE BLOCKING LIST AND MAKE
          THE FIRST PROCESS ON THE READY LIST THE RUNNING PROCESS

Denoting, for simplicity, the words included in this rule by the symbols s_1, s_2, s_3,.., we obtain the following formula:

IF $s_1 s_2 s_3 s_4 s_5$ AND $s_1 s_7 s_8 s_9 s_{10}$

THEN $s_{11} s_1 s_2 s_3 s_{12} s_1 s_{13} s_7$ AND $s_{14} s_1 s_{15} s_3 s_{16} s_1 s_6 s_7 s_2$

Each symbol of type s_j is read as a word, e.g. symbol s_3 is read as "PROCESS".

Note that in the rule explained ther are four clauses. For the formal description of this rule we denote these clauses by the symbols A, B, R, T respectively. Hence, we obtain:

IF A AND B THEN R AND T

The conjuctives appearing between the clauses and the word THEN we denote by simbol z_j. We assume the following code:
AND = z_2, OR = z_3, THEN = z_4. The connection between the beginning and ending of the rule will be denoted by symbol z_5. The space between words inside a given clause will be denoted by symbol z_1.

Transforming the above rule into a formal model of the initial KB, we assume that each clause, appearing in the rule, will be represented in computer memory by the symbol e_r, wher r is the index (r = 1,2,3,..). For example, the clause A will be represented by symbol e_1, B by e_2, R by e_3, T by e_4. Symbols e_1, e_2, e_3, e_4 are treated as values of the internal parameter "e" of the KB. Similarly as above, the clause appearing in the rule before the word THEN will be represented in computer memory by the symbol f_1, whereas the clause appearing after the word THEN will be represented by symbol hj. The symbols of the fype f_i and h_j are treated as values of the internal parameters "f" and "h", respectively. In the above example there is only one rule, hence $f_i = f_1$ and $h_j = h_1$. As we have three internal parameters of the KB, i.e. parameters "e", "f" and "h", we can distinguish three parts of the rule, denoted by symbols G(e), G(f), G(h). The structure of the above rule is shown in Fig. 1.

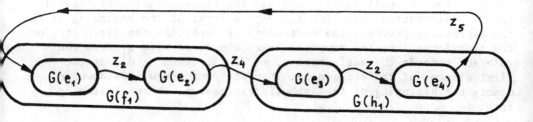

Fig. 1. A structure of the above rule.

According to the concept discussed in section 1, the initial KB containing the mentioned rule should be stored in computer memory in the form of a symbolic expression. Each word s_j of the rule is represented by the symbol d_k ($k = 1,2,3,..$). For this reason, the transformation of the rule into symbolic expression is associated with a translation of words, appearing in the rule, into symbols d_k. This translation depends on the building in the memory of an equivalent table which will contain the assignments of symbols d_k to wordt s_j of the rule. This table will be called a "dictionary". A structure of this dictionary is shown in Fig. 2.

the word s_j	symbol of the word in the symbolic expression	adress of the symbol d_k in memory
s_1 - THE	d_1	
s_2 - RUNNING	d_2	
s_3 - PROCESS	d_3	
s_4 - IS	d_4	
s_5 - BLOCKED	d_5	
s_6 - READY	d_6	
s_7 - LIST	d_7	
s_8 - OF	d_8	
s_9 - PROCESSES	d_9	
s_{10} - NONEMPTY	d_{10}	
s_{11} - MOVE	d_{11}	
s_{12} - TO	d_{12}	
s_{13} - MAKE	d_{13}	
s_{14} - FIRST	d_{14}	
s_{15} - ON	d_{15}	
s_{16} - BLOCKING	d_{16}	

Fig. 2. The equivalent table as a dictionary of words included in rules

Now we shall briefly explain the transformation of the rule under consideration into symbolic expressions. At the beginning of the transformation process, the dictionary is empty. As the first step of the transformation, the computer takes the first word s_1 from the rule and records the assignment $s_1 \rightleftharpoons d_1$ i.e. THE -- d_1^1, as the first element of the dictionary. Then the computer writes down in memory the beginning of the symbolic-expression, in the following form:

$$G^+ = {}^\Theta(d_1{}^1(z_1 e_1 f_1 \cdot \cdot$$

As the second step, the computer takes the second word from the rule, i.e. it takes s_2 = RUNNING, and checks whether this word is already included in the dictionary. If the word s_2 is not included in the dictionary, then the index k of the symbol d_k is increased by one, i.e. $d_k = d_2$, and in the second row of the dictionary the assignment s_2 -- d_2 is recorded. Then, the symbolic expression G^+ is extended by the term $d_2{}^2(z_1 e_1$ and obtains the following form:

$$G^+ = {}^0(d_1{}^1(z_1 e_1 f_1 d_2{}^2(z_1 e_1 \cdot$$

The third step and further steps of the above-mentioned transformation are similar to the second step. However, if a relevant word s_j of the rule is already included in the dictionary then an operation is performed which differs from that of the second step. In that case the column in the dictionary in which the given word s_j is included is found. From this column then the symbol d_k is read and recorded in symbolic expression. If the word AND is taken from the rule then this word is not translated into the symbol d_k. In this case, the computer increases the value e_r of the parameter "e" by one, i.e. the current value of "e" will be e_{r+1}. However, if the word THEN is read it is also not translated, but it means that the next part of the rule is $G(h)$, i.e. the current parameters are of the type "e" and "h". (see Fig. 1.)

The final result of the transformation is the following symbolic expression:

$$G^+ = {}^0(d_1{}^1(z_1 e_1 f_1 d_2{}^2(z_1 e_1 d_3{}^3(z_1 e_1 d_4{}^4(z_1 e_1 d_5{}^5($$
$$^5(z_2 e_1 f_1 d_1{}^6(z_1 e_2 f_1 d_6{}^7(z_1 e_2 d_7{}^8(z_1 e_2 d_8{}^9($$
$$^9(z_1 e_2 d_9{}^{10}(z_1 e_2 d_4{}^{11}(z_1 e_2 d_{10}{}^{12}(z_4 e_2 h_1 d_{11}{}^{13}($$
$$^{13}(z_1 e_3 h_1 d_1{}^{14}(z_1 e_3 d_2{}^{15}(z_1 e_3 d_3{}^{16}(z_1 e_3 d_{12}{}^{17}($$
$$^{17}(z_1 e_3 d_1{}^{18}(z_1 e_3 d_{13}{}^{19}(z_1 e_3 d_7{}^{20}(z_2 e_3 h_1 d_{14}{}^{21}($$
$$^{21}(z_1 e_4 h_1 d_1{}^{22}(z_1 e_4 d_{15}{}^{23}(z_1 e_4 d_3{}^{24}(z_1 e_4 d_{16}{}^{25}($$
$$^{25}(z_1 e_4 d_1{}^{26}(z_1 e_4 d_6{}^{27}(z_1 e_4 d_7{}^{28}(z_1 e_4 d_2{}^{29}($$
$$^{29}(z_5 e_4 f_1 d_1)^{29})^{28})^{27} \ldots)^2)^1)^0 \qquad (1)$$

Based on this symbolic expression we can draw a graph G', which may be treated as an image of the organization of the KB. This graph is shown in Fig. 3. The nodes of Graph G', labeled by the symboles d_i, represent words of the rule. The vertices of the graph represent relations between words of the rule. These vertices are labeled by symbolic values of the zype $z_i e_r$ of $z_i e_r f_l$ of $z_j e_r h_t$. In Fig. 3., for clarity of the drawing only five vertices are labeled.

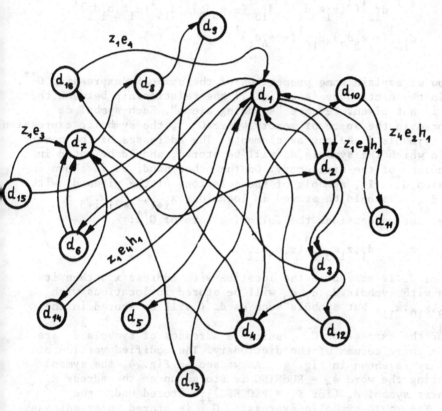

Figure 3. The graph G' derived from the expression G^+ (1)

In the practical use of this symbolic expression as a knowledge base, the expression G^+ must be transformed into another form denoted by symbol G^{++} below. Note that in the expression G^+ there are open brackets before which the same symbol d_j is placed, e.g. symbol d_2 appears on the following items: $...d_2 (^j...d_2 {}^{15} (...d_2 {}^{29} (... .$ This feature of the expression G^+ makes its utilization difficult. The transformation of the symbolic expression G^+ into the symbolic expression G^{++} depends on the arrangement of G^+ with respect to the symbols d_j. In G^{++} there will only be one open bracket $(^k$ assigned to each symbol d_j. The symbolic expression G^{++} derived from the expression G^+ has the following form:

$$G^{++} = {_{-}^{0}}(d_1{^1}(z_1e_1f_1d_2, z_1e_2f_1d_6, z_1e_4d_{15}, z_1e_3d_{13}, z_1e_4d_6,$$
$$z_1e_3d_2{^2}(z_1e_1d_3, z_5e_4f_1d_1, z_1e_3d_3{^3}(z_1e_3d_{12}, z_1e_4d_{16}',$$
$$z_1e_1d_4{^4}(z_1e_2d_{10}, z_1e_1d_5{^5}(z_2e_1f_1d_1)^5)^4)^3)^2)^1,$$
$$d_6{^1}(z_1e_2d_7, z_1e_4d_7{^2}(z_1e_4d_2, z_2e_3h_1d_{14}, z_1e_2d_8{^3}(z_1e_3h_1d_1)$$
$$^2)^1, d_{12}^{'}{^1}(^1(z_1e_3d_1)^1, d_{13}{^1}(z_1e_3d_7)^1, d_{14}{^1}(z_1e_4h_1d_1)^1,$$
$$d_{15}{^1}(z_1e_3d_7), d_{16}{^1}(z_1e_4d_1)^1)^0 \qquad (2)$$

Now we explain some properties of the symbolic expression G^{++}. Note that in the dictionary (see Fig. 2) the relationship between the symbols d_i is not given. Tey are "standing alone". Each symbol d_i will be stored in the space of memory where G^{++}, the symbolic expression whereto the symbols d_i belong as elements. The addresses of the memory locations in which the symbols d_i will be stored, should be noted in the third column of the dictionary. On the other hand, as is shown in the expression G^{++} (2), symbols of the relations of the given d_j with other d_{r1}, d_{r2},.. should be stored in locations $x_{i+1}, x_{i+2}, x_{i+3}$. For example, let us consider the following term of G^{++}:

$$\ldots d_2{^2}(z_1e_1d_3, z_5e_4f_1d_1, z_1e_3d_3{^3}(z_1e_3d_{12}, \ldots$$

If the symbol d_2 is stored in the location with address x_8, then its connections with symbols d_3, d_1, d_3 will be stored in locations with adresses x_9, x_{10}, x_{11}, but symbols such as d_3(will be stored in the location x_{12}.

For the expression G^{++}, suitable adresses of symbols d_i are noted in the third column of the dictionary. The modified version of the dictionary is shown in Fig. 4. As we see in Fig. 4, the symbol d_2 representing the word s_2 = RUNNING is stored under the adress x_5, while the next symbol d_3 (for s_3 = PROCESS) is stored under the adress x_{12}. The whole symbolic expression G^{++} is stored under adresses x_1 to x_{54}.

The symbolic expression G^{++} possesses features by which we may separate from it expression which represesnt the given clause of the rule. In other words, within the expression G^{++} we may find any clause of the given rule. This matter will be discussed in the next section.

word	symbol of word in symbolic expression	address of symbol d_j in memory
s_1	$d_1^1($	x_1
s_2	$d_2^2($	x_8
s_3	$d_3^3($	x_{12}
s_4	$d_4^4($	x_{16}
s_5	$d_5^5($	x_{19}
s_6	$d_6^1($	x_{22}
s_7	$d_7^2($	x_{26}
s_8	$d_8^3($	x_{30}
s_9	$d_9^4($	x_{32}
s_{10}	$d_{10}^1($	x_{35}
s_{11}	$d_{11}^2($	x_{37}
s_{12}	$d_{12}^1($	x_{40}
s_{13}	$d_{13}^1($	x_{43}
s_{14}	$d_{14}^1($	x_{46}
s_{15}	$d_{15}^1($	x_{49}
s_{16}	$d_{16}^1($	x_{52}

Figure 4. The modified version of the dictionary.

3. KNOWLEDGE ACQUISITION AND EXPANSION OF THE KNOWLEDGE BASE

Let us assume that knowledge extracted from the expertise of an expert
is the following rule:

RULE 2

    IF: THE RUNNING PROCESS IS BLOCKED
           AND THE READY LIST OF PROCESS IS EMPTY

    THEN: WAIT FOR THE UNBLOCKED PROCESS

This rule can be expressed as follows: IF A AND C THEN P. According
to the concept discussed in the first section, knowledge included in
this rule should be added to knowledge in the knowledge base. Since
the knowledge base in the memory is represented by a symbolic expression,
rule 2 must also be transformed into symbolic expression. However, the
computer does not know whether the knowledge included in this rule is
already included in the symbolic expressions of the KB. For this
reason it cannot build the symbolic expression of the type G^+ (see eq. 1)
for the newly acquired rule because it does not know what values of the
parameter "e" may be used. The computer only knows that for building
the symbolic expression of the KB the values $e_1, e_2, e_3, e_4, f_1, h_1$ were
used (because in the computer's memory there are suitable counters
for e, f, h.). Therefore the newly acquired rule is transformed, on the
basis of the existing dictionary, into the symbolic expression $\bar{G}^+$.

$$\bar{G}^+ = {}^0(d_1\,{}^1(z_1f_2d_2\,{}^2(z_1d_3\,{}^3(z_1d_4\,{}^4(z_1d_5\,{}^5(z_2f_2d_1\,{}^6($$
$$\quad {}^6(z_1f_2d_6\,{}^7(z_1d_7\,{}^8(z_1d_8\,{}^9(z_1d_9\,{}^{10}(z_1d_4\,{}^{11}(a_1d_{17}\,{}^{12}($$
$$\quad {}^{12}(z_2h_2d_{18}\,{}^{13}(z_1h_2d_{19}\,{}^{14}(z_1d_1\,{}^{15}(z_1d_1\,{}^{15}(z_1d_{20}\,{}^{16}(z_1d_3\,{}^{17}($$
$$\quad {}^{17}(z_5f_2d_1)^{17})^{16}\ldots)^1)^0 \qquad\qquad (3)$$

This expression is compared with the symbolic expression of the KB,
i.e. with G^{++} (2), in order to determine values of the parameter "e",
which should be assigned to the clauses of rule 2. We shall explain the
operation of the comparison of the $\bar{G}^+$ with G^{++} (2) by an example.
Example. Consider the part of $\bar{G}^+$ that represents the clause A of rule
2. This part, denoted by symbol $\bar{G}_1^+$ has the following form:

$$\bar{G}_1^+ = {}^0(d_1\,{}^1(z_1f_2d_2\,{}^2(z_1d_3\,{}^3(z_1d_4\,{}^4(z_1d_5\,{}^5(z_2f_2 \qquad (4)$$

ow we will consider an algorithm to compare $\bar{G}_1^+$ with the symbolic
xpression G^{++}. (eq. 2)
    1.   Take from $\bar{G}_1^+$ the first symbol $d_.$; this is symbol d_1 in (4).
    2.   Search the dictionary for the address of symbol d_1; this
         adress is denoted by x_1.
    3.   Having found address x_1, search in G^{++}(2) the term $d_1\,{}^1(\ldots;$
         this term has the form:

$$d_1\,{}^1(z_1e_1f_1d_2,z_1e_2f_1d_6,z_1e_4d_6,z_1e_4d_{15},z_1e_3d_{13},z_1e_3d_2$$

4. Take from $\bar{G}_1^+$ the denotation of the relation of d_1 with the next element d_j; this is $z_1 f_2 d_2$.

5. Search in the term $d_1^{\ 1}(\dots$ of G^{++} a relation with denotation $z_1 d_2$; the results of this search are $z_1 e_1 f_1 d_2$ and $z_1 e_3 d_2$. First relation $z_1 e_1 f_1 d_2$ is considered.

6. Combine relations $z_1 e_1 f_1 d_2$ and $z_1 f_2 d_2$ (as obtained in the fourth step of the algorithm). Result: $z_1 e_1 f_1 f_2 d_2$.

7. Build the beginning of the expression $_1 G_{acq.}^+$; this gives
$$_1 G_{acq.}^+ = {}^0(d_1{}^1(z_1 e_1 f_1 f_2 d_2.$$

8. Search in the dictionary the address of symbol d_2: i.e. x_8.

9. Having found address x_8, search the term $d_2(\dots$ in G^{++}. The algorithm finds $d_2{}^2(z_1 e_1 d_3, z_5 e_4 f_1, z_1 e_3 d_3$.

10. Take from $\bar{G}_1^+$ the denotation of the relation of d_2 with the next element d_j: $z_1 d_3$.

11. Search in the term $d_2{}^2(\dots$ of G^{++} a relation with denotation $z_1 d_3$. Relations $z_1 e_1 d_3$ and $z_1 e_3 d_3$ are found. First relation $z_1 e_1 d_3$ is looked at.

12. Check whether value e_1 in denotation $z_1 e_1 d_3$ is equal to the value of "e" as obtained in the fifth step; in the case under consideration these values are equal. Otherwise, if these values of "e" would not be equal, then a new value e_r, not already included in G^{++}, would be assigned to the first clause of rule 2.

13. Construct the expression $_1 G_{acq}^+$: this results in:
$$_1 G_{acq}^+ = {}^0(d_1{}^1(z_1 e_1 f_1 f_2 d_2{}^2(z_1 e_1 d_3.$$

The next steps of the algorithm are similar to those described above. As the final result, the following symbolic expression is obtained:
$$_1 G_{acq}^+ = {}^0(d_1{}^1(z_1 e_1 f_1 f_2 d_2{}^2(z_1 e_1 d_3{}^3(z_1 e_1 d_4{}^4(z_1 e_1 d_5($$
$$^5(z_2 e_1 f_1 f_2 \qquad\qquad\qquad\qquad (5)$$

Note that this symbolic expression has the same form as that part of the symbolic expression G^{++} (eq. 2), which represents the first clause A of rule 1. This similarity is denoted in the first and last term of the expression $_1 G_{acq}^+$ by the symbols f_1 and f_2. For this reason will only terms $z_1e_1f_1d_2$ and $z_2e_1f_1d_1$ be modified in the expression G^{++} when we perform the operation of combining G^{++} with $_1G^+_{acq}$. The modified forms will be $z_1e_1f_1f_2d_2$ and $z_2e_1f_1f_2d_1$, respectively.

Let us now take a look at the part of $\bar{G}^+$ that represents the clause C of rule 2. This part, denoted by the symbol $\bar{G}^+_2$, has the following form:

$$\bar{G}^+_2 = {}^0(d_1{}^1(z_1e_1f_1f_2d_2{}^2(z_1e_1d_3.$$

Comparing this expression with the symbolic expression G^{++} (2), we obtain:

$$_2G^+_{acq} = d_1{}^6(z_1e_2f_1f_2d_6{}^7(z_1e_2d_7{}^8(z_1e_2d_8{}^9(z_1e_2d_9{}^{10}($$

$$^{10}(z_1e_2d_4{}^{11}(z_1e_2f_2d_{17} \tag{7}$$

We can notice that the first words of clause C in rule 2 are the same as the first words of clause B in rule 1. However, the last word of clause C of rule 2 and the last word of clause B of rule 1 are different. This difference is denoted by symbol f_2 in the term

$$d_4{}^{11}(z_1e_2f_2d_{17} \text{ of } _2G^+_{acq} \text{ and by symbol } f_1 \text{ in the term}$$

$$d_4(z_1e_2f_1d_{10} \text{ of the expression } G^{++}.$$

The result of the comparison of the whole symbolic expression $\bar{G}^+$ with the symbolic expression G^{++} (2) is the following expression G^+_{acq}:

$$G^+_{acq} = {}^0(d_1{}^1(z_1e_1f_1f_2d_2{}^2(z_1e_1d_3{}^3(z_1e_1d_4{}^4(z_1e_1d_5{}^5($$

$$^5(z_2e_1f_1f_2d_1{}^6(z_1e_2f_1f_2d_6{}^7(z_1e_2d_7{}^8(z_1e_2d_8{}^9($$

$$^9(z_1e_2d_9{}^{10}(z_1e_2d_4{}^{11}(z_1e_2f_2d_{17}{}^{12}($$

$$^{12}(z_4e_2h_2d_{18}{}^{13}(z_1e_5h_2d_{19}{}^{14}(z_1e_5d_1{}^{15}($$

$$^{15}(z_1e_5d_{20}{}^{16}(z_1e_5d_3{}^{17}(z_1e_5f_2d_1)^{17})^{16}\ldots$$

$$\ldots)^1)^0 \tag{8}$$

Next the operation of combining expression G^{++} with expression G^+_{acq} is performed. As a result of performing this operation. the symbolic expression G^{++}, representing the KB, will be extended by the following part of the expression G^+_{acq}:

$$\ldots d_4{}^{11}(z_1e_2f_2d_{17}{}^{12}(z_4e_2h_2d_{18}{}^{13}(z_1e_5h_2d_{19}{}^{14}($$

$$^{14}(z_1e_5d_1{}^{15}(z_1e_5d_{20}{}^{16}(z_1e_5d_3{}^{17}(z_5e_5f_2d_1$$

$$)^{17})^{16}\ldots)^{12})^{11}\ldots$$

This expression represents the knowledge acquired by the knowledge base

from the rule 2. The extended symbolic expression G^{++}, representing
the extended knowledge base, denoted by $G^{++}_{ext.}$, has the following form:

$$G^{++}_{ext.} = {}^0(d_1{}^1(\underline{z_1 e_1 f_1 f_2 d_2}, \underline{z_1 e_2 f_1 f_2 d_6}, z_1 e_4 d_6, z_1 e_4 d_{15}, z_1 e_3 d_{13},$$
$$\underline{z_1 e_5 d_{20}}, z_1 e_3 d_2{}^2(z_1 e_1 d_3, z_5 e_4 f_1 d_1, z_1 e_3 d_3{}^3(z_1 e_3 d_{12}, z_1 e_3 d_{12},$$
$$z_1 e_4 d_{16}, z_5 e_5 f_2 d_1, z_1 e_1 d_4{}^4({}^4(\underline{z_1 e_2 f_1 d_{10}}, \underline{z_1 e_2 f_2 d_{17}}, z_1 e_1 d_5{}^5(z_2 e_1 f_1 d_1)$$
$$5)^4)^3)^2)^1, d_6{}^1(z_1 e_2 d_7, z_1 e_4 d_7{}^2(z_1 e_4 d_2, z_2 e_3 h_1 d_{14}, z_1 e_2 d_8{}^3($$
$$^3(z_1 e_2 d_9{}^4(z_1 e_2 d_4)^4)^3)^2)^1, d_{10}{}^1(z_4 e_2 h_1 d_{11}{}^2($$
$$^2(z_1 e_3 h_1 d_1)^2)^1, d_{12}{}^1(z_1 e_3 d_1)^1, d_{13}{}^1(z_1 e_3 d_7)^1, d_{14}{}^1($$
$$^1(z_1 e_4 h_1 d_1)^1, d_{15}{}^1(z_1 e_3 d_7)^1, d_{16}{}^1(z_1 e_4 d_1)^1, \underline{d_{17}{}^1(}$$
$$^1(z_4 e_2 h_2 d_{18}{}^2(z_1 e_5 h_2 d_{19}{}^3(z_1 e_5 d_1)^3)^2)^1, \underline{d_{20}{}^1(}{}^1\underline{z_1 e_5 d_3})^1)^0$$

$$(9)$$

In this expression the newly acquired terms are denoted by solid lines,
whereas the modified lines are denoted by broken lines. Note that
while the G^{++}_{ext} is built, some addresses in the dictionary (see Fig 4)
are modified.

4.   TRANSFORMATION OF A USER PROGRAM INTO THE INITIAL
KNOWLEDGE BASE

Let us suppose that we have an user program A_1 which will be stored
in the computer memory as an initial knowledge base. For simplicity,
let us consider a simple program written in Pascal (6), considering
a sorting. This program has the following form:

```
begin for i:= 2 to n do
    Begin for j:= n downto i do
    if a[j-1].key > a[j].key then
    begin x:= a[j-1] ; a[j-1]:= a[j]; a[j]:= x end
    end
end                                        (10)
```

The program A_1 kan be written in two parts, i.e. a structual part and
an operating part. First we will consider the structural part.
        The structural part of a user program is splitted into
components expresses in the form of clauses. For each clause, ccalled
structural components, an appropiate symbol f_n (n=1,2,3,..) is chosen
as a symbolic name for this component. The structural part of the
ser program A_1 (10), expressed in the form of a sequence of structural
components, is shown on the next page:

$$\text{begin } \underline{\text{for}} \text{ op } \underline{\text{do}} \text{ next } \underline{\text{end}} \leftrightarrow f_1 u_1 u_2,$$

$$\text{begin } \underline{\text{for}} \text{ op } \underline{\text{do}} \text{ next } \underline{\text{end}} \leftrightarrow f_1, u_1, u_2$$

$$\underline{\text{if}} \text{ op } \underline{\text{then}} \leftrightarrow f_2, u_1,$$

$$\underline{\text{begin}} \text{ op } \underline{\text{end}} \leftrightarrow f_3, u_2,$$

The word "op" denotes the operations included in the given structural component. The word "next" indicates the place of connection of the given structural component with other structural components. The symbol u_1 means that the given structural component f_n is connected with the next structural component at the position indicated by the word "next" or <u>then</u>. The symbol u_2 means that the given structural component f_n terminates with the word <u>end</u>.

Each type of structural component is stored in the knowledge base of the computer as a rule. Identical structural components are stored only once in the KB. In the structure of program A_1 we can distinguish three types of structural components, denoted by the symbolic names f_1, f_2, f_3. These components can be expressed as rules:

Rule 1: IF begin for op do next end THEN f_1, u_1, u_2

Rule 2: IF if op then THEN f_2, u_1

Rule 3: IF begin op end THEN f_3, u_2

Each rule will be stored in the KB as a symbolic expression. In this expression each word is represented by an appropriate symbol d_j. The assignment of symbols d_j to the words included in rules 1,2,3 will be stored as a table. This table, denoted by symbol $\bar{D}$, is shown in Fig. 5.

word	symbol of word in the symbolic expression	address of symbol d_j in memory
begin	d_1	x_1
for	d_2	x_4
op	d_3	x_8
do	d_4	x_{10}
next	d_5	x_{12}
end	d_6	x_{14}
if	d_7	x_{18}
then	d_8	x_{21}

Figure 5. Table $\bar{D}$ of assignments of symbols d_j to words describing the structure of program A_1.

Rule 1 can be expressed in the form of the following symbolic expression:

$$\vec{G}_1^+ = {}^0(d_1{}^1(z_1 f_1 d_2{}^2(z_1 f_1 d_3{}^3(z_1 f_1 d_4{}^4(z_1 f_1 d_5{}^5(z_1 f_1 d_6{}^6($$

$$^6(z_4 f_1 u_1 u_2)^6 \ldots)^1)^0 \qquad\qquad (12)$$

where the symbol z_1 denotes the space between the words, and symbol z_4 denotes THEN. The symbolic expressions derived from rules 2 and 3 have the following forms:

$$\tilde{G}_2^+ = {}^0(d_7{}^1(z_1 f_2 d_3{}^2(z_1 f_2 d_8{}^3(z_4 f_2 u_1)^3)^1)^2)^0 \qquad (13)$$

$$\tilde{G}_3^+ = {}^0(d_1{}^1(z_1 f_3 d_3{}^2(z_1 f_3 d_6{}^3(z_4 f_3 u_2)^3)^2)^1)^0 \qquad (14)$$

Note that in the symbolic expressions $\tilde{G}_1^+$, $\tilde{G}_2^+$, $\tilde{G}_3^+$ the same symbols d_j appear. According to the concept discussed in section 1 of this paper, the same elements of knowledge should be represented in the knowledge base by only one element. Therefore the expressions $\tilde{G}_1^+, \tilde{G}_2^+, \tilde{G}_3^+$ are transformed into one symbolic expression $\tilde{G}^+$:

$$\tilde{G}^+ = {}^0(d_1{}^1(z_1 f_1 d_2{}^2(z_1 f_1 d_3{}^3(z_1 f_1 d_4{}^4(z_1 f_1 d_5{}^5(z_1 f_1 d_6{}^6($$
$${}^6(z_4 f_1 u_1 u_2)^6 \ldots)^2)^1, d_7{}^1(z_1 f_2 d_3{}^2(z_1 f_2 d_8{}^3($$
$${}^3(z_4 f_2 u_1)^3)^2)^1, d_1{}^1(z_1 f_3 d_3{}^2(z_1 f_3 d_6{}^3(z_4 f_3 u_2)^3$$
$$)^2)^1)^0 \qquad (15)$$

The expression $\tilde{G}^+$ is then arranged on ascending elements d_j. The result of this arrangement is the symbolic expression $\tilde{G}^{++}$.

$$\tilde{G}^{++} = {}^0(d_1{}^1(z_1 f_3 d_3, z_1 f_1 d_2{}^2(z_1 f_1 d_3{}^3(z_1 f_3 d_6, z_1 f_2 d_8,$$
$$z_1 f_1 d_4{}^4(z_1 f_1 d_5{}^5(z_4 f_1 u_1 u_2, z_4 f_3 u_2)^6 \ldots)^1, d_7{}^1($$
$${}^1(z_1 f_2 d_3)^1, d_8{}^1(z_4 f_2 u_1)^1)^0 \qquad (16)$$

This expression is stored in the computer memory in the KB, as the representation of the initial set of structural components of user programs.

Now let us return to the sequence of the structural components of the program A_1, as shown before in the form of clauses in expression (11). This sequence can be expressed in the following form:

$$F_1^+ = f_1 u_1 u_2, f_1 u_1 u_2, f_2 u_1, f_3 u_2 \qquad (17)$$

As we see, there are two identical structural components in the program A_1, denoted by the same symbol f_1. In this case we apply the following principle:

P1: If in a given user program A_k two identical structural components appear, then the structural components of program A_1 are combined into groups, denoted by symbols $e_1, e_2, e_3, .$ which are treated as values of the parameter "e". In program A_1 there are two groups of structural components, i.e. $e_1(f_1)$ and $e_2(f_1, f_2, f_3)$. For this reason, the sequence F_1^+ (17) of structural components may be expressed in the following form:

$$F_1^{++} = e_1 f_1 u_1 u_2, e_2 f_1 u_1 u_2, e_2 f_2 u_1, e_2 f_3 u_2 \qquad (18)$$

The structural part of the program A_1 is stored in the initial knowledge base in the form of a symbolic expression. This expression can be derived from the sequence F_1^{++} (18). First, from the sequence F_1^+ the expression G_1 is derived.

$$G_1^+ = {}^0(f_1 {}^1(p_1 u_1 e_1 e_2 f_1 {}^2(u_1 e_2 e_2 f_2 {}^3(u_1 e_2 e_2 f_3 {}^4($$
$${}^4(u_2 e_2 f_3 p_1 e_2 f_1)^4)^3, u_2 e_2 f_1 e_1 f_1)^2, u_2 e_1 f_1)^1)^0 \quad (19)$$

Then, the expression G_1^+ is arranged with respect to the elements f_i and is thus transformed into the symbolic expression G_1^{++}:

$$G_1^{++} = {}^0(f_1 {}^1(u_1 p_1 e_1 e_2 f_1, u_2 e_1 f_1, u_2 e_2 f_1 e_1 f_1,$$
$$u_1 e_2 e_2 f_2 {}^2(u_1 e_2 e_2 f_3 {}^3(u_2 e_2 f_3 p_1 e_2 f_1)^3)^2)^1)^0 \quad (20)$$

The expression G_1^{++} is stored in memory as the part of the initial knowledge base that can be called "the set of program structures". In this set each program structure, stored in the KB, should be represented by an appropriate symbol p_i. For this reason the symbol p_1 is placed in the expression G_1^{++}; this indicates that the expression G_1^{++} concerns the program A_1.

In the symbolic expression G_1^{++}, any symbol f_n, placed before an open bracket, represents the structural component of the user program A_1. The term of the type $u_i e_r e_i f_s$ placed in the G_1^{++} after a given open bracket $f_n{}^n($ indicates the connection of the given structural component f^n with another structural component f_s. For example, the term:

$$\ldots f_2 {}^2(u_1 e_2 e_2 f_3 \ldots . \quad \text{means that the component}$$

to which the value e_2 is assigned, is connected with component f_3, that has the same value e_2 assigned to it. This term can be read as follows: "the structural component $e_2 f_2$ is connected with the structural conponent $e_2 f_3$ by the element u_1.". Similarly, the term

$$\ldots f_1 {}^1(\ldots u_2 e_2 f_1 e_1 f_1 \ldots \quad \text{is read as follows: "the structural component}$$

$e_2 f_1$ is connected by the element u_2 with its word end, and after this word there is an element of the structure belonging to the structural component $e_1 f_1$.".

On the basis of the symbolic expression G_1^{++}, the structure of the user program A_1 can be reproduced. For this purpose, the table F (with as contents f_n, the addresses of the f_n, the first d_j in the rule) should be stored in the knowledge base.

In order to determine the structure of program A_1, the terms with the symbol u_1 are read firstly from the expression G_1^{++}; then the terms containing the symbol u_2 are read. The result of this reading process is a sequence $\tilde{F}_1$,

$$F_1 = f_1 u_1 e_1, f_1 u_1 e_2, f_2 u_1 e_2, f_3 u_2 e_2, f_1 u_2 e_2, f_1 u_2 e_1 \quad (21)$$

The translation of the sequence F_1 into a sequence of clauses is realised using the knowledge included in the tables $\bar{F}$, $\bar{D}$ and in the set of structural components (see expression G^{++} (16)).

Now we will consider the operating part of program A_1. In the structural part of this program, expressed as a sequence of clauses (see expressions (11)), operations are represented by the word "op". On the basis of expressions (11) and (18), we can determine the operating part of program A_1 as the following sequence:

$$R_1^+ = e_1 f_1 r_1, e_2 f_1 r_2, e_2 f_2 r_3, e_2 f_3 r_4, e_2 f_3 r_5, e_2 f_3 r_6 \quad (22)$$

Symbols of type r_i, appearing in expression R_1^+, denote the operations "op" contained in the structural component. These operations are stored in the KB as a table R. Every row of this table contains: operation, symbol r_i of this operation, the address of symbol r_i in the KB. The operating part of program A_1, being the sequence of operations, is stored in the KB in the form of the symbolic expression H_1^+,

$$H_1^+ = {}^0(r_1 {}^1(p_1 e_1 f_1 r_2 {}^2(e_2 f_1 r_3 {}^3(e_2 f_2 r_4 {}^4(e_2 f_2 r_5 {}^5($$
$$ {}^5(e_2 f_2 r_6 {}^6(e_2 f_3 r_0)^6)^5 \ldots)^1)^0 \quad (23)$$

where symbol r_0 denotes the end of the sequence of operations included in program A_1. The expression H_1^+ is stored in the KB as the initial set of operations acquired from user program A_1.

5. ACQUISITION OF KNOWLEDGE FROM A USER PROGRAM

Now consider another user program A_2. We assume that the initial knowledge base does exist in the computer memory. We also assume that new elements of knowledge, included in program A_2, are to be extracted from this program and acquired by the computer for its KB. In this paper the knowledge extracted from program A_1 (see section 4) represents the initial knowledge base, whereas the knowledge contained in program A_2 stands for the additional knowledge to be acquired.

User program A_2 looks like this:

```
begin for i := 1 to n-1 do
  begin k := i; x := a[i]; j := i;
    for j := j + 1 to n do
      if a[j].key < x.key then
        begin k := j; x := a j end
      a[k] := a[i];   a[i] := x    end end        (24)
```

The structural part of this program, expressed as a sequence of structural components, has the following form:

1. <u>begin</u> <u>for</u> op <u>do</u> next <u>end</u> $\leftrightarrow$ u_1, u_2;
2. <u>begin</u> op next op <u>end</u> $\leftrightarrow$ u_1, u_2, u_3;
3. <u>for</u> op <u>do</u> $\leftrightarrow$ u_1;
4. <u>if</u> op <u>then</u> $\leftrightarrow$ u_1;
5. <u>begin</u> op <u>end</u> $\leftrightarrow$ u_2;   (25)

As we can see, these structural components do not yet have names of the f_n type. For this reason, each structural component is checked with the set of structural components, which is stored in the initial knowledge base in the form of the symbolic expression G^{++} (16) and the Table $\bar{D}$ (see fig. 5). Since the structural components 1,4,5 of program A_2 are already included in expression G^{++} (16), the names f_1, f_2, f_3 of these components are read from this expression. However, the structural components 2 and 3 of program A_2 are not contained in expression G^{++} and should be stored in the KB. For this purpose, structural components 2 and 3 (see expression (25)) are transformed into a rule format as follows:

Rule 4:   IF begin op next op end THEN f_4, u_1, u_2, u_3
Rule 5:   IF for op do THEN f_5, u_1

The symbol u_3, placed in rule 3, indicates a connection between the word "next" appearing in the rule and the word "op" placed after the word "next". Then the rules 4 and 5 are transformed into symbolic expressions $\tilde{G}_4^+$ and $\tilde{G}_5^+$,

$$\tilde{G}_4^+ = {}^0(d_1{}^1(z_1 f_4 d_3{}^2(z_1 f_4 d_5{}^3(z_1 f_4 d_3{}^4(z_1 f_4 d_6{}^5($$
$$ {}^5(z_4 f_4 u_1 u_2 u_3)^5 \ldots)^1)^0 \qquad (26)$$

$$\tilde{G}_5^+ = {}^0(d_2{}^1(z_1 f_5 d_3{}^2(z_1 f_5 d_4{}^3(z_4 f_5 u_1)^3 \ldots)^1)^0 \qquad (27)$$

The symbolic expressions $\tilde{G}_4^+$ and $\tilde{G}_5^+$ represent knowledge to be acquired in the domain of the structural components of user programs. This knowledge is added to the knowledge that is already stored in the KB in the form of the symbolic expression $\tilde{G}^{++}$. The result of this addition is the symbolic expression $\tilde{G}_{ext}^{++}$.'

$$\tilde{G}_{ext}^{++} = {}^0(d_1{}^1(z_1 f_4 d_3, z_1 f_3 d_3, z_1 f_1 d_2{}^2(z_1 f_5 d_3, z_1 f_1 d_3{}^3($$
$$ z_1 f_4 d_6, z_1 f_4 d_5, z_1 f_5 d_4, z_1 f_3 d_6, z_1 f_2 d_8, z_1 f_1 d_4{}^4($$
$$ z_4 f_5 u_1, z_1 f_1 d_5{}^5(z_1 f_4 d_3, z_1 f_1 d_6{}^6(z_4 f_4 u_1 u_2 u_3, z_4 f_1 u_1 u_2,$$
$$ z_4 f_3 u_2)^6)^5 \ldots)^1, d_7{}^1(z_1 f_2 d_3)^1, d_8{}^1(z_4 f_2 u_1)^1)^0$$

$$(28)$$

The expression G_{ext}^{++} represents the extended set of structural components.

The next step of the knowledge acquiring process is to determine that part of the structure of program A_2 that is not yet stored in the KB. As we now have symbols as names for the structural components of program A_2, we can express the structure of program A_2 as a sequence F_2^+,

$$F_2^+ = f_1 u_1 u_2, f_4 u_1 u_2 u_3, f_5 u_1, f_2 u_1, f_3 u_2 \qquad (29)$$

Sequence F_2^+ can be transformed into another form, denoted by symbol $\bar{F}_2^+$,

$$\bar{F}_2^+ = f_1 u_1, f_4 u_1, f_5 u_1, f_2 u_1, f_3 u_2, f_4 u_3, f_4 u_2, f_1 u_2 \qquad (30)$$

From sequence $\bar{F}_2^+$ the computer derives symbolic expression $\bar{G}_2^+$:

$$\bar{G}_2^+ = {}^0(f_1{}^1(p_2 u_1 f_4{}^2(u_1 f_5{}^3(u_1 f_2{}^4(u_1 f_3{}^5(u_2 f_3 f_4)^5$$
$$)^4)^3, u_3 f_4 f_5, u_2 f_4 f_1)^2, u_2 f_1)^1)^0 \qquad (31)$$

In order to determine the values e_r of the parameter "e", characterising a part of the structure of program A_2, the expression $\bar{G}_2^+$ is compared with the symbolic expression G_1^{++} (20) . As a result of this comparison, the structural components of program A_2 are divided into three groups: $e_1(f_1)$, $e_3(f_4 f_5)$ and $e_2(f_2, f_3)$. Notice that group $e_2(f_2, f_3)$ also belongs to group $e_2(f_1, f_2, f_3)$, appearing in the structure of program A_1 (see expression (18)).
On the basis of the above mentioned values of e_r of parameter "e", the expression $\bar{G}_2^+$ may be transformed into a symbolic expression G_2^+,

$$G_2^+ = {}^0(f_1{}^1(p_2 u_1 e_1 e_3 f_4{}^2(u_1 e_3 e_3 f_5{}^3(u_1 e_3 e_2 f_2{}^4($$
$$^4(u_1 e_2 e_2 f_3{}^5(u_2 e_2 f_3 p_2 e_3 f_4)^5)^4)^3, u_3 e_3 f_4 e_3 f_4,$$
$$u_2 e_3 f_4 e_1 f_1)^2, u_2 e_1 f_1)^1)^0 \qquad (32)$$

Then the expression G_2^+ is arranged in order of ascending elements f_n, and is transformed into the symbolic expression G_2^{++},

$$G_2^{++} = {}^0(f_1{}^1(u_2 e_1 f_1, p_2 u_1 e_1 e_3 f_4{}^2(u_2 e_3 f_4 e_3 f_4,$$
$$u_2 e_3 f_4 e_1 f_1, u_1 e_3 e_3 f_5{}^3(u_1 e_3 e_2 f_2{}^4(u_1 e_2 e_2 f_3$$
$$^5(^5(u_2 e_2 f_2 p_2 e_3 f_4)^5)^4)^3)^2)^1)^0 \qquad (33)$$

The expression G_2^{++} represents the knowledge to be acquired for the domain of program structures.
Next expression G_1^{++} (20) is combined with expression G_2^{++}. The result of this operation is a symbolic expression G_{ext}^{++}, representing the extended KB in the domain of program structures:

$$G_{ext.}^{++} = {}^0(f_1{}^1(u_1p_1e_1e_2f_1, u_2e_1f_1, u_2e_2f_1e_1f_1,$$
$$p_2u_1e_1e_3f_4, u_1e_2e_2f_2{}^2(u_1e_2e_2f_3{}^3(u_2e_2f_3p_1e_2f_1,$$
$$u_2e_2f_2p_2e_3f_4{}^4(u_3e_3f_4e_3f_4, u_2e_3f_4e_1f_1,$$
$$u_1e_3e_3f_5{}^5(u_1e_3e_2f_2){}^5){}^4){}^3){}^2){}^1){}^0 \qquad (34)$$

The symbol p_1 in expression $G_{ext.}^{++}$ enables the conputer to search the knowledge that is included in program A_1. The same counts for symbol p_2, that indicates the knowledge concerning program A_2. Moreover, in the KB exists a Table $P(p_i -- f_n r_k)$ which indicates the initial values of f_n and r_k in the expressions $G_{ext.}^{++}$ and $H_{ext.}^{++}$, for every user program.

The operating part of the user program can be considered in a similar manner to the structural part. Namely, the knowledge contained in the operating part of program A_2 can be added to the knowledge which is already stored in the KB. The final result of this procedure is a symbolic expression $H_{ext.}^{++}$. This symbolic expression represents the extended KB in the domain of operations that are included in user programs A_1 and A_2.

6. CONCLUSION

In this paper a new approach to the acquisition of knowledge and its integration into the knowledge base of the computer is introduced. The problems associated with the application of the presented solution deserve a separate discussion and should be considered in another paper. The main areas where such an application could be put to use are automated programming, decision support systems and expert systems.

Practical application of the presented solutions in a decision support system or expert system will give some important advantages. The main one is that the proposed description of an extended knowledge base, formulated as a set of symbolic expressions, enables the computer to search and extract any piece of knowledge present in its KB. It can for instance easily be proven that using the symbolic expression $G_{ext.}^{++}$ (8) (see section 3) the computer will find any clause that belongs to rule 1 or to rule 2. For example, when a question comes up that contains the clause R, the computer will generate an answer containing either the whole rule 1 or just clause A or R. When cluase P is included in a question, the computer will generate an answer that includes clauses A and C. Moreover, with symbolic expressions of the type $G_{ext.}^{++}$ in its memory, the computer can modify the knowledge contained in the KB, make inferences, and can create new clauses and new rules.

It is obvious that in the KB of decision support systems descriptions of situations, about which decisions are to be made, should be stored. These descriptions, expressed in natural language, can also be transformed into symbolic expressions. There do exist some relations between symbolic expressions representing descriptions of the mentioned situations, and symbolic expressions representing production rules. These relations, denoted by appropriate symboles, can be formulated as the mentioned symbolic expressions. When a user wants to use this system, he should give a description in natural language of the given situation. This discription is then translated into a symbolic expression. If such an expression is included in the appropriate part of the KB, then the computer will generate the adequate sequence of decisions.

Let us now consider the application of the presented solution in the domain of automated programming. In this paper, for simplicity, the acquisition of knowledge included in comments of user programs is not considered. We do know, however, that the comments included in an user program written in higher-lever language contain information about the task which will be executed by the computer. Such knowledge, expressed in natural language, can also be transformed into symbolic expressions, and then stored in an appropriata place in the KB. This part of the KB can be very important for an automated synthesis of a user program on the basis of knowledge included in a KB.

Let us now suppose that a computer has its own KB and presume also that in such a KB the knowledge, acquired from several user programs, is stored. In this case the KB consists of two parts; a part that contains specifications of tasks and another part that contains the algorithms for solving these tasks. Let us assume for instance that the user of this system wants to solve a task like sorting some numbers. The user presents a request to the system such as: "Sort n numbers from the least number to the greatest number". This clause is transformed by the computer into a symbolic expression, and then this expression is looked for in the first part of the KB. If it is found there, then the computer is able to solve the task presented by the user. In this case the computer answers that he is able to solve this task. The user then enters the data on which the task is to be performed. On the basis of the knowledge considering the given task in the second part of the KB, the compiler builds the required user program in Pascal. This program is then translated into machine language and executed.

However, if the specification of a given type of task is not included in the first part of the KB, the computer requires a user program for it. In this case the user has to write a program in Pascal. This program is then executed and the knowledge contained in it is stored in the KB in the same manner as is shown in section 5.

REFERENCES

1. Bose J.H., Personal Construct Theory and the Transfer
   of Human Expertise, ECAI-1984, Proceedings of 6th European
   Conference on Artificial Intelligence, (Pisa 1984)
   Elsevier Science Publishers B.V., North-Holland.
2. Clancey W,J., The Epistemology of a Rule-Based Expert System -
   a Framework for Explanation, Artificial Intelligence 20 (1983),
   Elsevier Science Publishers B.V. North Holland.
3. Kazimierczak J., Introduction to Synthesis of the Self-Organizing
   Operating System Nucleus, ECAI-1984, Proceedings of 6th European
   Conference on Artificial Intelligence, (Pisa 1984) Elsevier
   Science Publishers B.V., North-Holland.
4. Kazimierczak J., A Symbolic Manipulation on Graphs as a Method
   of Synthesis of a Self-Organizing Operating System Nucleus.
   Report 2/84, ICT, Technical University of Wroclaw, Wroclaw 1985
5. Wielinga B.J. and Breuker J.A., Interpretation of Verbal Data
   for Knowledge Acquisition, ECAI-1984, Proceedings of 6th European
   Conference on Artificial Intelligence, (Pisa 1984)
   Elsevier Science Publishers B.V., North-Holland.
6. Wirth N., Algorithms + Data Structures = Programs,
   Prentice-Hall, Inc., Englewood Cliffs, New Jersey, 1976.

ANALYSIS OF POTENTIAL FOR NEW PLACES OF BUSINESS

J.J.J. van Beek
BSO/Management Support bv
P.O. Box 8348
3503 RH UTRECHT
The Netherlands

ABSTRACT. A Dutch wholesale dealer found himself to be in the following nasty position. To increase his turnover he had to increase the number of places of business (selling points). On the other hand, the independent undertaker usually would not be able to do the funding himself and was found to fall back on the wholesale dealer. So every next place of business meant an increase in turnover, but also an increase of financial risk. To make the best of this situation, a number of analysts scouted for low risk, high profit situations. They used pen, paper, their eyes, their feet (to measure the competition's selling space) and their knowledge. And this is the keyword: knowledge. Most of the knowledge about how to find a promising opportunity was in the head of one man. His age was 63, which meant that - in the Netherlands - his pension was due within two years.
The problem was how to structure the extensive knowledge of this man, so that is could be stored in and interpreted by a computer. The solution was to build, together with this expert, an expert system, or from another point of view, a decision support system.
This paper will give an overview of how the system was built, what the major components were and how the system is used. Or, as the expert said after finishing the system, "It is nearly as good as I am".

INTRODUCTION

This article describes the system that was built by BSO/Management Support, a subsidiary company of the large Dutch software house BSO, the support decision making for a Dutch wholesale dealer.
The wholesale organisation was supplying a large number of grocery stores (more than 1000) and was planning to substantially increase this number. This is generally a very sensible thing to do, since more shops mean more turnover, which, given good cost control, means more profit.

The problem, however, was that the shops were run by 'independent' undertakers, who usually were not able to raise the necessary funds themselves. Logically, the consequence was that the financing consisted of bank

293

I. G. Sol et al. (eds.), Expert Systems and Artificial Intelligence in Decision Support Systems, 293–299.
© *1987 by D. Reidel Publishing Company.*

loans guaranteed by the wholesale dealer or directly by the dealer. So
every new store meant an extra financial risk.

The decision making situation may be described as the following: which
selling points should be allocated where, so that turnover is maximized
and risk is minimized.

The solution the company used until a few years ago was to have a number
of researchers (4 to 5) spot profitable situations and calculate the
risk and turnover.
This was, however, thought of as a moderate to poor solution for a number of reasons. First of all, every analysis was a case on its own and
not comparable with any other case. As a result, no statistics were
available and no objective measure could be produced for the quality of
the analysis.
Secondly, because it was quite a complex job consisting of a huge amount
of work, it was hard to be confident of the end results. Re-calculation
or trying out a few alternative ideas was nearly impossible.
And last, but certainly not least, the general opinion was that only
one of the researchers was grade A. The only problem with this man, was
that he was 63 and had only two years to go before retiring.

Summarizing, management was faced with three challenges:

1. Structure the analysis process so that analysis data and outcome
    should become comparable.
    As a consequence, statistics should be built up to increase the
    quality of standards used for the analysis. It should also be pos-
    sible to compare a number of alternative investments (shops) and
    choose the best.

2. Automate the process and with this, reduce the number of errors
    made during calculation and data input. This was felt to be a dif-
    ficult procedure, since a general belief was that calculations were
    rather complex (a lot of if-then rules), while also a high degree
    of flexilibity was required.
    Regular automation was seen as a non-viable solution.

3. Transfer - in a short time - all conscious (and if possible also
    the subconscious) knowledge from the expert's head to the organi-
    sation. Combining this with the two objectives above, the task was
    to build an automated system that held, not only the data and ex-
    periences of the expert mentioned, but also his reasoning ability
    relating to the analysis.

APPROACH

BSO/Management Support was asked to make a proposition for the above
stated objectives. They did, and the two companies agreed on the following scheme of actions:

a) BSO/Management Support, together with the wholesale dealer (about 50/50) was to build a prototype of the required system on a micro computer available at BSO.
   BSO was to supply a project leader and a prototyper, both for a part of their time.
   The wholesale company supplied the future systems co-ordinator as a co-builder and the (63 year-old) expert.

b) Since the prototype would, for a large part, be built by the users themselves, it was agreed upon that a five day course would be part of the project.
   This course would not only be attended by the two project partici-pants, but also by the management and the end users of the system (a group of all together 12 people).
   To involve the users in every phase of the project, the course con-sisted of information and data analysis, prototyping and APL, as this was the language used for the prototype.

c) Based on interviews, BSO was to produce the first architecture of the system. Next, the user was to modify and restructure the system. After this, BSO and the user were to iterate through 'think and build'.
   A total of three iterations was planned.

d) After acceptance of the final prototype, a conversion step was plan-ned. At the moment of planning the target computer was unknown. Later it was decided that this was going to be an IBM PC.

e) Finally a step was planned to make the prototype operational on the target machine. This step involved adding error checking and recove-ry, update and filing facilities, definition of procedures, authori-sation and organisation.

Overall, there was a strong feeling that flexibility and user friendli-ness of the system should be provided for in an extensive way.

For the man machine interface the choice fell on dynamic menus (menus dependent on what data has been typed in before) in combination with interactive data entry (input, see results, modify, etc.).

Flexibility was provided for in a constraint way. Since standardising the procedure without losing the possibility to specify case-specific data was a primary objective, the following was decided.
1. The main processing flow would be strict and not open to modifica-tion.
2. For all flows (main and sub) standard data values should be avail-able.
3. On all flows the user should be able to change standard data to specific values and accompany this modification with a remark.
4. On all subflows (usually output options) the user may modify the programs.

SYSTEM OVERVIEW

To support the argument that this system is an expert system, some insight in how it is structured and what it does is needed.

The system is composed of 6 functional modules, each of which will shortly be described hereafter.

I   Market module

For every potential establishment a case analysis has to be executed. The basis of this analysis is the estimation of the market size. To get an estimate of this, the market is divided into a primary and a secondary market. For each of the two the number of inhabitants is given over a period of 5 years. The system may now calculate the total amount of money to spend on groceries based on average values, which can be altered by the user.
If specific data about, e.g. what kind of neighbourhood, is available, this may be used to alter the outcome.

The end result of the market module is a good estimate of the total market size for groceries for the selling point under analysis.

II Competition module

Within the defined market all competition is entered in the system on a one by one basis.
For every competitor a large number of data may be specified. Some of these data are mandatory, such as square meters, number of checkouts, type of store (supermarket, drugstore, etc.), chain (AH, Hema, etc.) and so on.
Based on these data, the system will provide an estimate of the shops' turnover which, of course, may be modified by the user.

Three competitors are of special interest. First, there is a possible existing store, that will be taken over from every competitor. Because the competitors' type is known, a very interesting phenomenon occurs. By adding all partial turnovers (split up by assortment) the user may get an insight in what kind of shop formula might fit into that market. Also, if the shop formula is known, the specific percentages may be amended to match the partial turnovers.

The end result of the competition module is a very detailed estimate of the turnover of the investment (shop) under analysis.

III Investment module

To get a shop running, a substantial number of investments is needed. In the investment module all possible investments (and reinvestments) may be specified by the user.
The system will automatically take into account all kinds of aids

(investment, size, etc.) and will also calculate the different V.A.T. values.

All together this module has a lot of built in complexity, but presents itself to the user as rather straightforward.

IV   Finance module

Evidently investment should be financed. A number of options is open to the user. Bank loans, current account, wholesaler loan, owner capital etc.
Every type of financing has its own cost and limits.

The end result of this module is a financing scheme that should provide sufficient capital to carry out the specified investments.

V   Revenue account module

The next, and very important, module is the revenue account module. Here the cost of doing business is specified. A large number of these cost factors are more or less related to factors like the type of shop, assortment, whether there is an own butcher's or not, average amount spent at the check-out, etc., etc..

At the end of this module the user has a detailed overview of profit before taxation, as well as a turnover overview.

VI   Balance sheet/Profit and Loss/Ratios

The last module produces a five-year overview of properties and debts (balance sheets), of turnover and cost of turnover (profit and loss), of the expected cashflow and numerous ratios to give an insight in things like the pay back period, return on investment, discounted cashflow and so on.

From this point on the user may wish to go back to the finance module to use some of the cash(flow) to lower his loans. Also he might decide to start again at any other module and by iterating improve the quality of his analysis.

EXPERT SYSTEM?

Most people would agree that the system described in this article is a decision support system (DSS). Some would agree that that is an expert system.

From the viewpoint of BSO/Management Support, it is most certainly a DSS and BSO/Management Support argues as follows, that it may be called an expert system.

1. The system most surely implements knowledge, data and experience of
    a human expert into an automated system.

2. The system has no artificial intelligence subsystem to support
    things like natural language interfaces, rule definition facili-
    ties, or learning capabilities.
    These approaches were explicitly ruled out. The man machine inter-
    face is built up from dynamic menus and question and answer.
    How does this compare to a natural language interface?
    Well, a difficult menu is easier to understand than easy French.

    Rule definition is possible for subflows in the system and are open
    to the user who understands APL.

    Learning is implemented in a controlled way. By updating standard
    values and/or rules from the system manager's system (based on
    statistics, macro economics, etc.), the behavior of the system may
    change.
    Local learning was explicitly ruled out, as this would allow local
    versions of the system to grow apart.

    BSO/Management Support does not recognise man machine interface,
    rule definition or learning capabilities as determining factors for
    expert systems.

3. In operation, the system will co-operate with human beings. In this
    co-operation the user will be the steering party, but the system
    has the expert knowledge and data.
    Evidently this will result in optimal decision information.

CONCLUSION

Maybe the best way to conclude this description of a DSS that might be
called an expert system, is by stating a few simple facts.

-   The system was completely accepted by the expert, management and
    users, and is seen as a replacement for the expert.

-   The system can easily grow in data as well as in rules.

-   Development time was short (six months), cost low (Dfl 50.000,--).

-   It runs on a plain micro computer (IBM PC) and is built in a plain
    language (APL).

The following thesis might be defendable:

    "Experts are specialised ordinary people -
     Expert systems are specialised ordinary systems".

REFERENCES

Harmon P., King D., Expert Systems
John Wiley & Sons, Inc., New York, 1985

Buchanan B.G., Shortcliffe E.H..
Rule Based Expert Systems: the MYCIN Experiments of the Stanford
Neuristic Programming Project
Addison-Wesley, Reading, Massachusetts, 1984

Expert Systems and Micros
G.L. Simons, NCC Publications

Algorithms for Artificial Intelligence in APL2
Santa Teresa Technical Report, TR 03.281
Dr. James Brown et al. (to appear in May 1986)

Expert Systemen, proceedings NGI/SIC conferentie 16-12-1985
Sic-C16

THE SHAPING OF MANAGEMENT DECISION SCIENCE WITH INTELLIGENT TECHNOLOGY

Professor Charles H. Kriebel
Graduate School of Industrial Administration
Carnegie-Mellon University
Pittsburgh, PA 15213
USA

ABSTRACT. Technology has captured society's imagination and in the process the promise for enhanced productivity to the benefit of all. To management falls the responsibility to deliver on the promise and to capitalize on the best methods technology has to offer, recognizing that there are no "miraculous" solutions. This paper examines management decision as an evolutionary object of science with particular attention to computer-based, "intelligent technology." The shape of management decision science has emerged through the discipline of mathematics and the medium of information technology towards closer linkages between the fields of operations research and psychology/computer science-based problem solving paradigms in artificial intelligence. Despite cultural differences, the synergy is quite natural and the promise significant. We survey this evolution, caution the unwary on progress, and conjecture on the promise. The potential for impact and payoff is great, but de facto gains will take time and require substantial further work and understanding. Deja vu.

1. INTRODUCTION: THE PROLOG IS HISTORY

Technology has the potential to uplift our state of existence and to improve the standard of living throughout the world. Technology also holds the potential to destroy us -- little-by-little or all at once. In most respects technology is neutral; human beings determine which technology is developed and how it is applied. The principals responsible for delivering on the progress technology offers include scientists, engineers, and managers. Over time technology has changed the infrastructure of society, the organization of its institutions, and the conduct of processes within them. My focus in this essay is on the intervention of technology into the process of management.

New technology captures our imagination, especially through the popular media. "Newer technology.." often translates into "greater imagination." Last year the weekly trade periodical, Business Week, featured on the cover of one issue, a picture of the storybook character, The Scarecrow from The Wizard of Oz, smiling with a personal

H. G. Sol et al. (eds.), Expert Systems and Artificial Intelligence in Decision Support Systems, 301–315.
© *1987 by D. Reidel Publishing Company.*

computer on his lap under the bold title: "ARTIFICIAL INTELLIGENCE,
It's Here!" (see reference 2). I suspect this publicity helped to sell
extra copies of that week's issue of the magazine, but I'm not sure it
helped the cases of either scientists or managers in the field. The
incident, however, does serve to highlight the need for managing expectations (real or imagined) with respect to any new technology; and
artificial intelligence (or AI) is no exception.

I am neither an evangelist nor a doomsayer for the field of AI.
I believe I am an objective participant in the development of the field,
at least as it relates to the profession and process of management. Any
student in the field can tell you AI is not really "new" technology;
its origins date back at least thirty years or more -- including (re-
searched) applications to management problems (see 22). Actual research
on the potential of AI was one of the attractions that brought me to
Carnegie from M.I.T. over twenty years ago. This included not only the
pathbreaking work by A. Newell and H. Simon on "The General Problem
Solver (GPS)," but the thesis work by F. Tonge on "heuristic programming for assembly-line balancing" and the work by G. Clarkson on "simulating the portfolio decision behavior of a trust investment officer."
(See 5). Subsequently, one of my student, G. B. Bennett, building on
developments in operations research and his own industrial experience
extended Tonge's early efforts in his own thesis, "assembly-line balancing with a trainable heuristic." In my early research related to AI,
I have always believed that the guiding principle for systems design
was "synergy" (see 12, 13). Consequently, my remarks are those of a
management scientist with appropriate and proper emphasis on the "end
user" as manager -- professional and practitioner (see 9 and 22).

This conference opened on a philosophical question of choice in
methodology for modeling and design in inductive problem solving
systems. A distinction may be drawn between methods based primarily on
the paradigm of substantive rational behavior which are operations research (OR) dominant, and those based on the procedural rational behavior paradigm which can be viewed as AI dominant. That is, in the
latter case rationality depends on the procedure guiding behavior and
"intelligent" is defined by the process employed. Design considerations
involve the tradeoffs and balance desired.

Before I get into or ahead of the story, the conference explored
three areas of general interest: knowledge engineering, design environments, and applications. I will adopt a similar organization for discussion. In the next section, a brief summary of the evolution of
management decision science is provided. This leads into a description
of what can be called "the environment of intelligent technology."
Based on it, I propose some hypotheses on the current state of the field
and suggest some priorities on how to best shape progress into the
future. The essay concludes with some conjectures on what that future
might be.

2.   MANAGEMENT DECISION SCIENCE AND 'THE SHAPE OF AUTOMATION.'

In the conference announcement and "call for papers" the organizers reference Herbert A. Simon's 1965 book, <u>The Shape of Automation: For Men and Machines</u> (see 23), noting that this seminal work "breathes optimism" about the future. One of the major contributions it and subsequent work provided was the delineation of "The New Science of Management Decision" which added to our professional vocabularies the concepts of programmable and non-programmable decisions and structured and ill-structured problems.

Some ten years earlier building on work that originated (initially in Europe) during World War II, the Operations Research Society of America was founded. Shortly thereafter a sister society, The Institute of Management Sciences was organized to highlight the focus and emphasis on management problems. Although the notion of a "science of management" really began at the turn of the century with the early work by management and industrial engineers, these two organizations and their international brethern have contributed much toward achieving the reality. Not surprisingly their two major journals, <u>Management Science</u> and <u>Operations Research</u>, have experienced growing pains since their existence, in how they have attempted to organize the discipline in adolescence and in how they have sought to communicate with their memberships and their audience at large.

Today each journal is structured along two primary dimensions: underlying technique and functional management or problem application area. At the risk of oversimplification, one might remark that research articles along the first (technique) dimension tend to be more theoretical, abstract and technology-driven in nature, and that research articles along the second dimension tend to be more problem-driven and real world or institutional referenced. (However, the dichotomy is by no means as clear cut as this seems to imply.)

Progress in information technology, notably computers, has paralleled and been a catalyst for the development of management decision science as a field. Not surprisingly, increased computational power has facilitated the representation, formulation and solution of larger and more complex decision problems with the development of better algorithms and/or simulation methods. The world of the management decision scientist's laboratory has become a richer place, as more of the outside world has been able to enter and more relevant solutions have been able to leave. But how far have we been able to open the laboratory door? The answer depends on what the comparison makes reference to. For example, from thirty or twenty years ago? A lot. But, from what is still on the outside? Not enough, by a wide margin.

Without intending to sound trivial, most (not all) of what has been addressed still resides in Simon's well-structured problem, programmable decision domains. The reasons for this are obvious, however, exploration of alternative methods and approaches continues. The vehicle facilitating this investigation has been computer technology and in recent history this technology is becoming "intelligent."

3.   THE ENVIRONMENT OF 'INTELLIGENT TECHNOLOGY'

For clarification, the principal components of technology include:
computer hardware (and allied equipment or machines), programs or
software, people and infrastructure. Software can be further catego-
rized into applications programs, a system manager (which includes an
executive program or operating system), databases, model-bases and
knowledge bases. For example, Alter (see 1) classifies decision support systems (DSS) according to whether they are primarily data-oriented
(such as routine statistical analyses) or model-oriented (such as an
accounting system or one based on an optimization representation). My
point here is that all of these elements are included as components of
the technological environment.

Which components of technology can be considered "intelligent?"
Or more basically, what constitutes "intelligence" in this context? The
answer, alluded to earlier, is through a process model. Simon (24)
refers to this characterization as the "physical symbol system hypothesis." A physical symbol system (one that can deal with symbols or
patterns) requires the following capabilities: to read symbols or
patterns from some environment; to relate symbols to each other and
symbol structures (i.e., relational schemes associating the symbols);
to store symbols in some form of memory; to compare symbols and decide
whether a pair is the same or not based on some test; and to branch
(i.e., change processing control) based on a comparison test. A computer program is a physical symbol system in the sense of this characterization.

An elementary description of the properties of an intelligent
agent in terms of a symbol system involves its architecture and its
contents. Architecture is described by the "representation" employed,
the "access" methods, and "control." The domains of representation
include: objects and situations (a declarative representational form),
desires (i.e., goals, sub-goals and preferences), tasks (e.g., problem
spaces, cause symbols, operators), and procedures (e.g., select-and-
apply operators, for behavior, economics and planning). Access is required to "short-term knowledge" in the context of the current task and
to "long-term knowledge" as given by a knowledge base. Control is
required to focus attention and to resolve conflicts during the problem-
solving process.

Much of the recent work in AI has focused on the sub-field known
as "expert systems" (ES) and knowledge engineering (KE), often characterized by the specialized programming languages employed (such as rule-
based production systems). In (8) the authors describe what they call
"the anatomy of an ideal expert system" (see also 6,7,14,15,20 and 28).
They state the qualification "ideal" because no existing ES incorporates
all of their components (as of 1983).

> "The ideal expert system contains a language processor for
> problem-oriented communications between the user and the
> expert system; a 'blackboard' for recording immediate re-
> sults; a 'knowledge base' comprising facts as well as
> heuristic planning and problem-solving rules; an interpreter
> that applies these rules; a scheduler to control the order

of rule processing; a consistency enforcer that adjusts
previous conclusions when new data (or knowledge) alter
their bases of support; and a justifier that rationalizes
and explains the system's behavior" [i.e., of solution
progress and reasons in response to queries from the user].
(Reference 8, p. 18)

The "blackboard" provides a record of intermediate (and final) results
for three types of decision representation: the "plan" (the general
strategy for solving the problem, current goals, states, etc.), the
"agenda" (i.e., potential actions or rules scheduled to be executed),
and the "solution" (i.e., candidate decisions and hypotheses generated
thus far, and relational dependencies among decisions or links).

The authors (loc.cit., p. 14) further suggest the following generic
categories of knowledge engineering or expert system applications:

Interpretation -- Inferring situation descriptions from sensor data;
Prediction -- Inferring likely consequences of given situations;
Diagnosis -- Inferring "system" malfunctions from observables;
Design -- Configuring objects under constraints (i.e., descriptions
    in various relationships);
Planning -- "Designing" actions (i.e., for objects that perform
    functions);
Monitoring -- Comparing observations to "plan" vulnerabilities or
    flaws (e.g., constraint violation);
Debugging -- Prescribing remedies for malfunctions (typically a
    combination of "plan + design + prediction");
Repair -- Executing a plan to administer a prescribed remedy
    (typically a combination of "debug + plan + execution");
Instruction -- "Diagnosing, debugging and repairing "student
    behavior;
Control -- "Interpreting, predicting, repairing and monitoring"
    system behaviors.

Other classifications and descriptions of applications of KE or ES are
given in references (6,7,10,14 and 15).

If one were to attempt to generate a similar generic listing of
applications/methods/models/problems for the fields of operations research and management sciences based on the open literature and, say,
as given by the taxonomy employed by I.F.O.R.S. (International Federa-
tion of Operations Research Societies), we would obviously observe some
overlap but also notice more aggregative categories. For example, an
OR/MS listing would include: resource allocation (scheduling/sequencing
etc.), transportation/distribution, decision analysis, inventory, planning, bargaining/negotiation, investment, prediction/forecasting, accounting, strategy, information systems, and so on. Many of these no
doubt would also be focused on a decision aspect of problem solving,
i.e., choosing from among a set of alternatives according to a criterion, etc. However, this latter consideration is also integral to the
AI/ES process model as described above, so we require some other dimensions if we wish to juxtapose the two approaches for comparison.

At the risk of oversimplification, AI/ES models are primarily
symbolic in nature: they employ sumbols and declarative reasoning in
the form of relational schemes and forms or laws of action; the variables

typically range over logical relations and attributes; and their support systems are usually knowledge intensive (i.e., the knowledge bases contain large numbers of rules--on the order of 10^3). In contrast, OR/MS models are primarily quantitative in nature: they employ algebra and procedural reasoning in the form of mathematical relations, computational algorithms and heuristics; the variables typically range over numerical data and descriptive facts; and their support systems are usually computation and (factual) data intensive.

For comparison, suppose we define <u>computation</u> (or "search") as "the amount of knowledge employed per step in a process" (or, equivalently, "the number of times a rule is utilized in solving a problem"). Similarly, suppose <u>knowledge</u> is defined simply as "the number of rules stored in a knowledge base." Now envision a two-dimensional graph with "computation" plotted along the abscissa (x-axis) and "knowledge" plotted along the ordinate (y-axis). Points located close to the origin are "shallow" with respect to either dimension and points located away from the origin will be called "intensive," similarly. Newell (17) has suggested we can represent Architecture in Problem Solving on this graph as a rectangular hyperbola with respect to the origin, and the design question to be answered is the tradeoff between the search to find knowledge versus the amount of time it is used for computing. For example, many expert systems would be located towards the asymptote of the graph along the ordinate axis (i.e., some rules in a knowledge base are never used or used only once). In contrast, many OR/MS models (such as those based on a branch-and-bound algorithm) are along the opposite extremity of the graph--towards an asymptote of the abscissa (e.g., where a single rule may be employed hundreds or more times during a solution episode). Applications of management decision sciences, such as in decision support systems area, might be located across the entire graph or within this schematic framework.

The basic limitations of the current state of ES technology, such as those noted by B. Buchanan and R. Davis, have been well chronicled (e.g., 6) in the literature and do not require elaboration here--as have those of OR/MS technology in the extreme (e.g., 9,23,24 and 25). These include the narrow domain of expertise considered, the limitations of available knowledge representation languages, fragile behavior (they do not perform well at the boundaries of their knowledge base), laborious construction and maintenance, and the requirement for a dominant expert or "knowledge czar," as well as a knowledge expert to operate the system (see 6). But, there are also classes of problems which remain notoriously "wicked" for AI researchers.

One of these classes of problems is <u>pattern recognition</u>, expecially in the realm of human vision. Early in the history of AI the "vision problem" solution was considered a summer research project for graduate students by some academics. We have been much humbled by subsequent research on the complexity of this issue. Consider an infant who within a few months after birth can recognize its mother from among a vast complex array of visual and aural stimuli. We are at best just beginning to understand the array of phenomena involved. Another class of "wicked problems" are those involving human <u>judgment</u>. For example, consider the context of selecting an appropriate (or ideal) wine with dinner and the host of subtleties brought to bear. Or more simply (superficially) a teenager's preference for a brandname soft drink--could he/she explain their preferences, notwithstanding their convictions? A third difficult class of problems for AI systems is the familiar area of context understanding, especially with respect to language and human communication. We recognize that natural language requires much more than lexical content; it needs concepts about "expectations" and "conceptual dependencies," etc. But we are still groping for good theories (e.g., see 15 and 18).

Where does the field stand in intelligent technology and what should be the priorities for research in management decision science? These questions are addressed next.

4. SOME HYPOTHESES ASSERTED

In an attempt to bring some order to this discourse, I will advance five hypotheses which I believe are in the process of being confirmed by the experience of the past two decades, but are not proven by any stretch of the imagination. The hypotheses are also not necessarily original (I am confident variations on them exist in the literature, although I haven't explicitly sought out citations), and I expect colleagues will philosophically (or otherwise) take exception. I offer them as hypotheses for discussion and debate.

4.1 'AI does not seek to replicate the human brain.'

Much of the early criticism of AI was rooted in the perceived claims by those working in the field of AI that their research was a "replication of God's handiwork." There is no question that the basic research in AI concerned the search for knowledge in understanding human cognition and problem solving processes in humans, but this is significantly different from the popular criticism. Science, whether "natural" or "artificial" (see 22), seeks understanding, knowledge and truth about phenomena; the concept of "intelligence" is not unique in this respect, the human problem-solver is a principal research instrument, and there is nothing "sinister" about the research quest.

The aforementioned "symbol processing system hypothesis," it was argued, is a sufficient condition for a process to exhibit intelligent behavior--nothing more, nothing less. (Note: M. Minsky in (15) advances a comparable argument in the "principle of sparseness" with respect to representation.) Given the assertion, one should observe (extreme) caution in attempts to extrapolate interpretations and inferences from one domain to the other. This caveat is paramount in situations for proposing change in human (organizational) systems based on AI systems behavior.

4.2 'Expert's knowledge provides the key to expert performance.'

This hypothesis may be less controversial than its predecessor. The key here is the "knowledge base." Early research in AI and experience

with general problem solving approaches (see 5) or theories were disappointing in the sense that the "methods" employed were "too weak."
That is, the more general the approach, the more diminished the efficiency in problem solving, and the less significant the results (consequences) in terms of specific problem domains. This experience provides a rationale, in part, for the recent focus on ES as an alternative design paradigm, and has reinforced the fact that the expert's knowledge, as encoded in the knowledge base, dominates other components of the ES (such as the "inference engine") as the principal determinant of performance.

4.3 'Some "hard problems" may be impossible.'

This hypothesis may sound "defeatist" for a "purist" in the field, however, I believe negative results (i.e., "impossibilities") are as productive in this field as they have been in mathematics (although we don't often share the luxury of a "proof."). I alluded to some "wicked problems" above which may be "impossible" within your (or your offspring's) lifetime. This should not be taken as a commitment to pessimism, but rather a recognition of reality. For example, new directions in AI research are investigating "learning inference structures" and "thinking" as researchable (dynamic) issues (see 17 and 18), and I have little doubt that computing power gains will ameliorate classes of non-polynomially bounded computational problems in OR (so called "NP complete" problems). Moreover, some distinguished professionals feel communication with "alien intelligence" from outer-space is well within our (conceptual) technical capabilities (see Minsky, and other references he cites, in 15). But, there is a need to recognize, and indeed appreciate the limitations of our technology--we have a responsibility to be honest with our "patrons" and with ourselves. Although this is oblique to the message of this essay, and (with the author) I am not an advocate of a particular political position on policy, I commend Parnas' assessment of the technical "limitations" for the Strategic Defense Initiative by the United States (see 19). What are the policy implications for AI research funding in the U.S.? Is the program "impossible?"

4.4 'Keep expectations realistic.'

This hypothesis (or admonition) is in rebuttal to an over-enthusiastic press (e.g., 2), but I believe it is appropriate advice regardless of whether one is a consumer or a supplier of new technology (e.g., 21). The pitfalls of "oversell" need no elaboration, and inflated claims on potential capabilities are a disservice to the science. AI and ES have made significant progress in recent years and research in the field (in both academia and industry) has become much more intense. However, according to all informed sources the science is not on the brink of major "breakthroughs" and advances come one step at a time. Humility appears to be a desired hallmark in promulgating results.

4.5 'Keep the human as a component of the problem-solving system.'

I believe some time ago Dr. Fred Brooks of the University of North Carolina coined the phrase "intelligence amplification" as an alternative to the conventional denotation of AI. The basic idea here is to employ intelligent technology more in a DSS mode, than as a replacement for the individual--the concept of "dialectic programming" is also relevant in this context (see 12). As I've said years past (opt.cit.), I couldn't agree more! It is most unlikely that managers (in the full sense of that term) will ever be replaced by computer systems. Routine, programmable decisions will increasingly become programmed, of course, but the manager's job is always expanding. Hence, a continuing and symbiotic partnership between manager and system is inevitable. Recognition of this fact should do much to enhance the design of future systems.

For example, Jordan (11) relates the following interesting anecdote. In the early 1950's an industrial engineer named Fitts published a paper which included two lists of tasks; one list contained things machines do well and the other listed things humans do well. According to Jordan, this paper delayed the development of industrial automation by at least a decade. Why? Because for the next ten years, engineers devoted much of their efforts attempting to move tasks from the list for humans to the list for machines. They ignored the very real potential for symbiosis. The combinations of both, working together, could have produced a more desirable alternative.

5.   CONJECTURES ON PRIORITIES

If you grant me the license of the preceding hypotheses, I now turn attention to the question of research priorities for management decision science and intelligent technology. Although by no means exhaustive, again five areas come to mind.

5.1 'Cost/Benefit/Impact Evaluation.'

To contribute to the welfare of society resources and technology must be managed effectively. Industry has spent billions of dollars on information technology and anticipates spending more billions. What has been the economic impact? The answer to this question remains surprisingly elusive. In point of fact, we do not have good methods or data for developing an answer. The senior management of most organizations demands ROI (return on investment) calculations for any capital investments. But existing accounting systems do not accommodate information systems technology costs or returns, and for the most part software development costs are expensed. There is no general agreement on how to define, let alone measure, the benefits from information technology (see 27).

Basic research in this general area is sorely needed (4). The default to simplistic concepts like ROI just doesn't work. Nonetheless, unlike the experimental ES in the laboratory, any industrial ES must

pass the test of clear need <u>and</u> economic benefit, besides the usual
criteria applied to choice of an application domain (10). A comparable
justification is required in the case of computer-assisted management
decisions employing OR/MS models.

5.2 'Software Engineering for Development of Large Systems.'

For more than 25 years we have known that our system analysis, design,
and programming methods are inadequate for large projects (19). A
common thrust of research results in software engineering has been to
reduce the amount of information that a programmer must remember when
checking and changing a program in a system. Computer scientists have
been able to demonstrate, and in some cases prove (e.g., structured programming), sound principles to guide software development. But implementing software engineering and enforcing its practice is not easy, and
it is known that broad experience with similar systems is necessary to
design good, reliable software (19). This experience is expensive and
difficult to accumulate in the case of large systems. Software continues to be a bottleneck in systems development and issues of productivity, quality, maintainability and adaptability will require extensive applied, empirical research.

The anticipated spread of industrial ES expand the set of conventional development issues. For example, unlike laboratory models, the
industrial ES will require interfaces with conventional systems--to
access existing programs, large databases and to communicate with the
underlying computer system (10). Issues concerning test, validation,
specification, integrity, and portability present new challenges for
programming technology. A large gap currently exists between desired
and available technologies for knowledge acquisition, knowledge representation, and efficient inference mechanisms. We need to close the
gaps through fundamental research and development based on successes
and failures in industry experience (10).

5.3 'Build Researched-Concensus for Design.'

With the increase in notoriety, we are beginning to see (or hear about)
more ES being developed--even though it seems the same set of systems
is always cited. Indeed, the availability of commercial ES programming shells (you provide the knowledge base of expertise) and list processing language machines has made the task of developing an ES somewhat simpler than it used to be. If we assume some experience is beginning to emerge might we not ask: What have we learned? Is this experience, even within an organization, being monitored and recorded?
Is there a researched-concensus among ES professionals on good principles for design?

Certainly, there are some things we know to avoid and advice is
available, but it is not clear how much of it is an outgrowth of research
and experience with industrial ES. Beyond the fact of recency or new-
ness, one problem here is industry confidentiality--both within the
commercial AI industry and in general. That is, the former are in a
rush to develop viable products for sale and the latter are not anxious

to divulge "trade secrets." Hong (10) suggests there are identifiable phases in the life cycle of an industrial ES after the domain has been defined and development begun. The initial prototyping phase extends up to six months; during it a fraction of the knowledge base, a skeleton inference engine and preliminary tools are implemented. The next phase of further development ranges from several months to a year; more rules are added to the knowledge base to improve coverage accompanied by more tools development. The ES is then "field tested" for another few months to a year immediately followed by a rapid growth in the size of the knowledge base--the number of rules doubling, tripling, and more. This increase is partially due to the knowledge engineer's mastery of the domain, recognition of missing expertise and the need to ready the ES for actual use. The final phase is field use and a continuously grow-ing ES as rules keep being added, usually to accommodate a greater variety of conditions. This growth requires efforts to evaluate the additions and to maintain the system, as it becomes more complex and cumbersome. Maintenance becomes a dominant problem at this point.

Some research is underway to better understand how ES design can be "streamlined" and learning rule development can be incorporated (17), but much more work is necessary. For the most part actual ES design remains an "art form," and we need to share experience and research re-sults to bring it into a discipline.

5.4 'Employ Joint Technology for Enhanced System Performance.'

Just as man and computer can be a symbiotic system in consort, joint technology has the same potential. I continue to wonder about confer-ence panels and papers with titles such as "AI vs. DSS," or "AI vs. OR," or "ES vs. DSS vs. OR," and so forth. Why versus? Is a forced choice necessary, or even desirable? These manufactured debates on non-issues in my opinion serve little constructive purpose, except perhaps to ex-pose "strawmen," and they remind me of a similar phenomena in the late 1960's. Some of you may recall, at that time the debate was "time-sharing vs. batch processing." What experience taught us about that issue was to re-learn the economic principle of comparative advantage, that is, either type of computing may be superior contingent on the task. I believe the same principle applies to intelligent technology and it is not a matter of ideology. (I address communications consider-ations below.)

The opportunity for technological synergy, indeed to exploit the interdisciplinary reality of management, has been recognized for some time (9,12,22). Successful applications of individual technologies are manifest; those employing combinations of AI/ES and OR/MS and allied technologies are less plentiful as documented in the literature. Further research into comparative advantages, design tradeoffs and field study descriptions of industry experience will serve to make this case more apparent. Of particular interest is empirical data on the interplay and integration of intelligent and management technologies. We can learn from one another, productively.

5.5 'Develop New and Better Communications Channels Across Professions.'

One aspect I side-stepped in the previous conjecture regarding "A vs. B" as an issue, is the "us vs. them" variation. In the OR/MS literature much has been written on the problem of "implementation," particularly as it may pertain to "managers vs. management scientists" and the differences in cultures, perspectives and so on. A significant literature provided by the behavioral scientists has contributed much to the normative resolution of this issue, and to the understanding of organizational change and intervention. But, what about the conflict of "territorial disputes" between professional groups? Alas, the situation is less sanguine and the disputes are often unprofessional.

Since its birth, the AI/ES "camp" has been an outgrowth of computer science, whereas the OR/MS "camp" has evolved from management engineers and applied mathematicians. The early "dialogue" of communication between these two groups can perhaps be best described as "talking at one another" rather than "talking to one another." That is, for communication to occur, each group has to "listen" (and comprehend the message) at least some fraction of the time during the discourse; they can't simply talk (lecture) all of the time. Unfortunately, the "keep talking, we know the answer" syndrome has been dominant, until recently.

Today, I think each professional group recognizes the potential for learning from the other camp, if both are to more effectively serve the ultimate consumer, management. As professionals, we need to encourage and provide opportunities to enhance this potential for better communication. At a minimum it will serve to short-circuit blind attempts to "reinvent the wheel" and rediscover the real problems. It will facilitate a better understanding of the problem and true comparative advantages. It will serve to diminish misconceptions about "job security" and professional integrities, not to mention status. Most importantly, we can learn from one another and enhanced communication among professionals will better serve management, and ultimately society in general. I believe the grass roots effort for this sort of endeavor should begin with the professional societies and allied organizations which include academia and industry. Let's communicate!

6.   CONCLUSIONS.

Clearly, we haven't reached the boundaries of computer capabilities today and we may not even be close to the limits. In pondering the microcomputer revolution of the last decade, it is not inconceivable to imagine another 10^x gain in computing over the next decade. The emerging intelligent technology holds great potential for management, but it is only in its infancy and we should proceed with caution on any claims of virility. Experience to date has already shown that ES can have a tendency to turn into "vaporware" (21). The economics of technology is moving in the right direction, but the ultimate payoff must end up with management. Most of us are painfully aware of the monumental challenges we face in that domain (16).

The science of management decision is indeed being reshaped by developments in intelligent technology and in historical perspective this process has only begun. I am certain each of us shares the excitement, as agents who are influencing the evolution and contributing to the outcomes for the next generation.

REFERENCES

1. Alter, S. L., Decision Support Systems: Current Practices and
   Continuing Challenges (Addison-Wesley, Reading, MA, 1980).

2. Anon., 'Artificial Intelligence -- It's Here!', Business Week
   (July 9, 1984), 54-62.

3. Barr, A. and E. A. Feigenbaum (eds.), The Handbook of Artificial
   Intelligence, Vol. 1 (William Kaufmann, Inc., Los Altos, CA,
   1981).

4. Chismar, W. G. and C. H. Kriebel, 'A Method for Assessing the
   Economic Impact of Information Systems Technology on Organizations,'
   in Proceedings of the Sixth International Conference on Information Systems (Indianapolis, Indiana, forthcoming December 1985).

5. Ernst, G. and Allen Newell, GPS: A Case Study in Generality and
   Problem Solving (Academic Press, NY, 1969).

6. Gevarter, W. B., 'Expert systems: limited but powerful,' IEEE
   Spectrum 26, no. 8(August 1983), 39-45.

7. Harmon, P. and D. King, Expert Systems: Artificial Intelligence
   in Business (John Wiley & Sons, Inc., NY, 1985).

8. Hayes-Roth, F., D. A. Waterman and D. B. Lenat, (ed.), Building
   Expert Systems (Addison-Wesley, Reading, MA, 1983).

9. Hertz, D. B., New Power for Management: Computer Systems and
   Management Science (McGraw-Hill, NY, 1969).

10. Hong, S. J., 'Knowledge Engineering in Industry,' Research Report,
    RC10330 (#45958), IBM T. J. Watson Research Center, Yorktown
    Heights, NY (January 12, 1984).

11. Jordan, N., 'Allocation of Functions Between Man and Machine in
    Automated Systems,' Journal of Applied Psychology, 47 (1963),
    161-5.

12. Kriebel, C. H., 'Perspectives on Information Processing in Manage-
    ment Information Systems,' Saertryk of Ehvervsokonomist Tridsskrift
    (Nr. 4, 1969), 229-247; reprinted in W. Goldberg (ed.), Behavioral
    Approaches to Modern Management, Vol. 1 (Gothenberg Studies in
    Business Administration, Gothenberg, Sweden, 1970), 183-200.

13. Kriebel, C. H., 'MIS Technology: A View of the Future,' in
    Spring Joint Computer Conference Proceedings, 40 (A.F.P.S. Press,
    Montvale, NJ, 1972), 1173-1180.

14. Lenat, D. B. and R. Davis, Knowledge-Based Systems in AI (McGraw-Hill, NH, 1981).

15. Lemmons, P., 'Artificial Intelligence,' Byte, 10, no. 4 (April 1985), 125-330.

16. McFarlan, F. W. (ed.), The Information Systems Research Challenge (Harvard Business School Press, Boston, MA, 1984).

17. Newell, A., 'Some New Directions in Expert System Research,' OR Seminar, G.S.I.A. and Department of Computer Science, Carnegie-Mellon University, Pittsburgh, PA (November 1985).

18. Nickerson, R. S. (Chair), Research Needs on the Interaction Between Information Systems and Their Users: Report of a Workshop (October 1983), Committee on Human Factors, Commission on Behavioral and Social Sciences and Education, National Research Council, Washington, DC.

19. Parnas, D. L., 'Software Aspects of Strategic Defense Systems: Views,' American Scientist, 73, (September-October 1985), 432-440.

20. Rich, E., Artificial Intelligence (McGraw-Hill, NY, 1983).

21. Salerno, L. M.,'What happened to the computer revolution?' Harvard Business Review, 63, no. 6 (November-December 1985), 129-138.

22. Simon, H. A., The Sciences of the Artificial (MIT Press, Cambridge, MA, 1969).

23. Simon, H. A., The New Science of Management Decision (revised edition), Prentice Hall, Inc., Englewood Cliffs, N.J., 1977.

24. Simon, H. A., 'AI -- The Reality and the Promise,' 1.1 - 1.17, in Colloquium Proceedings: Artificial Intelligence -- Opportunities and Limitations in the 80's (November 7, 1984) Miami, FL.; Sponsored by the University of Miami, Intelligent Computer Systems Research Institute, Coral Gables, FL.

25. Sol. H. G., 'Paradoxes Around DSS,' Working Paper 1985, Center for Information Systems, Department of Informatics, Delft University of Technology, The Netherlands.

26. Sprague, R. H. and E. D. Carlson, Building Effective Decision Support Systems (Prentice-Hall, Englewood Cliffs, N.J., 1982).

27. Strassmann, P. A., Information Payoff: The Transformation of Work in the Electronic Age (Free Press, NY, 1985).

28. Whinston, P. H., Artificial Intelligence (Addison-Wesley, Reading, MA, 1977).

A

Abbot-monk problem 181
Ackoff 118
adaptable responsive systems 72
adaptive responsive systems 72
adaptive design process 48
AI
  as a tool 69
  frames 219
  heuristics 3
  history 11
  inference under uncertainty 60
  knowledge representation 49
  semantic nets 219
  progress in 79, 302
AI & OR
  relations between 11
  views of 11
AI-techniques; role of simulation in 194
algorithm design 80
algorithms 271
Alter 24
Alvey report 242
analysis; linguistic exploratory 137
Anthony 58,60
APL 142,295
aspect
  discriminating nature of an 156
  context of an 157
ASPES 228, 235
automated programming 290
automated reasoning 139
automation
  describing 69,70

B

Barr and Feigenbaum 230
Basden 228
bayesian inference 199
Belew 26
Bellman 16
Bennett 302
biased information 66
Blending problem; LP-model 122
Blumenthal 63
Bonczek 2, 25, 31
Bonnet 234
Bosman 35
Bosman and Sol 31, 43
Bots 138
bounded rationality 37
Bramer 229
Bright 70